Focus on GRAMMAR 2B

FOURTH EDITION

Focus on GRAMMAR 2B

FOURTH EDITION

Irene E. Schoenberg

FOCUS ON GRAMMAR 2B: An Integrated Skills Approach, Fourth Edition

Pearson Education, 10 Bank Street, White Plains, NY 10606

Staff credits: The people who made up the *Focus on Grammar 2B, Fourth Edition*
team, representing editorial, production, design, and manufacturing, are Elizabeth Carlson,
Tracey Cataldo, Aerin Csigay, Dave Dickey, Christine Edmonds, Nancy Flagmann, Ann France,
Lise Minovitz, Barbara Perez, Robert Ruvo, Debbie Sistino, and Kim Steiner.

Cover image: Shutterstock.com
Text composition: ElectraGraphics, Inc.
Text font: New Aster

PEARSON LONGMAN ON THE **WEB**

Pearsonlongman.com offers online
resources for teachers and students. Access
our Companion Websites, our online catalog,
and our local offices around the world.

Visit us at **pearsonlongman.com**.

Printed in the United States of America

ISBN 10: 0-13-216926-6
ISBN 13: 978-0-13-216926-4

8 16

ISBN 10: 0-13-216927-4 (with MyLab)
ISBN 13: 978-0-13-216927-1 (with MyLab)

1 11

CONTENTS

Welcome to *Focus on Grammar*

Now in a new edition, the popular five-level *Focus on Grammar* course continues to provide an integrated-skills approach to help students understand and practice English grammar. Centered on thematic instruction, *Focus on Grammar* combines controlled and communicative practice with critical thinking skills and ongoing assessment. Students gain the confidence they need to speak and write English accurately and fluently.

NEW for the FOURTH EDITION

VOCABULARY

Key vocabulary is highlighted, practiced, and recycled throughout the unit.

PRONUNCIATION

Now, in every unit, pronunciation points and activities help students improve spoken accuracy and fluency.

LISTENING

Expanded listening tasks allow students to develop a range of listening skills.

UPDATED CHARTS and NOTES

Target structures are presented in a clear, easy-to-read format.

NEW READINGS

High-interest readings, updated or completely new, in a variety of genres integrate grammar and vocabulary in natural contexts.

NEW UNIT REVIEWS

Students can check their understanding and monitor their progress after completing each unit.

MyFocusOnGrammarLab

An easy-to-use online learning and assessment program offers online homework and individualized instruction anywhere, anytime.

Teacher's Resource Pack   One compact resource includes:

THE TEACHER'S MANUAL: General Teaching Notes, Unit Teaching Notes, the Student Book Audioscript, and the Student Book Answer Key.

TEACHER'S RESOURCE DISC: Bound into the Resource Pack, this CD-ROM contains reproducible Placement, Part, and Unit Tests, as well as customizable Test-Generating Software. It also includes reproducible Internet Activities and PowerPoint® Grammar Presentations.

THE *FOCUS ON GRAMMAR* APPROACH

The new edition follows the same successful four-step approach of previous editions. The books provide an abundance of both controlled and communicative exercises so that students can bridge the gap between identifying grammatical structures and using them. The many communicative activities in each Student Book provide opportunities for critical thinking while enabling students to personalize what they have learned.

- **STEP 1: GRAMMAR IN CONTEXT** highlights the target structures in realistic contexts, such as conversations, magazine articles, and blog posts.
- **STEP 2: GRAMMAR PRESENTATION** presents the structures in clear and accessible grammar charts and notes with multiple examples of form and usage.
- **STEP 3: FOCUSED PRACTICE** provides numerous and varied controlled exercises for both the form and meaning of the new structures.
- **STEP 4: COMMUNICATION PRACTICE** includes listening and pronunciation and allows students to use the new structures freely and creatively in motivating, open-ended speaking and writing activities.

Recycling

Underpinning the scope and sequence of the *Focus on Grammar* series is the belief that students need to use target structures and vocabulary many times, in different contexts. New grammar and vocabulary are recycled throughout the book. Students have maximum exposure and become confident using the language in speech and in writing.

Assessment

Extensive testing informs instruction and allows teachers and students to measure progress.

- **Unit Reviews** at the end of every Student Book unit assess students' understanding of the grammar and allow students to monitor their own progress.
- Easy to administer and score, **Part and Unit Tests** provide teachers with a valid and reliable means to determine how well students know the material they are about to study and to assess students' mastery after they complete the material. These tests can be found on MyFocusOnGrammarLab, where they include immediate feedback and remediation, and as reproducible tests on the Teacher's Resource Disc.
- **Test-Generating Software** on the Teacher's Resource Disc includes a bank of *additional* test items teachers can use to create customized tests.
- A reproducible **Placement Test** on the Teacher's Resource Disc is designed to help teachers place students into one of the five levels of the *Focus on Grammar* course.

COMPONENTS

In addition to the Student Books, Teacher's Resource Packs, and MyLabs, the complete *Focus on Grammar* course includes:

Workbooks Contain additional contextualized exercises appropriate for self-study.

Audio Program Includes all of the listening and pronunciation exercises and opening passages from the Student Book. Some Student Books are packaged with the complete audio program (mp3 files). Alternatively, the audio program is available on a classroom set of CDs and on the MyLab.

THE *FOCUS ON GRAMMAR* UNIT

Focus on Grammar introduces grammar structures in the context of unified themes. All units follow a **four-step approach**, taking learners from grammar in context to communicative practice.

STEP 1 GRAMMAR IN CONTEXT

This section presents the target structure(s) in a natural context. As students read the **high-interest texts**, they encounter the form, meaning, and use of the grammar. **Before You Read** activities create interest and elicit students' knowledge about the topic. **After You Read** activities build students' reading vocabulary and comprehension.

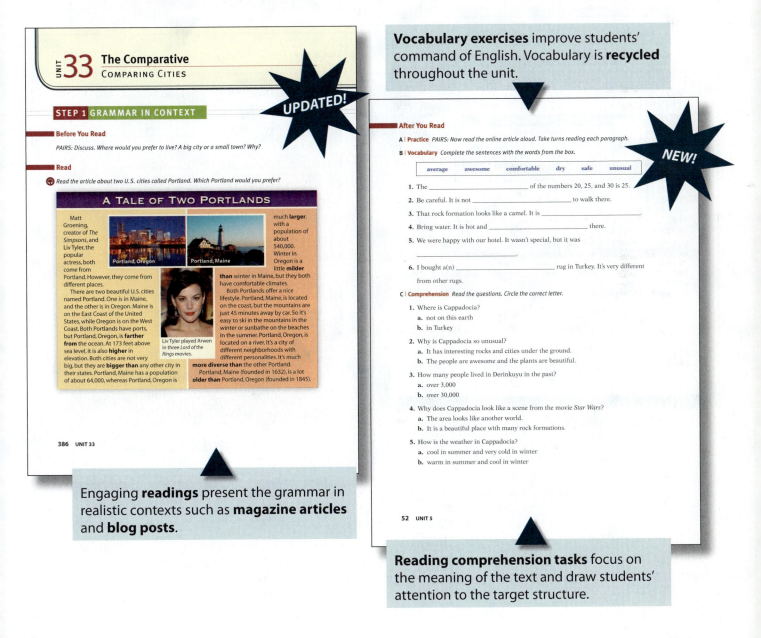

Vocabulary exercises improve students' command of English. Vocabulary is **recycled** throughout the unit.

Engaging **readings** present the grammar in realistic contexts such as **magazine articles** and **blog posts**.

Reading comprehension tasks focus on the meaning of the text and draw students' attention to the target structure.

This section gives students a comprehensive and explicit overview of the grammar with detailed **Grammar Charts** and **Grammar Notes** that present the form, meaning, and use of the structure(s).

Grammar Charts present the structure in a clear, easy-to-read format.

Grammar Notes give concise, simple **explanations** and **examples** to ensure students' understanding.

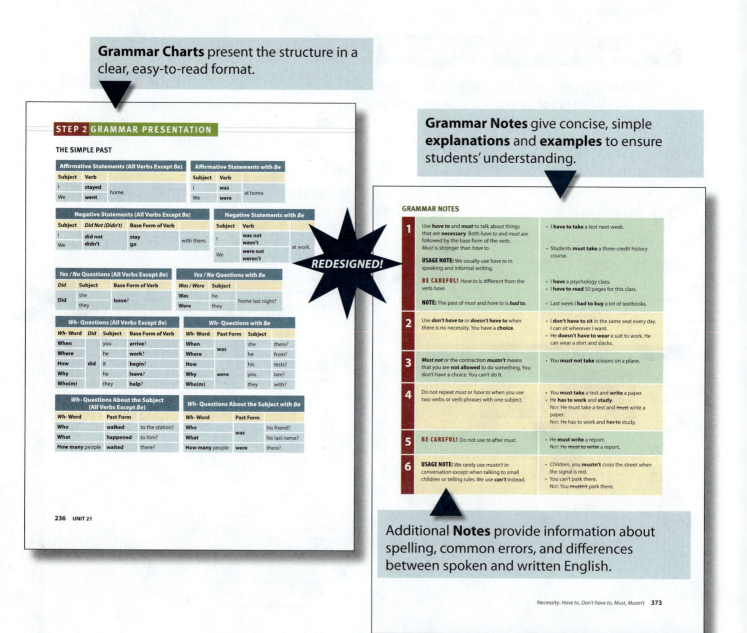

REDESIGNED!

Additional **Notes** provide information about spelling, common errors, and differences between spoken and written English.

STEP 3 FOCUSED PRACTICE

Controlled practice activities in this section lead students to master form, meaning, and use of the target grammar.

Discover the Grammar activities develop students' recognition and understanding of the target structure before they are asked to produce it.

A **variety of exercise types** engage students and guide them from recognition and understanding to accurate production of the grammar structures.

An **Editing** exercise ends every Focused Practice section and teaches students to find and correct typical mistakes.

STEP 3 FOCUSED PRACTICE

EXERCISE 1: Discover the Grammar

Underline the simple present. Circle the present progressive. Underline twice all non-action verbs.

Raisa has a new phone with a lot of great features. She likes her phone a lot. Her phone keeps her in touch with her friends wherever she is. Right now Raisa is texting friends. They are making plans for the evening. She and her friends often text. They don't talk much on the phone. They also connect through Facebook®. Raisa often adds new friends to her site. Sometimes she doesn't know them very well. Raisa's mother, Olga, worries about that. Olga doesn't use social networks. She prefers to talk on the phone or connect through email.

EXERCISE 2: Simple Present; Non-Action Verbs; Present Progressive *(Grammar Notes 1–5)*

Complete the conversation with the words in parentheses. Use the simple present or present progressive. Use contractions when possible.

A: What _____*are*_____ you _____*doing*_____?
                1.   2. (do)

B: I _____ my messages. Look. That's my friend from high school.
        3. (check)

She _____ three kids now. They _____ happy birthday to
        4. (have)   5. (sing)
their father.

A: Oh. That's nice.

B: _____ you _____ social networking sites?
        6.   7. (use)

A: No, I _____. I _____ to email my friends. I _____
        8.   9. (prefer)   10. (think)
it's more personal. Also, I _____ there are privacy features in social
                            11. (know)
networking sites, but I _____ about my privacy.
                        12. (worry)

Simple Present and Present Progressive; Non-Action Verbs **189**

EXERCISE 4: Comparison of Adjectives *(Grammar Notes 1–7)*

Complete the paragraph with the adjectives in parentheses. Use the comparative form.

You are choosing between two cities to live in, Los Angeles or Glendale. You aren't sure which is a _____*better*_____ choice. Los
                                1. (good)
Angeles is a much _____ city than
                    2. (big)
Glendale, and it has all the problems of big
cities. Los Angeles is _____ than
                        3. (polluted)
Glendale, and traffic is _____.
                            4. (bad)

Rodeo Drive, Los Angeles

The streets of downtown Los Angeles are

_____ too. However, Los Angeles is much _____ than Glendale.
5. (busy)   6. (exciting)
Los Angeles has a great night life. Glendale
is much _____ at night. Both
            7. (quiet)
cities have the same great climate. It's hard
to compare housing costs. Some parts of Los
Angeles are _____ than Glendale
            8. (more / expensive)
and other parts are _____. Both
                    9. (less / expensive)
cities are close, so if you make a mistake, you
can always move.

Bicycle trail, Glendale, California

EXERCISE 5: Editing

Correct the sentences. There are seven mistakes. The first one is already corrected. Find and correct six more.

1. Our new apartment is ^more comfortable than our old one.

2. Florida is more hotter than Maine.

3. Oregon is far north than California.

4. A motorcycle is more fast than a bicycle.

5. Traffic at 8:00 A.M. is more heavy than traffic at 10:00 A.M.

6. The climate in Portland, Oregon, is mild than the climate in Anchorage, Alaska.

7. The location of Jake's apartment is more convenient than his sister.

394 UNIT 33

This section provides practice with the structure in **listening** and **pronunciation** exercises as well as in communicative, open-ended **speaking** and **writing** activities that move students toward fluency.

Listening activities allow students to hear the grammar in natural contexts and to practice a range of listening skills.

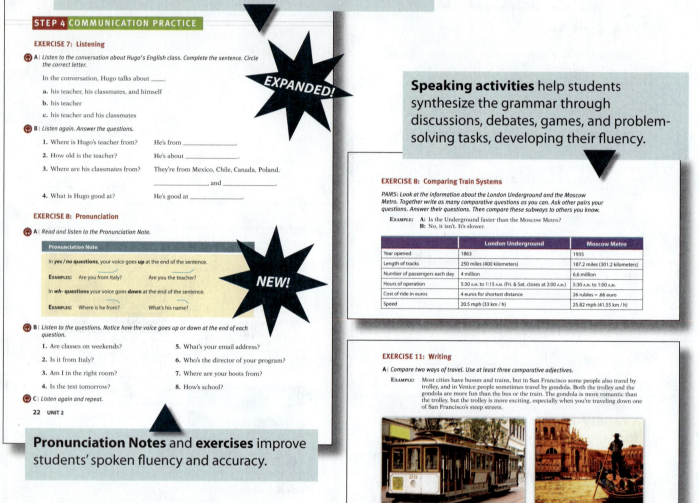

STEP 4 COMMUNICATION PRACTICE

EXERCISE 7: Listening

A | *Listen to the conversation about Hugo's English class. Complete the sentence. Circle the correct letter.*

In the conversation, Hugo talks about _____.

a. his teacher, his classmates, and himself

b. his teacher

c. his teacher and his classmates

B | *Listen again. Answer the questions.*

1. Where is Hugo's teacher from? He's from _____.

2. How old is the teacher? He's about _____.

3. Where are his classmates from? They're from Mexico, Chile, Canada, Poland, _____, and _____.

4. What is Hugo good at? He's good at _____.

EXERCISE 8: Pronunciation

A | *Read and listen to the Pronunciation Note.*

> **Pronunciation Note**
>
> In *yes / no questions*, your voice goes **up** at the end of the sentence.
>
> **EXAMPLES:** Are you from Italy? Are you the teacher?
>
> In *wh- questions* your voice goes **down** at the end of the sentence.
>
> **EXAMPLES:** Where is he from? What's his name?

EXPANDED!

NEW!

B | *Listen to the questions. Notice how the voice goes up or down at the end of each question.*

1. Are classes on weekends?

2. Is it from Italy?

3. Am I in the right room?

4. Is the test tomorrow?

5. What's your email address?

6. Who's the director of your program?

7. Where are your boots from?

8. How's school?

C | *Listen again and repeat.*

22 UNIT 2

Pronunciation Notes and **exercises** improve students' spoken fluency and accuracy.

Speaking activities help students synthesize the grammar through discussions, debates, games, and problem-solving tasks, developing their fluency.

EXERCISE 8: Comparing Train Systems

PAIRS: Look at the information about the London Underground and the Moscow Metro. Together write as many comparative questions as you can. Ask other pairs your questions. Answer their questions. Then compare these subways to others you know.

EXAMPLE: **A:** Is the Underground faster than the Moscow Metro?
B: No, it isn't. It's slower.

	London Underground	Moscow Metro
Year opened	1863	1935
Length of tracks	250 miles (400 kilometers)	187.2 miles (301.2 kilometers)
Number of passengers each day	4 million	6.6 million
Hours of operation	5:30 A.M. to 1:15 A.M. (Fri. & Sat. closes at 2:00 A.M.)	5:30 A.M. to 1:00 A.M.
Cost of ride in euros	4 euros for shortest distance	26 rubles = .66 euro
Speed	20.5 mph (33 km / h)	25.82 mph (41.55 km / h)

EXERCISE 11: Writing

A | *Compare two ways of travel. Use at least three comparative adjectives.*

EXAMPLE: Most cities have busses and trains, but in San Francisco some people also travel by trolley, and in Venice people sometimes travel by gondola. Both the trolley and the gondola are more fun than the bus or the train. The gondola is more romantic than the trolley, but the trolley is more exciting, especially when you're traveling down one of San Francisco's steep streets.

B | *Check your work. Use the Editing Checklist.*

> **Editing Checklist**
>
> Did you . . . ?
> ☐ use comparative adjectives correctly
> ☐ check your spelling

NEW!

Writing activities encourage students to produce meaningful writing that integrates the grammar structure.

An **Editing Checklist** teaches students to correct their mistakes and revise their work.

Unit Reviews give students the opportunity to check their understanding of the target structure. **Answers** at the back of the book allow students to monitor their own progress.

UNIT 33 Review

Check your answers on page UR-7.
Do you need to review anything?

NEW!

A | *Circle the correct words to complete the sentences.*

1. She is **more / much** younger than he is.
2. It is colder **then / than** it was yesterday.
3. This singing group is **more popular / popular more** than the other one.
4. The traffic is **more worse / worse** now than it was an hour ago.
5. Which city has a **high / higher** elevation, Bogota or Mexico City?
6. Which city has a **better / more good** transportation system, Quebec or Vancouver?
7. Is your car more comfortable than your **brother / brother's**?

B | *Look at the chart. Make comparisons. Use the words in parentheses.*

	New City	Sun City
Bus fare	$2.00	$3.00
Cup of coffee	$1.20	$1.50
Average home	$200,000	$300,000
Average income	$65,000	$90,000

1. _____
   (bus / expensive)

2. _____
   (cup of coffee / cheap)

3. _____
   (average home / less / expensive)

4. _____
   (average income / high)

C | *Correct the paragraph. There are nine mistakes.*

We moved to the countryside, and we're mu[...]
larger, and the air is cleaner and polluted less. [...]
and vegetables are more cheap. The people are [...]
is more bad; it's much more long, but we listen [...]
more good.

Extended writing tasks help students integrate the grammar structure as they follow the steps of the **writing process.**

PART XI From Grammar to Writing
THE ORDER OF ADJECTIVES BEFORE NOUNS

1 | *Complete the sentences with the words in parentheses.*

1. I saw a _____ on Main Street.
   (funny / monkey / brown / little)

2. Maria wore a _____.
   (red / dress / beautiful / silk)

2 | *Study this information about the order of adjectives before nouns. When you use adjectives, write them in this order.*

1	1. opinion	2. size	3. shape	4. age	5. color	6. origin	7. material	8. noun
	beautiful	big	square	new	red	French	silk	scarf

2 We use adjectives to describe nouns. Descriptions make writing more lively. They also help the reader form mental pictures. When **several adjectives** come before a noun, they follow a **special order.**
• I saw a **beautiful young** woman.
NOT: I saw a ~~young beautiful~~ woman.

3 Use **and** to connect adjectives from the same category.
• The shirt was cotton **and** polyester.
• The blouse was red **and** white.

3 | *Complete the sentences with the words in parentheses. Use the correct order.*

1. He ate a(n) _____ pear.
   (brown / big / Asian)

2. His cashmere coat was not as expensive as her _____
   (Italian / new / leather / black)
   _____ jacket.

3. They bought three _____ bowls.
   (silver / beautiful / Mexican)

SCOPE AND SEQUENCE

UNIT	READING	WRITING	LISTENING
1 page 2 **Grammar:** Present of *Be*: Statements **Theme:** Famous People	An article: *Famous Couples*	Sentences about a famous person or talented friend or relative	Occupations and countries of famous people
2 page 13 **Grammar:** Present of *Be*: *Yes / No* Questions and *Wh-* Questions **Theme:** First Day of School	A conversation: *Arriving in Class*	Questions about a language school	A conversation about an English class
3 page 25 **Grammar:** Past of *Be*: Statements, *Yes / No* Questions, *Wh-* Questions **Theme:** First Jobs	An illustrated story: *A boy's first job*	An email to a friend about your weekend	Phone messages
PART I **From Grammar to Writing,** page 36 Capitalization			
4 page 40 **Grammar:** Count Nouns and Proper Nouns **Theme:** Photographs and Photographers	An article: *A Photographer and a Photo*	A paragraph about a photo of a person you know	A conversation about a family gathering
5 page 51 **Grammar:** Descriptive Adjectives **Theme:** Cave Homes	An online article: Cappadocia, Turkey	A paragraph about an interesting place	A telephone conversation about a vacation
6 page 60 **Grammar:** Prepositions of Place **Theme:** Locations	An online posting and a conversation: *At the Museum*	An invitation to a party with directions	Locations of countries
PART II **From Grammar to Writing,** page 70 Connecting with *And* and *But*			
7 page 72 **Grammar:** Imperatives; Suggestions with *Let's*, *Why don't we . . . ?* **Theme:** Long Life	An online article: *Secrets to a Long Life*	An advertisement for a hotel in Ikaria, Greece	An advertisement for a spa

SPEAKING	PRONUNCIATION	VOCABULARY	
Pair Discussion: Occupations *Class Discussion*: Talented People	Tips for *he, she, he's,* and *she's*	athlete busy exciting	famous husband talented
Pair Activity: Asking and Answering Questions *Role Play*: Meeting at a Party	Rising intonation in *yes / no* questions Falling intonation in *wh-*questions	by the way excuse me on time	right room
Guided Conversation: Describing the Weather *Group Discussion*: The First Day of School	Extra pronounced syllable in negative forms of *be* Clipped /t/ sound in *wasn't, weren't*	a big deal boring busy	make money still
Game: Describing Things *Game*: Comparing Choices	Sound of plurals: /s/, /z/, /ɪz/	all over almost be born	holiday special striking
Group Discussion: Asking Questions about a Place	Syllable stress	average awesome comfortable	dry safe unusual
Game: Guessing Countries *Game*: Describing Locations	Stressed words for emphasis	appointment be free cafeteria	flight rest room sculpture
Pair Activity: Making Suggestions for You and Another Person *Pair Activity*: Giving Advice *Pair Activity*: Giving Directions	Linking sound in *don't + you*	advice dead island	nap pray secret

SPEAKING	PRONUNCIATION	VOCABULARY	
Pair Discussion: Likes and Dislikes *Group Discussion*: Clothing Customs of the World	Third person singular ending /s/, /z/, or /ɪz/	alone companies cute	middle school senior teenager
Pair Discussion: Comparing Habits and Personality *Game*: Find Someone Who . . . *Game*: What's in Your Backpack?	Linking sound in *does it* and *does he*	bother easygoing messy neat	outgoing private stay up wake up
Pair Survey: Sleeping Habits *Group Survey*: Sleeping Habits *Pair Activity*: Information Gap	Consonant clusters with /r/ and /l/	author guest nightmares	remember unfortunately

SPEAKING	PRONUNCIATION	VOCABULARY	
Pair Activity: Comparing Pictures of a Street *Game*: Tic Tac Toe	Homophones: *there, their,* and *they're*	amusement park attraction get away include	indoor international market one of a kind
Class Activity: Asking about Family Photos *Game*: Find Someone Who . . .	Ending sounds with possessives: /z/, /s/, /ɪz/	back composition grade	handwriting recognize
Game: Find Someone Who . . . *Game*: What Can Your Group Do?	Reduced vowel in *can* when followed by base form verb Stressed vowel in *can't*	be surprised genius intelligent	invent professor
Information Gap: Asking Questions about a Website	Vowel sounds /eɪ/ and /ɛ/	especially gain lose	overweight pound

SPEAKING	PRONUNCIATION	VOCABULARY	
Game: Describing a Classroom Photo	Unstressed -*ing* ending in the present progressive	competition extracurricular give up	top tough wealthy
Role Play: Talking about Movies *Pair Activity*: Describing Pictures for a Partner to Draw	Stressed final syllable in abbreviations	catch a cold classic cough	favorite fever scene
Pair Discussion: Guessing About People *Group Activity*: Survey	Intonation to express emotions	connect constantly improving	minor waterproof
Pair Discussion: Talking About your Weekend *Game*: Truths or Lies	Final sound with simple past verbs: /d/, /t/, or /ɪd/	bumpy canceled freezing	landed picked up
Group Activity: A Memory Game *Group Discussion*: A Wonderful and Terrible Day	Vowel sounds /æ/ and /ɛ/	appeared border lucky	shout suddenly terrible
Pair Discussion: Describing a Performance or Event	/dʒ/ and /y/ sounds	author be out mystery	play poem

SPEAKING	PRONUNCIATION	VOCABULARY	
Group Activity: A Quiz Show *Pair Discussion*: What Were You Like as a Child? *Information Gap*: Guess the Musician	/ɝ/ and /ɔ/ and the consonant cluster /kt/	admire be based on illustrated	noticed statue
Pair Discussion: Preferences *Game*: What Do I Do? *Pair Activity*: Problem Solving	Unstressed sound /əv/ in *of* Linking of consonant with *of*	avoids can't stand competitive	dress clothes personality predictable
Information Gap: Inventions	Stress on first syllable in compound nouns	accepted came up with comes after	invented rejected
Pair Discussion: Changes in Your Life	Reduced pronunciation of *going to* "gonna"	against announced be worth it	in my opinion increased tuition
Group Activity: Survey *Class Survey*: In the Future *Class Activity*: Making Predictions	Linking between subject pronoun and *will*	common disappear meal	spend time vegetarian
Pair Discussion: Describing Plans	Stress on numbers ending in *-ty* and *-teen*	commute entire flooding highways	mild predicted storm
Class Activity: Cooking Class Presentation *Group Discussion*: Your Favorite Restaurant	Schwa sound /ə/ in the indefinite article	atmosphere delicious main course	menu reservation service

UNIT	READING	WRITING	LISTENING
28 page 321 **Grammar:** *How much / How many,* Quantifiers, *Enough,* Adverbs of Frequency **Theme:** Desserts, Cooking, and Baking	A conversation: Desserts	A paragraph describing desserts	A conversation about a recipe
29 page 334 **Grammar:** *Too much / Too many, Too* + Adjective **Theme:** The Right Place to Live	An online article: Three U.S. cities	An email of complaint to a newspaper about an aspect of city life	A conversation about apartment rentals
PART IX From Grammar to Writing, page 344 A Business Letter			
30 page 348 **Grammar:** Advice: *Should, Ought to, Had better* **Theme:** Dos and Don'ts of the Business World	An online article: Global Business	A paragraph of advice to a businessperson about a culture that you know well	A conversation about travels to Japan
31 page 360 **Grammar:** Requests, Desires, and Offers: *Would you, Could you, Can you . . . ?, I'd like . . .* **Theme:** Neighbors	A message board: Problems with neighbors	Two email requests to neighbors	A telephone conversation between neighbors
32 page 370 **Grammar:** Necessity: *Have to, Don't Have to, Must, Mustn't* **Theme:** Rules at School	A conversation: Requirements for a history class	A paragraph about an elementary school where you grew up	Advice from a college counselor to a student
PART X From Grammar to Writing, page 382 Expressing and Supporting an Opinion			
33 page 386 **Grammar:** The Comparative **Theme:** Comparing Cities	An article: *A Tale of Two Portlands*	A paragraph comparing two ways to travel	A conversation about city improvements

SPEAKING	PRONUNCIATION	VOCABULARY	
Class Survey: Eating Habits *Information Gap*: Recipes *Group Presentation*: Desserts	/aʊ/ sound	in season ingredients neighborhood	prepare pretty good taste
Role Play: Living Situations *Group Discussion*: Describing Your City	/t/, /θ/, and /ð/ sounds	climate crime free time	housing pollution unemployment
Pair Discussion: Gift Giving *Group Discussion*: Body Language	Reduction of /t/ sound after *shouldn't* before a verb	business receptions confusion consider	customs insult
Group Survey: Making Requests *Role Play*: Making Polite Requests *Pair Activity*: Offering Invitations *Role Play*: Offering Invitations and Making Requests	Vowel sound /ʊ/ in *would*; Reduced forms of *would you* /wʊdʒə/ and *could you* /kʊdʒə/	be hurt go away lend me a hand	post a message selfish
Class Discussion: School Rules *Class Survey*: Preventing Cheating	Stress and unstress in *have to* or *has to*	average due final hard copy	midterm outline pass percent
Pair Activity: Comparing Train Systems *Pair Discussion*: Making Comparisons *Class Discussion*: Comparing Cities	Unstressed vowel in *than*	be located coast diverse mild	personality port sea level ski

UNIT	READING	WRITING	LISTENING
34 page 399 **Grammar:** Adverbs of Manner **Theme:** Public Speaking	A blog: *Public Speaking*	A paragraph describing a sports event	Tips for giving a speech
35 page 408 **Grammar:** *Enough*, *Too / Very*, *As* + Adjective + *As*, *Same / Different* **Theme:** Proms and Parties	A conversation: High school prom dates	A paragraph comparing two friends or two events	A discussion between two managers
36 page 421 **Grammar:** The Superlative **Theme:** Penguins	An online article: *The Penguin*	A paragraph about animals in the zoo, literature, or movies	A quiz show
PART XI From Grammar to Writing, page 433 **The Order of Adjectives Before Nouns**			

SPEAKING	PRONUNCIATION	VOCABULARY	
Group Game: A Chain Story *Pair Discussion*: A Sports Event	Intonation to express emotions	applause appreciated audience facts	jokes polite seriously
Pair Activity: Describing Yourself *Class Survey*: Comparing Similarities	Unstressed vowel in *as . . . as*	I'm a loser I'm not going to make a fool of myself I'm not his type Making excuses No one can get a word in edgewise	
Group Survey: Animals	Unstressed *-est* syllable in superlatives	centimeter explorer extinct feathers	inch kilogram pound species

ABOUT THE AUTHOR

Irene E. Schoenberg has taught ESL for more than two decades at Hunter College's International English Language Institute and at Columbia University's American Language Program. Ms. Schoenberg holds a master's degree in TESOL from Columbia University. She has trained ESL and EFL teachers at Columbia University's Teachers College and at the New School University. She has given workshops and academic presentations at conferences, English language schools, and universities in Brazil, Chile, Dubai, El Salvador, Guatemala, Japan, Mexico, Nicaragua, Peru, Taiwan, Thailand, Vietnam, and throughout the United States.

Ms. Schoenberg is the author of *Talk about Trivia*; *Talk about Values*; *Speaking of Values 1: Conversation and Listening*; *Topics from A to Z*, Books 1 and 2; and *Focus on Grammar 2: An Integrated Skills Approach*. She is the co-author with Jay Maurer of the *True Colors* series and *Focus on Grammar 1: An Integrated Skills Approach*. She is one of the authors of *Future 1: English for Results* and *Future 3: English for Results*.

ACKNOWLEDGMENTS

I gratefully acknowledge the many reviewers for their suggestions and comments. There are many people at Pearson who have contributed to the development and production of this edition. I would like to thank them all, in particular:

- The people in production who helped carry the project through: **Rhea Banker** and especially **Robert Ruvo** for his indefatigable efforts.
- **Lise Minovitz**, the supervising editor, for her expert guidance and unflagging energy in keeping a very complex project on target.
- **Debbie Sistino**, the series director, who, in addition to managing the entire series, was always available to answer any of my questions.
- **Joanne Dresner** for her original vision and guidance of the *Focus on Grammar* series.
- My editors of the first three editions for helping to bring the books to fruition.
- **Ann France**, for her attractive new design, and **Aerin Csigay** and **Kim Steiner** for great photos that make the pages come alive.
- Above all, I'm most grateful to my editor **Kim Steiner**. Her dedication to the project, her brilliant solutions to problems, her creativity, her availability and her eye for detail, have made working on the revised edition a joy.
- Finally, I thank my family for their love and understanding: **Harris**, **Dan**, **Dahlia**, **Jonathan**, and **Olivia**.

REVIEWERS

We are grateful to the following reviewers for their many helpful comments:

Aida Aganagic, Seneca College, Toronto, Canada; **Aftab Ahmed**, American University of Sharjah, Sharjah, United Arab Emirates; **Todd Allen**, English Language Institute, Gainesville, FL; **Anthony Anderson**, University of Texas, Austin, TX; **Anna K. Andrade**, ASA Institute, New York, NY; **Bayda Asbridge**, Worcester State College, Worcester, MA; **Raquel Ashkenasi**, American Language Institute, La Jolla, CA; **James Bakker**, Mt. San Antonio College, Walnut, CA; **Kate Baldrige-Hale**, Harper College, Palatine, IL; **Leticia S. Banks**, ALCI-SDUSM, San Marcos, CA; **Aegina Barnes**, York College CUNY, Forest Hills, NY; **Sarah Barnhardt**, Community College of Baltimore County, Reisterstown, MD; **Kimberly Becker**, Nashville State Community College, Nashville, TN; **Holly Bell**, California State University, San Marcos, CA; **Anne Bliss**, University of Colorado, Boulder, CO; **Diana Booth**, Elgin Community College, Elgin, IL; **Barbara Boyer**, South Plainfield High School, South Plainfield, NJ; **Janna Brink**, Mt. San Antonio College, Walnut, CA; **AJ Brown**, Portland State University, Portland, OR; **Amanda Burgoyne**, Worcester State College, Worcester, MA; **Brenda Burlingame**, Independence High School, Charlotte, NC; **Sandra Byrd**, Shelby County High School and Kentucky State University, Shelbyville, KY; **Edward Carlstedt**, American University of Sharjah, Sharjah, United Arab Emirates; **Sean Cochran**, American Language Institute, Fullerton, CA; **Yanely Cordero**, Miami Dade College, Miami, FL; **Lin Cui**, William Rainey Harper College, Palatine, IL; **Sheila Detweiler**, College Lake County, Libertyville, IL; **Ann Duncan**, University of Texas, Austin, TX; **Debra Edell**, Merrill Middle School, Denver, CO; **Virginia Edwards**, Chandler-Gilbert Community College, Chandler, AZ; **Kenneth Fackler**, University of Tennessee, Martin, TN; **Jennifer Farnell**, American Language Program, Stamford, CT; **Allen P. Feiste**, Suwon University, Hwaseong, South Korea; **Mina Fowler**, Mt. San Antonio Community College, Rancho Cucamonga, CA; **Rosemary Franklin**, University of Cincinnati, Cincinnati, OH; **Christiane Galvani**, Texas Southern University, Sugar Land, TX; **Chester Gates**, Community College of Baltimore County, Baltimore, MD; **Luka Gavrilovic**, Quest Language Studies, Toronto, Canada; **Sally Gearhart**, Santa Rosa Community College, Santa Rosa, CA; **Shannon Gerrity**, James Lick Middle School, San Francisco, CA; **Jeanette Gerrity Gomez**, Prince George's Community College, Largo, MD; **Carlos Gonzalez**, Miami Dade College, Miami, FL; **Therese Gormley Hirmer**, University of Guelph, Guelph, Canada; **Sudeepa Gulati**, Long Beach City College, Long Beach, CA; **Anthony Halderman**, Cuesta College, San Luis Obispo, CA; **Ann A. Hall**, University of Texas, Austin, TX; **Cora Higgins**, Boston Academy of English, Boston, MA; **Michelle Hilton**, South Lane School District, Cottage Grove, OR; **Nicole Hines**, Troy University, Atlanta, GA; **Rosemary Hiruma**, American Language Institute, Long Beach, CA; **Harriet Hoffman**, University of Texas, Austin, TX; **Leah Holck**, Michigan State University, East Lansing, MI; **Christy Hunt**, English for Internationals, Roswell, GA; **Osmany Hurtado**, Miami Dade College, Miami, FL; **Isabel Innocenti**, Miami Dade College, Miami, FL; **Donna Janian**, Oxford Intensive School of English, Medford, MA; **Scott Jenison**, Antelope Valley College, Lancaster, CA; **Grace Kim**, Mt. San Antonio College, Diamond Bar, CA; **Brian King**, ELS Language Center, Chicago, IL; **Pam Kopitzke**, Modesto Junior College, Modesto, CA; **Elena Lattarulo**, American Language Institute, San Diego, CA; **Karen Lavaty**, Mt. San Antonio College, Glendora, CA; **JJ Lee-Gilbert**, Menlo-Atherton High School, Foster City, CA; **Ruth Luman**, Modesto Junior College, Modesto, CA; **Yvette Lyons**, Tarrant County College, Fort Worth, TX; **Janet Magnoni**, Diablo Valley College, Pleasant Hill, CA; **Meg Maher**, YWCA Princeton, Princeton, NJ; **Carmen Marquez-Rivera**, Curie Metropolitan High School, Chicago, IL; **Meredith Massey**, Prince George's Community College, Hyattsville, MD; **Linda Maynard**, Coastline Community College, Westminster, CA; **Eve Mazereeuw**, University of Guelph, Guelph, Canada; **Susanne McLaughlin**, Roosevelt University, Chicago, IL; **Madeline Medeiros**, Cuesta College, San Luis Obispo, CA; **Gioconda Melendez**, Miami Dade College, Miami, FL; **Marcia Menaker**, Passaic County Community College, Morris Plains, NJ; **Seabrook Mendoza**, Cal State San Marcos University, Wildomar, CA; **Anadalia Mendoza**, Felix Varela Senior High School, Miami, FL; **Charmaine Mergulhao**, Quest Language Studies, Toronto, Canada; **Dana Miho**, Mt. San Antonio College, San Jacinto, CA; **Sonia Nelson**, Centennial Middle School, Portland, OR; **Manuel Niebla**, Miami Dade College, Miami, FL; **Alice Nitta**, Leeward Community College, Pearl City, HI; **Gabriela Oliva**, Quest Language Studies, Toronto, Canada; **Sara Packer**, Portland State University, Portland, OR; **Lesley Painter**, New School, New York, NY; **Carlos Paz-Perez**, Miami Dade College, Miami, FL; **Ileana Perez**, Miami Dade College, Miami, FL; **Barbara Pogue**, Essex County College, Newark, NJ; **Phillips Potash**, University of Texas, Austin, TX; **Jada Pothina**, University of Texas, Austin, TX; **Ewa Pratt**, Des Moines Area Community College, Des Moines, IA; **Pedro Prentt**, Hudson County Community College, Jersey City, NJ; **Maida Purdy**, Miami Dade College, Miami, FL; **Dolores Quiles**, SUNY Ulster, Stone Ridge, NY; **Mark Rau**, American River College, Sacramento, CA; **Lynne Raxlen**, Seneca College, Toronto, Canada; **Lauren Rein**, English for Internationals, Sandy Springs, GA; **Diana Rivers**, NOCCCD, Cypress, CA; **Silvia Rodriguez**, Santa Ana College, Mission Viejo, CA; **Rolando Romero**, Miami Dade College, Miami, FL; **Pedro Rosabal**, Miami Dade College, Miami, FL; **Natalie Rublik**, University of Quebec, Chicoutimi, Quebec, Canada; **Matilde Sanchez**, Oxnard College, Oxnard, CA; **Therese Sarkis-Kruse**, Wilson Commencement, Rochester, NY; **Mike Sfiropoulos**, Palm Beach Community College, Boynton Beach, FL; **Amy Shearon**, Rice University, Houston, TX; **Sara Shore**, Modesto Junior College, Modesto, CA; **Patricia Silva**, Richard Daley College, Chicago, IL; **Stephanie Solomon**, Seattle Central Community College, Vashon, WA; **Roberta Steinberg**, Mount Ida College, Newton, MA; **Teresa Szymula**, Curie Metropolitan High School, Chicago, IL; **Hui-Lien Tang**, Jasper High School, Plano, TX; **Christine Tierney**, Houston Community College, Sugar Land, TX; **Ileana Torres**, Miami Dade College, Miami, FL; **Michelle Van Slyke**, Western Washington University, Bellingham, WA; **Melissa Villamil**, Houston Community College, Sugar Land, TX; **Elizabeth Wagenheim**, Prince George's Community College, Lago, MD; **Mark Wagner**, Worcester State College, Worcester, MA; **Angela Waigand**, American University of Sharjah, Sharjah, United Arab Emirates; **Merari Weber**, Metropolitan Skills Center, Los Angeles, CA; **Sonia Wei**, Seneca College, Toronto, Canada; and **Vicki Woodward**, Indiana University, Bloomington, IN.

SIMPLE PAST

UNIT 18 Simple Past: Affirmative and Negative Statements with Regular Verbs
TRAVEL

STEP 1 GRAMMAR IN CONTEXT

Before You Read

Discuss the question.

- In which countries are these tourist attractions? (See answers on page 202.)

Read

Read a message from Karen to Dahlia and Dahlia's answer. What city did Karen visit?
(See answer on page 202.)

WALL
FRIENDS
PHOTOS

Karen van der Broek

Hi Dahlia,

You were so right! This city is awesome.

Yesterday morning Julian and I **watched** foot-volley on Ipanema Beach. The players were great. Then in the afternoon we **visited** Sugarloaf. What a view! In the evening we **enjoyed** a delicious meal at a churrascuria (a barbecued meat restaurant).

Our flight here was the only bad part of the trip. It was bumpy, and we **didn't land** until 11:30 at night. But someone from the hotel **picked** us **up**, and we **arrived** at the hotel before 1:00 A.M. Everyone here is helpful, and our room is beautiful. The weather is great. I **didn't need** to pack my umbrella or my jacket.

Say hi to everyone at the office.

Love, Karen

Dahlia Gold

Hey Karen,

I'm glad *you're* having such a great time. It's freezing here. Yesterday it **snowed** all day, and last week it **rained**.

I **stayed** late Monday and Tuesday preparing for the spring conference. I **dined** on sandwiches from the vending machines downstairs. Then guess what happened? Mr. Grimes **canceled** the conference.

So enjoy every minute of your vacation.

—Miss you.

Love, Dahlia

WALL
FRIENDS
PHOTOS

After You Read

A | Practice *PAIRS: Now read the messages aloud. Take turns.*

B | Vocabulary *Complete the sentences with the words from the box.*

bumpy	canceled	freezing	landed	picked / up

1. Our flight was very _____. I felt sick during the flight.

2. Our airplane _____ on time. I was glad the flight was over.

3. Someone from the hotel _____ us _____.

4. It's _____ in this room. I need a sweater.

5. I ordered french fries and a shake but then I _____ my order because I

need to diet.

C | Comprehension *Make the false statements true.*

              watched

1. Karen and Julian ~~played~~ foot-volley on Ipanema Beach.

2. Karen and Julian enjoyed dessert at a café.

3. Karen and Julian's plane arrived in the afternoon.

4. The people at the hotel were unhelpful.

5. Mr. Grimes attended the spring conference.

THE SIMPLE PAST: STATEMENTS WITH REGULAR VERBS

Affirmative Statements		Negative Statements		
Subject	Base Form of Verb + -ed	Subject	*Did Not*	Base Form of Verb
I He She It We You* They	land**ed**. arrive**d**. cri**ed**.	I He She It We You* They	did not didn't	land. arrive. cry.

*You can be both singular and plural subjects.

Past Time Markers		
Yesterday	*Ago*	*Last*
yesterday **yesterday** morning **yesterday** afternoon **yesterday** evening	two days **ago** a week **ago** a month **ago** a year **ago** a couple of days **ago**	**last** night **last** Monday **last** week **last** summer **last** year

GRAMMAR NOTES

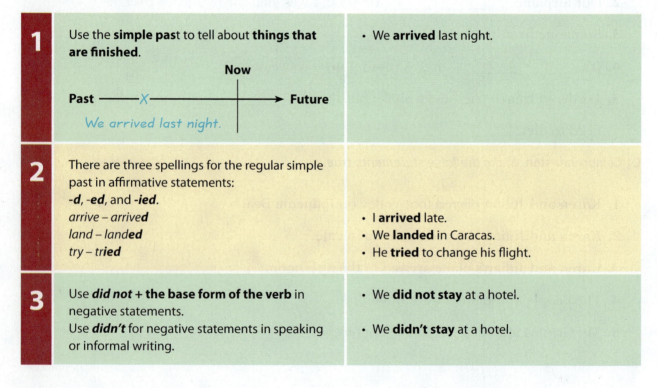

1	Use the **simple past** to tell about **things that are finished**.	• We **arrived** last night.

2	There are three spellings for the regular simple past in affirmative statements: -**d**, -**ed**, and -**ied**. *arrive – arrived* *land – landed* *try – tried*	• I **arrived** late. • We **landed** in Caracas. • He **tried** to change his flight.

3	Use *did not* + **the base form of the verb** in negative statements. Use *didn't* for negative statements in speaking or informal writing.	• We **did not stay** at a hotel. • We **didn't stay** at a hotel.

4	The **verb form** is the **same for all subject pronouns**.	• **I visited** Seoul. • **She visited** Mexico City. • **They visited** Madrid.
5	**Time markers** usually come at the beginning or end of a sentence.	• **Yesterday** I studied. • I studied **yesterday**.
	You can use **yesterday** alone. You can also use it before *morning*, *afternoon*, or *evening*.	• I visited my friends **yesterday**. • I visited my friends **yesterday evening**.
	Use **ago** after a length of time.	• I started this class a month **ago**.
	Use **last** before words like *night*, *week*, or *year*.	• I arrived here **last** month.

REFERENCE NOTE
For complete simple past spelling and pronunciation rules, see Appendix 10 on page A-10.

STEP 3 FOCUSED PRACTICE

EXERCISE 1: Discover the Grammar

A | *Underline the simple past affirmative verbs. Circle the simple past negative verb. Then write the base form of the verb next to each sentence.*

Base Form

1. We arrived in Washington, D.C., last Friday.   *arrive*

2. Yesterday afternoon we walked around the National Zoo.   _____

3. Some friends invited us for dinner last night.   _____

4. Ana baked a cheesecake yesterday morning.   _____

5. The cheesecake didn't look good, but it tasted delicious.   _____, _____

6. Miguel cooked enchiladas.   _____

7. The enchiladas looked delicious, but they didn't taste good.   _____, _____

8. We visited Dupont Circle with Ana and Miguel.   _____

9. An hour ago I called and thanked them for a wonderful evening.   _____, _____

B | *Write the five time markers in Part A.*

_____, _____, _____,

_____, _____

Simple Past: Affirmative and Negative Statements with Regular Verbs   **201**

EXERCISE 2: Affirmative Statements

(Grammar Notes 1, 2, 4)

Complete the sentences with the verbs from the box. Use the simple past form.

~~borrow~~	cook	land	walk
cancel	hug	visit	watch

1. We _____borrowed_____ a guidebook from our friends.

2. His plane _____ on time.

3. Yesterday she _____ the art museum.

4. He _____ a meal for us. It was terrific.

5. I'm tired. I _____ up a lot of hills in San Francisco this morning.

6. The airlines _____ many flights because of bad weather.

7. Two nights ago they _____ a movie.

8. Everyone _____ and kissed us when we left.

EXERCISE 3: Negative Statements

(Grammar Notes 3–4)

Underline the verb in the first sentence. Then complete the second sentence with the negative simple past form of the verb.

1. He <u>stayed</u> with friends. He _____didn't stay_____ at a hotel.

2. I wanted coffee. I _____ tea.

3. It rained in the morning. It _____ in the afternoon.

4. She only invited you. She _____ your whole family.

5. He helped you. He _____ me.

6. I watched a movie. I _____ the news.

7. He picked her up from the airport. He _____ her

   _____ from the train station.

EXERCISE 4: Affirmative and Negative Statements
(Grammar Notes 2–3)

Complete Camila's travel notes with the verbs in parentheses. Use the simple past.

Carlos and I _____arrived_____ in San
       1. (arrive)

Francisco last Wednesday night at 9:00. The

next day it _____, but the weather
       2. (rain)

_____ us from sightseeing.
  3. (stop / not)

We _____ our umbrellas and
     4. (carry)

_____ at Fisherman's Wharf. Then the
  5. (shop)

rain _____, so we _____
    6. (stop)   **7. (climb)**

Telegraph Hill. We _____ around there a bit, and then we _____ a
        8. (walk)   **9. (board)**

bus to Baker Beach. We _____ the sun set next to the Golden Gate Bridge, and
        10. (watch)

we _____ to the ocean waves. I was so tired. I _____ to stay out. I
   11. (listen)   **12. (want / not)**

_____ to go back to our hotel. On the way home we _____ to eat,
 13. (want)   **14. (need)**

though. Chinatown was the perfect spot. We _____ a "bird's nest" and red bean
        15. (order)

soup. It was delicious. Everything in San Francisco was amazing.

EXERCISE 5: Past Time Markers
(Grammar Note 5)

Complete the conversations. Use **last** *or* **ago**, *or* **yesterday.**

1. **BEN:** Were you away?

   SAM: Yes, I was in Mexico City _____last_____ week.
         a.

   BEN: Oh. I was there a couple of months _____. By the way, Ian called
              b.

   me _____ night. He wants us to meet for lunch.
      c.

2. **STEVE:** Where is Demetrios? I never see him anymore!

   ALLY: I know. He's always traveling. He was in Montreal _____
                a.

   weekend. He was in Prague _____ month. And two months
         b.

   _____ he visited his family in Greece.
    c.

   STEVE: Where is he now?

   ALLY: I'm not sure. I called him _____ but he didn't answer.
           d.

EXERCISE 6: Simple Past and Simple Present Statements

(Grammar Notes 1–6)

Complete the conversations with the words in parentheses. Use the simple past or simple present.

1. **A:** When do you usually travel?

   B: We usually _____*travel*_____ in the summer, but last year we _____

   (travel)   *(travel)*

   in the fall.

2. **A:** Does John like guided tours?

   B: No. He _____ most guided tours, but he _____ the one

         (like / not)   *(like)*

   yesterday in Chicago.

3. **A:** When does that restaurant open?

   B: It usually _____ at 7:00 A.M., but it _____ until 7:30

           (open)   *(open / not)*

   today.

4. **A:** Do you travel on business a lot?

   B: No, I don't. I usually _____ on business, but last month I

                     (travel / not)

   _____ twice on business.

   (travel)

5. **A:** When do you start work?

   B: I usually _____ at 9:00, but I _____ at 8:00 this morning

           (start)   *(start)*

   because I was very busy.

6. **A:** Does Jade always take the bus?

   B: She usually _____ a bus or train, but this week she

               (take)

   _____ public transportation. She _____ a car.

   (use / not)   *(rent)*

7. **A:** Where do you have lunch?

   B: I usually _____ something from home, but last Friday was a

           (bring)

   co-worker's birthday, so five of us _____ in a Thai restaurant.

                                       (eat)

EXERCISE 7: Editing

Correct the postcard. There are six mistakes. The first mistake is already corrected. Find and correct five more.

Dear Ilene,

Paris is unbelievable at night! It's 10 P.M., and I'm
writing to you from a café. We arrived here ~~ago two days~~. *two days ago*
Paul's friend Pierre picks^ed us up. We toured the city during
the day, and at night we did walked along the Seine
River. Today we dining in Montmartre, and we visited the
Louvre Museum. I not like the food in Montmartre, but
I did loved the area.

We hope all is well with you. Don't work too hard.

Love,

Michelle and Paul

To:
Ilene Carson
85 Maple Street
Plymouth, DE 19905
USA

STEP 4 COMMUNICATION PRACTICE

EXERCISE 8: Listening

A | *Listen to the conversation. Write **T** (**True**) or **F** (**False**) for each statement. Then correct the false statements.*

  Japan
__F__ **1.** Marta visited ~~Mexico~~.

____ **2.** Marta stayed with friends.

____ **3.** Marta stayed at a traditional Japanese inn.

____ **4.** Marta rented a car.

____ **5.** Marta didn't enjoy her trip.

ryokan

B | *Listen again. Write the amount of time.*

1. Marta was in Japan: _____

2. Marta stayed in a ryokan: _____

3. Marta visited Kyoto: _____

4. Marta and her friend talked about Marta's trip: _____

EXERCISE 9: Pronunciation

 A | *Read and listen to the Pronunciation Note.*

> **Pronunciation Note**
>
> Regular simple past verbs end in three sounds: / **d** /, / **t** /, or / **ɪd** /.
>
> **EXAMPLES:** He arriv<u>ed</u> late. / **d** /
> They work<u>ed</u> at a hotel. / **t** /
> We wait<u>ed</u> a long time. / **ɪd** /

 B | *Listen to the sentences. Check (✓) the final sound of each verb.*

Last weekend, . . .	/ t /	/ d /	/ ɪd /
1. I watched TV.	✓		
2. I rented a movie.			
3. I listened to music.			
4. I played a sport.			
5. I visited friends.			
6. I worked.			

C | *PAIRS: Ask your partner what he or she did last weekend. Then tell your partner what you did. Use the verbs in Part B or other regular simple past verbs.*

> **EXAMPLE:** **A:** What did you do last weekend, Zofiya?
> **B:** I listened to music at a concert in the park.

EXERCISE 10: Game: Truths and Lies

A | *On a separate piece of paper, write five things you did on your last trip. Four of them are true, and one is a lie. Use five verbs from the unit. Use the past tense.*

> **EXAMPLE:** On my last trip, . . .
>
> 1. I toured Seattle.
> 2. I rented a car.
> 3. I stayed with friends.
> 4. I visited the Space Needle.
> 5. It rained every day.

B | *GROUPS: Take turns reading your sentences. Guess which one is not true.*

> **EXAMPLE:** **A:** On my last trip, I toured Seattle. I rented a car. I stayed with friends. I visited the Space Needle. It rained every day.
> **B:** I think "I rented a car" is not true. You don't drive!

EXERCISE 11: Writing

A | *Write about a city you would like to visit. Imagine you traveled to that city last summer. Write a postcard to a classmate about the trip. Use the words from the box, the simple past, and at least two time markers.*

arrive	like	shop	travel	walk
enjoy	rent	stay	visit	watch

EXAMPLE:

Hola Jack,

Guadalajara is amazing. I landed here four days ago. I stayed at a hotel the first night. Then Hugo invited me to stay with his family.

Yesterday morning we visited the palace and rented a horse-drawn carriage. In the afternoon I shopped for ceramics. Now I can't buy anything else unless I buy another suitcase.

See you soon.

Emily

To:
Jack Spence
10 Arbor Lane
Alexandria, VA
22315

Guadalajara

B | *Check your work. Use the Editing Checklist.*

Editing Checklist

Did you . . . ?
☐ use the simple past with regular verbs correctly
☐ check your spelling

A | Circle the correct words to complete the sentences.

1. I **watch / watched** TV last night.

2. We **did visit / visited** Chile last summer.

3. He picked her up from work **an hour ago / last hour**.

4. **Last night / A night ago** I stayed home.

5. Our plane **didn't land / no landed** on time.

B | Complete the sentences with the verbs in parentheses. Use the simple past.

1. I'm helping them now. I _____ helped _____ them last week too.
   (help)

2. She's staying with me. Last year I _____ stayed _____ with her.
   (stay)

3. It snowed during the night, but it _____ did not snow _____ in the morning.
   (snow / not)

4. She only asked you. She _____ did not ask _____ him.
   (ask / not)

5. We wanted to fly first class. We _____ didn't want _____ to fly coach.
   (want / not)

C | Complete the sentences with the verbs from the box. Use the simple past affirmative or negative.

cancel	enjoy	play	rain	stay

1. My boss _____ canceled _____ the conference. He's trying to save money.

2. She _____ didn't stay _____ late at work. She needed to get home to her children.

3. I didn't need my umbrella. It _____ didn't rain _____.

4. We _____ played _____ soccer for three hours. It was a lot of fun.

5. He _____ didn't enjoyed _____ the movie. It was very boring.

D | Read the paragraph. Find the five mistakes.

Hello from London. Our friends did invited us here for a week. We're having a great time. Yesterday we visit Big Ben, and we tour the Royal Palace. This morning we watch the Changing of the Guard. We wanted to shop this afternoon, but we didn't. The prices were high, but we are enjoyed looking at the store windows.

Simple Past: Affirmative and Negative Statements with Irregular Verbs

You Never Know

Before You Read

Some people say, "In life, you never know what will happen." What does that mean?

a. Life never changes.　　　　**b.** Life has surprises.

Read

Read this Chinese folktale.

You Never Know What Will Happen

A long time ago there lived a poor Chinese peasant.[1] One day a beautiful horse appeared on his farm. When the peasant's friends **saw** the horse they **said**, "How lucky you are!"

The peasant answered, "You never know what will happen."

Two days later the horse **ran** away. The peasant's friends **came** and **said**, "What a terrible thing. How unlucky you are! The fine horse **ran** away." The peasant **didn't get** excited. He simply **said**, "You never know what will happen."

Exactly one week later the horse returned. And it **brought** three other horses. When the peasant's friends **saw** the horses they **said**, "Oh. You are so lucky. Now you have four horses to help you." The peasant looked at them and once again **said**, "You never know what will happen."

The next morning the peasant's oldest son **was** in the field.[2] Suddenly one of the horses **ran** into him, and the boy **fell** to the ground. He **was** badly hurt. He **lost** the use of his leg. Indeed, this **was** terrible, and many people **came** to the peasant and expressed their sadness for his son's misfortune. But again the peasant simply **said**, "You never know what will happen."

[1] *peasant:* person who works on a farm
[2] *field:* large grassy area

A month after the accident, soldiers **rode** into the village. They shouted, "There is a problem along the border! We are taking every healthy young man to fight." The soldiers **took** all the other young men, but they **didn't take** the peasant's son. All the other young men **fought** in the border war, and they all died. But the peasant's son lived a long and happy life. As his father **said**, you never know what will happen.

After You Read

A | Practice *PAIRS: Read the folktale again aloud. Take turns reading paragraphs.*

B | Vocabulary *Complete the sentences with the words from the box.*

appeared	border	lucky	shouted	suddenly	terrible

1. I didn't like the story because it had a(n) ___terrible___ ending.

2. He showed his passport to cross the ___border___ into Mexico.

3. We didn't expect the rain. The weather changed ___suddenly___.

4. It's a folktale about a(n) ___luck___ man. Good things always happen to him.

5. He ___shouted___, but nobody heard him.

6. A beautiful red bird ___appeared___ on my window sill.

C | Comprehension *Number the events in the order they occurred (1 to 6).*

___2___ A week later the horse came back with three other horses.

___1___ A horse appeared on a peasant's land. Two days later it ran away.

___3___ The next morning one of the horses ran into the peasant's son; he was hurt.

___4___ A month later soldiers rode into the village.

___6___ The other young men died. The peasant's son lived a long, happy life.

___5___ The soldiers took all the healthy young men to fight, but they didn't take the peasant's son.

SIMPLE PAST: IRREGULAR VERBS—AFFIRMATIVE AND NEGATIVE STATEMENTS

Affirmative Statements		
Subject	Verb	
I You He We	**bought rode saw**	the horses.

Negative Statements			
Subject	*Did Not / Didn't*	Base Form of Verb	
I You He We	**did not didn't**	**buy ride see**	the horses.

Be: Affirmative Statements		
Subject	*Was / Were*	
She	**was**	lucky.
They	**were**	unlucky.

Be: Negative Statements		
Subject	*Was / Were not*	
I	**was not**	home.
We	**were not**	nearby.

Contractions	
was not → **wasn't**	
were not → **weren't**	

GRAMMAR NOTES

1 Many common verbs are irregular. **Irregular past verbs** do not add *-ed*. They often look different from the base form.

- We **saw** a beautiful horse. (**see**)
- They **went** to work. (**go**)
- She **came** late. (**come**)
- He **brought** a friend to school. (**bring**)
- He **ate** a big lunch. (**eat**)

2 For **negative statements** in the past, use *did not* + **base form of the verb** (except for *be*). Use the short form *didn't* for speaking and informal writing.

BE CAREFUL! Do not use the simple past form after *didn't*.

- They **did not see** him.
- She **did not eat** lunch.
- They **didn't** see him.

Nот: They didn't ~~saw~~ him.
They didn't ~~ate~~ lunch.

3 The **past tense of be** is *was* or *were*. The **negative** is *was not* or *were not*. Use *wasn't* and *weren't* for speaking and informal writing.

- I **was** at the library last night.
- They **were not** home this morning.
- It **wasn't** late.
- They **weren't** in Mexico City.

4 We use *was* or *were* + *born* to tell when or where people were born.

- I **was born** in Nicaragua.
- She **was born** in 1989.

REFERENCE NOTES
See Appendix 11, page A-11 for a list of irregular past forms.
See Unit 18, pages 200–201, and Unit 20, pages 222–223 for more about the simple past.

EXERCISE 1: Discover the Grammar

Circle the verbs in the past. Then write the verbs and the base form of each verb in the chart.

I have two brothers. My older brother (was) a great student. He (brought) home prizes and (won) awards. My younger brother (felt) bored by school. He never (did) well. My parents (worried) about him. Then in his second year of high school, he had a great chemistry teacher. He (became) interested in chemistry. He (began) to study hard. He's now a chemistry professor at a university. So, you never know what will happen.

Past	Base Form
was	be
brought	bring
felt	feel
worried	worry
had	have
became	become
began	begin
did	do
won	win

EXERCISE 2: Simple Past: Irregular Verbs

(Grammar Notes 1–3)

Complete the paragraph with the words in parentheses. Use the simple past.

Abe _____was_____ nine when his mother died in 1818. His family
_____1. (be)_____

_____had_____ very little money and lived in a log cabin with one room. Still,
_____2. (have)_____

Abe _____went_____ to school. He _____grew_____ strong and very tall. He
_____3. (go)_____ _____4. (grow)_____

_____split_____ wood for money, then he _____taught_____ himself the law and
_____5. (split)_____ _____6. (teach)_____

_____began_____ a law firm. For a short time, he _____was_____ a soldier, but he
_____7. (begin)_____ _____8. (be)_____

___didn't see___ any action. He _____came_____ home, _____gave_____ speeches,
_____9. (see / not)_____ _____10. (come)_____ _____11. (give)_____

and _____ran_____ for political office. People ___made fun___ of him because he
_____12. (run)_____ _____13. (make fun)_____

was so tall, but he ___did let___ it bother him. He _____became_____ president of
_____14. (let / not)_____ _____15. (become)_____

the United States and _____led_____ the country during a difficult civil war. His army
_____16. (lead)_____

_____won_____ the war. He _____became_____ one of the most admired American
_____17. (win)_____ _____18. (become)_____

presidents in history. His name, as you guessed, _____was_____ Abraham Lincoln.
_____19. (be)_____

EXERCISE 3: Simple Past: Irregular Verbs

(Grammar Notes 1–4)

Complete the paragraphs with the words in parentheses. Use the simple past.

James Earl Jones _____*was born*_____ in Mississippi in 1931. At five his family moved

1. (be born)

to Michigan. Soon after that, he _____began_____ to stutter. For many years he

2. (begin)

_____did say_____ more than a few words. In high school a teacher tried to help him. After

3. (say / not)

Jones _____wrote_____ a poem, this teacher _____made_____ him read it aloud. Jones

4. (write) · **5. (make)**

_____knew_____ the poem by heart, and he _____said_____ it without stuttering. It

6. (know) · **7. (say)**

_____was_____ his first success at public speaking. Later, Jones _____got_____ a

8. (be) · **9. (get)**

scholarship to the University of Michigan. At first, he

studied medicine, but then he changed to theater.

After college, he _____went_____ to New York. He

10. (go)

_____didn't has_____ money, and he _____did_____

11. (have / not) · **12. (do)**

all sorts of jobs to pay his bills. After a few years, people

_____saw_____ his talent. He _____became_____ a

13. (see) · **14. (become)**

famous and admired

actor. Maybe you

know his deep,

powerful voice. It

is the voice of Darth Vader in the *Star Wars* movies and

Mufasa in *The Lion King*.

In 2009 Jones _____won_____ a Lifetime

15. (win)

Achievement Award of the Screen Actors Guild. Jones's

life is amazing when you think that as a child, speaking

_____was_____ his biggest challenge. So in life you

16. (be)

never know what will happen.

EXERCISE 4: Simple Past: Irregular Verbs

(Grammar Notes 1–4)

Complete each paragraph with the words from the box. Use the simple past.

~~be born~~	become	begin	be / not	read

Joanne Kathleen _____*was born*_____ in 1965 in England. She _____*began*_____ writing
                                    1.   **2.**
at the age of five, and she always _____*read*_____ a lot. She majored in French at the
                                              3.
university and _____*became*_____ a bilingual secretary. But she _____*wasn't*_____ very
                              4.   **5.**
good at it.

begin	go	have	teach

At 26, she _____*went*_____ to Portugal. She _____*taught*_____ English there. At this
                        6.   **7.**
time she first _____*began*_____ working on a story about a boy with special powers named
                          8.
Harry. She met a journalist in Portugal. They married and _____*had*_____ a daughter in
                                                                              9.
1993. Unfortunately, the marriage ended in divorce.

be	give	have / not	sell	want / not	write

She moved to Scotland to be near a sister and finish

her book. In Scotland life _____*w*_____ hard
                                      10.

because she _____*didn't have*_____ much money. She tried
                        11.

to sell her book, but the publishers _____*did want*_____
                                                  12.

it. She finally _____*sold*_____ her book for about
                        13.

$4,000. Several months later, an American company

_____*gave*_____ her money to write full time. Soon
        14.

her book became a bestseller. She _____*wrote*_____
                                              15.

several more Harry Potter books. Today, J. K. Rowling is

rich and famous. So you never know what will happen.

Actor Daniel Radcliffe, star of *Harry Potter*

EXERCISE 5: Editing

Correct the sentences. There are nine mistakes. The first mistake is already corrected.
Find and correct eight more.

>   *was*
> My grandfather ^ born in Peru. He had an older brother and sister. Their dad
>
>   *didn't have*
> (my great-grandfather) were a dreamer. The family have ~~not~~ much money.
>
> When my grandfather was 13, his mother did ~~did~~ died and his dad remarried.
>
>   *didn't*   *d*
> My grandfather ~~no~~ like his stepmother so he move in with his sister and her
>
>   *left*   *began*
> husband. All three ~~leave~~ for America. They did ~~begin~~ a small business. They
>
>   *grew*
> worked hard, and the business ~~grow~~. Today my sister and I direct the
>
> company.

EXERCISE 6: Listening

A | *Listen to Paul's story. Answer the question. Circle the correct letter.*

The story is about _____.

    a. a father and son   **b.** a man and his grandfather

B | *Listen again and complete the sentences.*

1. Paul's grandfather gave him a(n) _____*blanket*_____.

2. After a couple of years it _____ _____ good.

3. Paul's mother made it into a(n) _____ _____.

4. Then the _____ _____ tore.

5. His mother made it into a(n) _____ _____.

6. Paul _____ the _____.

7. He felt _____.

8. His friends said, "_____ _____ _____."

9. Paul didn't _____ about it. He _____ about it instead.

10. Many years later Paul's _____ found the story.

Simple Past: Affirmative and Negative Statements with Irregular Verbs   **215**

EXERCISE 7: Pronunciation

A | *Read and listen to the Pronunciation Note.*

> **Pronunciation Note**
>
> The / æ / sound, as in **have**, is slightly more open than the / ɛ / sound, as in **bed**.
>
> To pronounce the / ɛ / sound, keep your mouth open and your lips spread. Keep your tongue low in your mouth. Touch the lower front teeth lightly with the tip of your tongue.

B | *Listen to the / æ / sound in the underlined words. Then repeat the sentences.*

1. The story <u>happened</u> in China.
2. A Chinese peasant's horse <u>ran</u> away.
3. It came <u>back</u> with three more horses.
4. The son lived a <u>happy</u> life.
5. The peasant <u>laughed</u> and said, "You never know what will <u>happen</u>."

C | *Listen. Check (✓) if the underlined word has the / æ / sound or the / ɛ / sound.*

	/ æ /	/ ɛ /
1. They <u>had</u> a hard life.	✓	☐
2. The boy's <u>head</u> hurt from his fall.	☐	☐
3. He told us the <u>end</u> of the story.	☐	☐
4. We liked the story <u>and</u> the movie.	☐	☐
5. The <u>man</u> was lucky.	☐	☐
6. The <u>men</u> fought on the border.	☐	☐

EXERCISE 8: A Memory Game

GROUPS: Sit in a circle. Take notes. The first student tells one thing he or she did last weekend. The next student tells what the first one did and then what he or she did. Continue until every student speaks.

EXAMPLE: ANN: I went to the movies.

JOE: Ann went to the movies, and I read a book.

EXERCISE 9: Discussion

SMALL GROUPS: Tell about a wonderful day and a terrible day. Use **First, Then,** *and*
After that.

EXAMPLE: I had a wonderful day. First, I saw my grandmother. Then, I went to the park. After that, I rented a video.
Yesterday I had a terrible day. First, I got up late. Then, I broke my glasses. After that, I lost my keys.

EXERCISE 10: Writing

A | *Write your autobiography. The year is now 2066. Think about these questions as you write.*

- Where and when were you born?
- Where did you go to school?
- What did you do in your free time?
- What did you become? (businessperson, etc.) Why?
- Where did you live?
- Did you marry? Did you have children?
- Did you travel?
- Did you become rich or famous?
- Did you make a difference in the world?
- Were you happy?

EXAMPLE: Right now I'm celebrating my eightieth birthday with my four children, their children, and their children's children. I am a lucky man. I was born in 1980 in Korea. My family didn't have much money, but we were hardworking. I was the fourth of five children. My parents were . . .

B | *Check your work. Use the Editing Checklist.*

Editing Checklist

Did you . . . ?
☐ use the simple past of irregular and regular verbs correctly
☐ check your spelling

A | Complete the sentences with the verbs in parentheses. Use the simple past.

1. One day a fox _____saw_____ some delicious grapes.
   (see)

2. He _____was_____ hungry, and he _____wanted_____ the grapes.
   (be)   (want)

3. He _____tried_____ to reach the grapes, but they were too high.
   (try)

4. He _____got_____ angry and said, "I really _____didn't want_____ them anyway."
   (get)   (want / not)

B | Complete the paragraph with the verbs from the box. Use the simple past.

| become | find | keep | steal | use / not |

A lucky man _____lfound_____ a pot of gold. He _____kept_____ the pot of gold in

a hole in the ground of his garden. A jealous worker _____stolen_____ the gold from

the man. The man _____became_____ upset. But a neighbor laughed because the man

_____didn't use_____ the gold. He just enjoyed counting it.

C | Complete the sentences with the verbs in parentheses. Use the affirmative or negative form.

1. The concert was terrible. I _____didn't stay_____ until the end.
   (stay)

2. He _____lost_____ his keys. He needs to get a new set of keys.
   (lose)

3. We _____ran_____ 5 miles yesterday. We're practicing for a big race.
   (run)

4. We _____saw_____ him in school. Was he sick?
   (see)

5. It _____took_____ him a long time to get to school. I wonder why?
   (take)

D | Correct the sentences. There are four mistakes.

1. William Sidney Porter ~~was~~ born in North Carolina in 1862.

2. He was a famous American short story writer. He wrote under different names, but he did became best known as O. Henry.

3. His stories were had surprise endings.

4. O. Henry had many talents, but he did get into trouble and spent time in prison.
   got

Simple Past: *Yes/No* and *Wh-* Questions
INTERVIEWS

STEP 1 GRAMMAR IN CONTEXT

Before You Read

PAIRS: Read these lines by the greatest writer in the English language. Who wrote these famous lines? In what play did he write them?

- "Romeo, Romeo! Wherefore art thou Romeo?"
- "Parting is such sweet sorrow."

William Shakespeare wrote these words in the play *Romeo and Juliet*. Altogether Shakespeare wrote between 37 and 38 plays and many poems.

Leonardo DiCaprio starred in the 1996 movie version of *Romeo and Juliet*

Read

Read a radio talk show interview between English professor Robert Gibbons and Carla Jonas.

CARLA: Thank you for coming today Professor Gibbons. I see your new book ***Who Wrote the Greatest Plays of All?*** is out. It's about Shakespeare, right?

PROFESSOR GIBBONS: Yes, it is. It's about Shakespeare and the time period he lived in.

CARLA: So, **why did you write the book?**

PROF: I wanted to explore some questions we have about Shakespeare and his life. Shakespeare probably wrote all the plays and poems that we say he did, but we don't know for sure. You see, Shakespeare's life is a mystery. There are many things we don't know about him. And the questions are interesting.

(continued on next page)

Carla: Well, what can you tell us about him? **When was Shakespeare born?**

Prof: He was born in 1564 in Stratford-on-Avon, but we don't know the exact date.

Juliet's castle, Castle Vecchio

Carla: What about his family?

Prof: His father was a landowner and a town leader. His mother was the daughter of a wealthy landowner. But his father was illiterate.[1]

Carla: **Did Shakespeare go to school?**

Prof: Yes, but we don't know too much about Shakespeare's education because there is no paper trail.[2] We think he went to grammar school.[3] But he did not attend a university. He probably studied Latin and Greek. But . . . **was his education good enough? How did Shakespeare learn to write so well? Did he really write the plays himself**, or **did someone else write them for him?**

Carla: What do you mean?

Prof: At that time, many people wrote under a different name, a pen name. Some people think that Shakespeare's friend, Ben Jonson, wrote the plays.

Carla: That's interesting. I have a question about Shakespeare. He wrote many plays about English kings and queens. **How did he know so much about the life of royalty?**[4] He wasn't in that class.[5]

Prof: That's a good question. We think he read about them. We're pretty sure the story of *Macbeth* and parts of *King Lear* came from a book by Raphael Holinshed. That book tells all about English, Scottish, and Irish kings. Still . . . we don't know, **was Shakespeare the writer?** And could one person write so many great works? Most scholars[6] believe Shakespeare was the author. We think he was a man of great genius and imagination . . . but perhaps it was someone else. We may never know for certain.

Carla: Such interesting points! I'm looking forward to reading your book, Professor. For those of you who like a good mystery, buy Professor Mark Gibbons's new book, *Who Wrote the Greatest Plays of All?* And Professor, thank you for coming here today.

Prof: And thank you, Carla, for inviting me.

---

[1] *illiterate:* not able to read or write
[2] *paper trail:* a written record
[3] *grammar school:* basic English schooling for boys in the 1500s
[4] *royalty:* a king, queen, and their family
[5] *class:* a group of people classified by income and education
[6] *scholar:* someone who studies a subject deeply

After You Read

A | Practice *PAIRS: Now read the interview aloud.*

B | Vocabulary *Complete the sentences with the words from the box.*

author	be out	mystery	play	poem

1. Shakespeare wrote the _____ *Romeo and Juliet* between the years 1591

   and 1595.

2. Shakespeare is the _____ of between 37 and 38 plays.

3. Nobody knows Shakespeare's exact birthday. It's a(n) _____.

4. The words in that _____ are beautiful, but they don't rhyme.

5. When will that new book about *Romeo and Juliet* _____?

   I'd like to read it.

C | Comprehension *Read the questions. Circle the correct letter.*

1. Where was Shakespeare born?
   a. London   **b.** Stratford-on-Avon

2. When was he born?
   a. 1654   **b.** 1564

3. Did his parents come from poor families?
   a. Yes, they did.   **b.** No, they didn't.

4. Did Shakespeare attend a university?
   a. Yes, he did.   **b.** No, he didn't.

5. What was *Macbeth* the name of?
   a. a play by Shakespeare   **b.** a town in England

6. Do most scholars believe that Shakespeare wrote all of his plays?
   a. Yes, they do.   **b.** No, they don't.

Stratford-on-Avon

THE SIMPLE PAST: *YES / NO* AND *WH-* QUESTIONS AND ANSWERS

Yes / No Questions

Did	Subject	Base Form of Verb
Did	I you he she it we they	help?

Short Answers

Affirmative			Negative		
Yes,	you I he she it you they	did.	No,	you I he she it you they	didn't.

Wh- Questions

Wh- Word	*Did*	Subject	Base Form of Verb
What		I	ask?
Where		you	go?
When	did	he	write?
Why		we	leave?
Who		you	call?
How long		they	stay?

Answers

You asked about his name.
I went to the library. (To the library.)
He wrote at night, after work. (At night, after work.)
We went someplace else.
We called the doctor. (The doctor.)
They stayed for an hour. (For an hour.) (An hour.)

Wh- Questions about the Subject

Wh- Word	Past Form of Verb	
Who	wrote	*Romeo and Juliet?*
What	happened	in the play?

Answers

William Shakespeare did.
Romeo and Juliet fell in love.

GRAMMAR NOTES

1 *Yes / No* questions in the simple past have the same form (*Did* + subject + base form) for regular and irregular verbs.

The verb *be* is the one exception.

REGULAR VERB
- **Did** you **call** your classmate?

IRREGULAR VERB
- **Did** you **write** your report?
- **Was** Shakespeare an actor?

2 Most *wh-* questions in the past begin with the **question word** followed by *did* + **the subject** + **the base form** of the verb.

- **What did** he **write**?
- **Why did** he **write**?
- **Where did** he **write**?
- **Who did** he **work** for?

3	*Wh-* questions in the past **do not use** *did* when the **question is about the subject.**	**SUBJECT** • Shakespeare wrote *Romeo and Juliet.* **Q: Who wrote** *Romeo and Juliet?* **A:** William Shakespeare. Not: **Q:** Who ~~did write~~ *Romeo and Juliet?*
4	We usually give **short answers** to *yes / no* and *wh-* questions, but we can also give **long answers**. **NOTE:** *Yes / No* **questions** use **rising** intonation. *Wh-* **questions** use **falling** intonation.	**Q:** Did you work yesterday? **A:** Yes. or Yes, I did. or Yes, I worked yesterday. • Did you hear the story? • What did you think about it?

STEP 3 FOCUSED PRACTICE

EXERCISE 1: Discover the Grammar

A | *Underline all the base form verbs.*

1. Did you watch a Shakespeare play last summer?

2. What did you see?

3. Did anyone go with you?

4. Did you understand it?

5. Did you enjoy it?

6. Did you read the whole play?

B | *Match the questions with the responses from the box. Write the responses.*

> **a. I read *Hamlet*.** ［hæmlət］ 书柄 →small than village
> **b. William Shakespeare.**
> **c. Yes, I saw it three times.**
> **d. No, I didn't. I got it at the library.**

1. **A:** What did you read for English class?

   B: _a_____

2. **A:** Who wrote it?

   B: _b_____

3. **A:** Did you buy the book?

   B: _d_____

4. **A:** Did you see the movie?

   B: _c_____

EXERCISE 2: Simple Past: *Yes / No* Questions

(Grammar Note 1)

Write **yes / no** questions in the simple past. Use the verb from the first sentence.

1. I read all his plays. _____*Did*_____ you _____*read*_____ them too?

2. We enjoyed the movie. _____*Y*_____ you _____*enjoy*_____ it too?

3. The movie had good acting. _____*Y*_____ it _____*have*_____ a good story?

4. I didn't understand everything. _____*Y*_____ she _____*understand*_____ everything?

5. We didn't like the ending. _____*"*_____ he _____*like*_____ the ending?

6. I expected a happy ending. _____*"*_____ you _____*expect*_____ a happy ending?

7. We saw a review online. _____*Did*_____ they _____*see*_____ the review online?

EXERCISE 3: Simple Past: Short Answers

(Grammar Note 4)

Complete the conversations with the simple past. Write affirmative or negative short answers.

1. **A:** Did you finish your homework?

   B: _____*Yes, I did.*_____ I finished it before dinner.

2. **A:** Did they go to the movies?

   B: _____*No, they didn't*_____. They stayed home and watched TV.

3. **A:** Did I call too late?

   B: _____*No, I didn't*_____. I'm usually up at this hour.

4. **A:** Did we get any mail?

   B: _____*Yes, we did*_____. We got our tickets for *King Lear*.

5. **A:** Did the package arrive?

   B: _____*Yes, it did*_____. It just came.

6. **A:** Did you buy the DVD?

   B: _____*No, I didn't*_____. I plan to buy it next weekend.

7. **A:** Did she lose her phone?

   B: _____*Yes, she did*_____. She thinks she left it on the bus.

EXERCISE 4: Simple Past Questions

(Grammar Notes 1–3)

Sherryl Woods is a best-selling romance and mystery writer. She <u>has written more than 100 books that are available in over 20 countries</u>. Read the interview. Complete the questions with the words in parentheses. Use the simple past.

I = INTERVIEWER

SW = SHERRYL WOODS

(speech bubble: When will David ask me to marry him? Only Sherryl Woods knows!)

I: _____<u>When did you write</u>_____ your first
<u>1. (When / you / write)</u>
book?

SW: In 1980. It came out in 1982.

I: _____<u>Did you always want</u>_____ to be a
<u>2. (you / always / want)</u>
writer?

SW: No, I didn't. For many years I wanted to be a

graphic artist.

I: _____<u>Were you</u>_____ always good
<u>3. (be / you)</u>
at writing?

SW: Well, my first-grade teacher wrote, "Sherryl is good at everything except making up

stories."

I: _____<u>Did you like</u>_____ your first-grade teacher?
<u>4. (you / like)</u>

SW: I can't remember.

I: _____<u>When did you start</u>_____ to write?
<u>5. (When / you / start)</u>

SW: After I graduated from college, I became a journalist.

I: <u>How long did you work</u> as a journalist?
<u>6. (How long / you / work)</u>

SW: I worked for newspapers for 14 years.

I: <u>Why did you start</u> writing romance novels?
<u>7. (Why / you / start)</u>

SW: Romances were new when I started. I read one and said, "I can do this too."

I: <u>who helped you</u> the most?
<u>8. (Who / help / you)</u>

SW: My agent did. She was there for me from the beginning.

I: <u>How did you feel</u> when your books became popular?
<u>9. (How / you / feel)</u>

SW: I felt terrific. I remember the first time I saw someone with my book. I said, "That's

my book." The woman looked at me and said, "No, it's not. It's mine." I said, "No, no,

no. It's my book. I wrote it."

EXERCISE 5: Editing

John Steinbeck was a great American writer. Correct the questions and answers about him. There are ten mistakes. The first mistake is already corrected. Find and correct nine more.

Q: When John Steinbeck ~~was~~ *was* born?

A: He *was* born in 1902.

Q: Where *he* was born?

A: He was born in Salinas, California.

Q: Where did he studied writing?

A: He studied writing at Stanford University.

Q: *Did* He graduate from Stanford?

A: No, he didn't.

Q: *Did* Does he marry?

A: Yes, he did. He married in 1930.

Q: When *did* he published *Tortilla Flat*?

A: In 1936.

Q: What year did *The Grapes of Wrath* come out?

A: In 1938. It was his best book.

Q: What *was* were it about?

A: It was about a family who lost their farm and became fruit pickers in California.

Q: Did he *win* won many prizes?

A: Yes, he did. He won a Pulitzer Prize and a Nobel Prize in Literature.

Q: When did he died?

A: He died in New York in 1968.

EXERCISE 6: Pronunciation

 A | *Read and listen to the Pronunciation Note.*

> **Pronunciation Note**
>
> When you pronounce / ʤ / as in **jump**, place the tip of your tongue high and pulled back from the teeth.
>
> When you pronounce / **y** / as in **young**, the center of your tongue slides up toward the front of your mouth.
>
> **EXAMPLES:** / ʤ / jet
> / **y** / yet

B | *Listen and repeat the sentences.*

1. I like yellow.
2. I like Jell-O.™
3. He's going to Yale.
4. He's going to jail.
5. There's no juice.
6. There's no use.

C | *PAIRS: Your partner says a sentence from Part A. Read a sentence from the list below that follows your partner's sentence.*

1. Why? Did he rob a bank?
2. I do too. It's delicious.
3. Do I need to buy some?
4. You mean we can't change anything?
5. That's a great university.
6. It's my favorite color, too.

D | *Listen to the sentences. Underline the / ʤ / sounds and circle the / y / sounds that you hear.*

1. His initials are J. S.

2. He's good at storytelling, and some say he's a genius.

3. Does the J stand for Jack or John?

4. What year was he born?

5. We saw the movie *The Grapes of Wrath* yesterday.

6. At what age did he write his first book?

7. The language is not so difficult to understand.

8. Steinbeck wrote, "A journey is like marriage."

EXERCISE 7: Listening

A | Listen to the conversation between Jon and Elena. Then read the questions. Circle the correct letter.

1. What movie did Jon see last night?
   a. *I Love Shakespeare*
   b. *Shakespeare in Love*

2. Where did it take place?
   a. in London
   b. in Rome

3. When did it take place?
   a. in the 1500s
   b. in the 1600s

B | Listen again. Complete the sentences about the play Romeo and Juliet.

Romeo and Juliet fell _____. They couldn't _____

because _____. In the last scene, they _____.

EXERCISE 8: Describing a Performance or Event

PAIRS: Name a play, a movie, a concert, a TV show or an athletic event you attended. Your partner asks wh- questions and yes / no questions about the event.

> EXAMPLE: **A:** I saw the play *West Side Story*.
> **B:** What was it about?
> **A:** It was a play about two people who fell in love.
> **B:** When did it take place?
> **A:** In the 1950s.

EXERCISE 9: Writing

A | Work in small groups. Complete the chart with names of famous people from the past.

Artists	Writers	Musicians	Scientists / Inventors	Actors	Athletes

B | *Write 10 questions about one of the people from Part A. Use the words in parentheses.*

1.   *Where was Leonardo diCaprio born?*
     (Where / he or she / born?)

2.   _____
     was
     (When / he or she / born?)

3.   _____
     (Where / he or she / grow up?)

4.   _____
     (What / he or she / do in his or her free time?)

5.   _____
     (he or she / have / a happy childhood?)

6.   _____
     (he or she / travel?)

7.   _____
     (he or she / work hard?)

8.   _____
     (he or she / make a lot of money?)

9.   _____
     (YOUR QUESTION)

10. _____
     (YOUR QUESTION)

C | *Check your work. Use the Editing Checklist.*

Editing Checklist
Did you . . . ? ☐ use *yes/no* and *wh-* questions with the simple past correctly ☐ check your spelling

Check your answers on page UR-4.

Do you need to review anything?

A | Write **yes** / **no** questions with the verbs in parentheses. Use the simple past.

1. _____ *did* (they / go to the theater)

2. _____ (she / get there by bus)

3. _____ (you / have good seats)

4. _____ *Did* (he / understand everything) ?

5. _____ *did* (we / miss the beginning)

6. _____ (it / have a happy ending)

B | Complete the questions with the words in parentheses. Use the simple past.

1. _____ *did you see* (what play / see / you) ?

2. _____ *did* (where / you / see / it) ?

3. _____ *was* (how long / be / the show) ?

4. _____ *Did* (you / enjoy / the performance) ?

5. _____ *wer* (who / be / the stars) ?

6. _____ *Did* (you / go out / after the show) ?

7. _____ *did* (Where / you / go) ?

8. _____ *did* (What / you / order) ?

C | Correct the sentences. There are six mistakes.

1. Where he *did* go last night?

2. What *did* saw he? *see*

3. Did he enjoyed it?

4. Who *did* he met*e*?

5. When *did* they go?

6. Who did pay for it?
paid

From Grammar to Writing

PUNCTUATION II: THE EXCLAMATION POINT (!), THE HYPHEN (-), QUOTATION MARKS (". . .")

1 | *What's wrong with the sentences? Discuss them with a partner.*

1. You're kidding

2. She's 21 years old

3. He said I love you

4. He worked for many years before he became rich. Then he invest

    ed his money and became even richer.

2 | *Study this information about punctuation.*

The exclamation point (!) Use the exclamation point after **strong, emotional statements**. (Don't use it too often.)	• What a surprise! • You're kidding! • How wonderful!
The hyphen (-) **a.** Use a hyphen in **compound numbers** from twenty-one to ninety-nine. **b.** Use a hyphen **at the end of a line** when dividing a word. Words must be divided by syllables. (Check your dictionary if you are unsure.)	• There were **twenty-two** students in the class. • We visited them at the **begin-ning** of the year.
Quotation marks (". . .") Use quotation marks **before** and **after the exact words** of a speaker. Use a comma before the quote.	• She said, "I just love your new sweater."

3 | *Add the correct punctuation to the sentences in Exercise 1.*

Whose Baby Is It?

Solomon was a king. He lived about 3,000 years ago. Everyone came to Solomon because he was very wise.

One day two women approached King Solomon. One carried a baby. The woman said, We live nearby and had our babies three days apart. Her baby died in the night, and she changed it for mine. This baby is really mine.

The other woman said, No! That woman is lying. That's my baby.

The two women started arguing. They continued until King Solomon shouted, Stop!

He then turned to his guard and said, Take your sword and chop the baby in two. Give one part to this woman and the other to that one. The guard pulled out his sword. As he was about to harm the baby, the first woman screamed, No! Don't do it. Give her the baby. Just don't kill the baby.

King Solomon then said, Now I know the real mother. Give the baby to the woman who has just spoken.

5 | *Work in small groups. Follow the steps.*

1. Think about these questions. Take notes.
- What was your favorite story as a child?
- When did you first hear it? Who told it to you? Why did you like it?

2. Tell your story to your group.

3. Write your story. When you are finished, read your story twice. First pay attention to the story. Next pay attention to the grammar and punctuation.

6 | *Exchange papers with a partner. Did your partner follow the directions? Correct any mistakes in grammar and spelling.*

7 | *Talk to your partner. Discuss the mistakes you made. Then rewrite your own paper and make any necessary changes.*

8 | *Hang your story on the wall. Go around and read the stories of your classmates.*

VII

VERB REVIEW AND CONTRAST AND EXPANSION

Simple Past Review
BIOGRAPHIES

Before You Read

PAIRS: Look at the words in the box. Tell your partner about people or pets with these qualities. Tell why.

generous	innovative	loyal	powerful
hardworking	loving	passionate	understanding

EXAMPLE: My cousin is very passionate about his work. He's an architect and spends hours working on projects.

Read

Read the article about a very unusual dog.

A Loyal Friend

Many people say dogs are loving and loyal. For one dog named Hachiko that description is especially true. He **won** the hearts of people all over the world because of his love and faithfulness to his master.

Hachiko **was** an Akita Inu dog. Akita Inus are large dogs from Japan. Hachiko **was born** in 1923. His owner, Ueno, **was** a professor at Tokyo University. Every morning Ueno and Hachiko **walked** to the Shibuya train station together. Every evening Hachiko **met** Ueno at the station. This routine **continued** for a couple of years. One evening, however, Hachiko **went** to the station, but Ueno **didn't get** off the train. That day, Ueno **was** at work when he suddenly **had** a cerebral hemorrhage[1] and died.

Hachiko **didn't know** what to do. He **looked** everywhere for Ueno. He **was** very sad, and he **missed** his master a lot. Every day for nine years he **went** to the train station and **waited** for his master's return. After a while people at the station **noticed** the dog and **began** to bring him food. They **admired** his loyalty. In 1934 they **hired** a well-known sculptor to build a statue of Hachiko. Hachiko **was** there when the statue was unveiled. A year later, in 1935, Hachiko **died**.

After Hachiko's death, Ueno's students **wrote** articles about the amazing dog. People **wrote** books about him. In 2004 Leslie Newman **wrote** and Machiyo Kodaira **illustrated** *Hachiko Waits*. This book **received** many awards. In 2009 Richard Gere **starred** in a movie based on Hachiko's life.

These days when people are near the Shibuya train station in Tokyo, they often say, "Let's meet at the statue of Hachiko!"

One thing is certain. Hachiko's life will not be forgotten.

[1] *cerebral hemorrhage:* bleeding in the brain

After You Read

A | Practice *PAIRS: Now read the article aloud. Take turns reading each paragraph.*

B | Vocabulary *Circle the letter of the best meaning for the words in* blue.

1. I **noticed** that he had a good memory.
   a. forgot   b. saw

2. When I'm away from home, I **miss** my brothers.
   a. wish to be with   b. don't think about

3. He **illustrated** a children's book.
   a. wrote   b. drew pictures for

4. The movie **is based on** the book.
   a. comes from ideas in   b. is different from

5. I **admire** his ability in art. He is a very good sculptor.
   a. think highly of   b. admit

6. There is a stone **statue** of our first president in front of the park.
   a. figure that looks like a person   b. painting that looks like a person

C | Comprehension *Read the questions. Circle the correct letter.*

1. What kind of dog is Hachiko?
   a. a Collie   b. an Akita Inu

2. What did Hachiko's master do?
   a. He was a professor.   b. He was a train conductor.

3. When was Hachiko born?
   a. in 1934   b. in 1923

4. Where did Hachiko wait for his master every evening?
   a. at the university   b. at the train station

5. What did Hachiko do after Ueno died?
   a. He waited for Ueno at the train   b. He looked for Ueno at the university.
      station.

6. Why did people admire Hachiko?
   a. He was loyal and patient.   b. He was strong and powerful.

7. What is *Hachiko Waits*?
   a. a story based on Hachiko's life   b. a TV show based on Hachiko's life

THE SIMPLE PAST

Affirmative Statements (All Verbs Except *Be*)

Subject	Verb	
I	**stayed**	home.
We	**went**	

Affirmative Statements with *Be*

Subject	Verb	
I	**was**	at home.
We	**were**	

Negative Statements (All Verbs Except *Be*)

Subject	*Did Not (Didn't)*	Base Form of Verb	
I	**did not**	**stay**	with them.
We	**didn't**	**go**	

Negative Statements with *Be*

Subject	Verb	
I	**was not** **wasn't**	at work.
We	**were not** **weren't**	

Yes / No Questions (All Verbs Except *Be*)

Did	Subject	Base Form of Verb	
Did	she they	**leave**?	

Yes / No Questions with *Be*

Was / Were	Subject	
Was	he	home last night?
Were	they	

Wh- Questions (All Verbs Except *Be*)

Wh- Word	*Did*	Subject	Base Form of Verb	
When		you	**arrive**?	
Where		he	**work**?	
How	**did**	it	**begin**?	
Why		he	**leave**?	
Who(m)		they	**help**?	

Wh- Questions with *Be*

Wh- Word	Past Form	Subject	
When		she	there?
Where	**was**	he	from?
How		his	tests?
Why	**were**	you	late?
Who(m)		they	with?

Wh- Questions About the Subject (All Verbs Except *Be*)

Wh- Word	Past Form	
Who	**walked**	to the station?
What	**happened**	to him?
How many people	**waited**	there?

Wh- Questions About the Subject with *Be*

Wh- Word	Past Form	
Who		his friend?
What	**was**	his last name?
How many people	**were**	there?

GRAMMAR NOTES

1	Use the **simple past** to tell about **something that happened in the past**. For all verbs except *be*, the simple past form is the same for all persons.	• **He liked** that book. • **We liked** that book. • **I liked** that book.
2	**Regular verbs** end in *-d*, *-ed*, or *-ied*. Many common verbs are **irregular** in the past.	• They **noticed** the dog. • He **missed** his master. • He **worried** about him. • She **wrote** a book. • He **had** a special dog.
3	For **negative statements** use *did not (didn't)* + **the base form of the verb**.	• He **did not know** him. • He **didn't know** him.

4	For *yes / no* questions use *Did* + subject + the base form of the verb.	DID SUBJECT BASE FORM • **Did** you **see** the dog? • **Did** they **go** to work?

5	Most *wh-* questions use a *wh-* question word and *yes / no* question order.	WH- WORD DID SUBJECT BASE FORM • **What** did he do? • **Where** did she go? • **Who** did he marry? • **How** did he do it?

6	**Questions about the subject** use statement word order. They do not use *did*.	SUBJECT VERB SUBJECT • **Who helped** him? His **friend** did. NOT: Who ~~did~~ helped him? NOT: Who ~~did help~~ him?

7	The verb *be* has **different forms** from all other verbs. **BE CAREFUL!** Do not use *did* or the base form of the verb for questions or negative statements with *be*.	**STATEMENTS** • He **was** happy. • They **weren't** happy. **QUESTIONS** • **Was** he in a movie? • **Were** you in the audience? • Where **were** they? Who **was** on TV? NOT: ~~Did they were~~ famous? NOT: He was ~~be~~ a loyal dog.

REFERENCE NOTES

For a more complete discussion of the past, see Unit 18, page 201, Unit 19, page 211, and Unit 20, page 222.
For a list of irregular verbs see Appendix 11, page A-11.
For pronunciation and spelling rules for the simple past of regular verbs, see Appendix 10, pages A-10–A-11.

EXERCISE 1: Discover the Grammar

Read the conversation. Then write the sentences (both statements and questions) that use the past on the lines below.

BORIS: Who's the man in the picture?

TEACHER: George Washington. He was the first president of the United States.

BORIS: When was that?

TEACHER: He became the president in 1789.

RODRICA: How long was he president?

TEACHER: For eight years.

RODRICA: Was he a good leader?

TEACHER: Yes, he was. And before he became president, he led the army during the American Revolution.

BEKIR: He sounds a lot like Ataturk. Kemal Ataturk was the father of modern Turkey. He was also a great soldier and leader. He gave Turkey many things including a modern alphabet. Now spelling is easy in Turkish.

TEACHER: Well, George Washington didn't do anything about the English alphabet. Spelling is still hard in English.

EUN YOUNG: King Sejong gave Korea an alphabet. He was one of Korea's greatest leaders.

JOSÉ: In South America, Simón Bolívar led many countries to independence. He didn't change our alphabet, but spelling is not so hard in Spanish.

Sentences with *Be* in the Past	Sentences with Other Verbs in the Past
1. *George Washington was the first president of the United States.*	1. *He became the president in 1789.*
2. _____	2. _____
3. _____	3. _____
4. _____	4. _____
5. _____	5. _____
6. _____	6. _____
7. _____	7. _____

EXERCISE 2: Affirmative and Negative Statements

(Grammar Notes 1–2, 7)

Complete the paragraph with the words in parentheses. Use the correct form of the simple past.

Pierre Omidyar _____was born_____ in Paris, France. His parents
1. (be / born)

_____were_____ from Iran. His mother _____was_____
2. (be)   **3. (be)**

a professor, and his father _____practiced_____ medicine. His
4. (practice)

family _____moved_____ to the United States when Omidyar
5. (move)

_____turned_____ six years old. He _____went_____ into the
6. (turn)   **7. (go)**

field of computer science. At age 28, Omidyar _____wrote_____
8. (write)

the computer code for eBay. eBay _____became_____ extremely
9. (become)

successful. In July 2008, eBay _____had_____ shares that were
10. (have)

worth $4.45 billion. In 2004 Omidyar _____started_____ the Omidyar Foundation. In
11. (start)

2005, Omidyar and his wife _____gave_____ $100 million to the foundation. The money
12. (give)

will help poor people in developing countries. In 2010, Omidyar _____joined_____
13. (join)

40 billionaires. They all _____promised_____ to give away at least half of their money
14. (promise)

before they die.

EXERCISE 3: Affirmative and Negative Statements

(Grammar Notes 1–3, 7)

Read the article. Complete the sentences with the words in parentheses. Use the correct form of the simple past. recluse [ˈrɛkluːs] n. 隐士; 隐居者 a 隐居的

Recluse Leaves Millions

Anne Schreiber _____was_____ a recluse. Recluses live apart from other people.
1. (be)

Anne Schreiber never _____married_____. She also never _____had_____ close friends.
2. (marry)   **3. (have)**

She _____lived_____ alone in a tiny studio apartment and _____weared_____ the same
4. (live)   **5. (wear)**

outfit every day—a black coat and a black hat. For many years she _____worked_____
6. (work)

for the tax department of the U.S. government. She _____was_____ an auditor. She
7. (be) 审计员

_____made_____ sure people paid their taxes. However, she _____didn't like_____ to pay
8. (make)   **9. (like / not)**

taxes. She _____didn't like_____ to pay for anything.
10. (like / not)

(continued on next page)

As a young woman, Anne _____followed_____ the suggestions of a brother and
11. (follow)

_____invested_____ all her money in his company. His company _____went_____

12. (invest)   **13. (go)**

bankrupt, and she _____lost_____ her life savings. She _____didn't forgive_____ her

14. (lose)   **15. (forgive / not)**

brother. Anne _____started_____ investing again in 1944 when she _____was_____

16. (start)   **17. (be)**

49 years old. This time she _____used_____ her own ideas. By investing well, she

18. (use)

_____turned_____ $5,000 into $22,000,000. She _____did_____ better than the biggest

19. (turn)   **20. (do)**

businessmen. But she _____didn't want_____ her relatives to know she had so much money

21. (want / not)

because she _____didn't want_____ to give them any of it. And she didn't. Anne Schreiber

22. (want / not)

_____died_____ in 1995 at the age of 101. She _____left_____ her money to

23. (die)   **24. (leave)**

universities to help poor, bright women get an education.

EXERCISE 4: Simple Past: Questions and Answers   *(Grammar Notes 1–7)*

A | *Read the article. On the next page, write **wh-** questions that the underlined words answer.*

When you think of basketball, do you think of Michael

Jordan, LeBron James, Shaquille O'Neal . . . or Dr. James

Naismith? Dr. Naismith? Who was he? What did he do for

basketball?

James Naismith was born <u>in Ontario, Canada</u>, <u>in 1861</u>.

         1.   **2.**

He was a good athlete and a good student. He always

loved <u>school</u>.

    3.

Dr. Naismith earned <u>four</u> degrees, including one in medicine. But his biggest

    4.

Basketball team around 1900

contribution to the world did not come from his work as a

medical doctor. <u>In the winter of 1891</u> he worked as a gym

    5.

instructor in Massachusetts.

His students were <u>active and hard to control</u>. He wanted them

    6.

to play an indoor sport <u>because it was too cold to play outdoors</u>.

    7.

He invented the game of <u>basketball</u>. It became an instant success

    8.

in the United States. Soon it spread to other countries.

1. _Where was James Naismith born?_
2. _when was James Naismith born?_
3. _what did he always love?_
4. _How many degrees did he earn?_
5. _when did he work as a gym instructor?_
6. _How were his student?_
7. _why did he want them to play an indoor sport)_
8. What game _did he invent ?_ ?

B | *Write* **yes / no** *questions about James Naismith with the given words. Use the correct form. Then write short answers.*

1. be / he good at sports?

   Q: _Was he good at sports?_

   A: _Yes, he was._

2. be / he a good student?

   Q: _____

   A: _____

3. he / finish college?

   Q: _____

   A: _____

4. he / become a lawyer?

   Q: _____

   A: _____

5. he / invent the game of volleyball?

   Q: _____

   A: _____

EXERCISE 5: Editing

Correct the conversation. There are eleven mistakes. The first mistake is already corrected. Find and correct ten more.

1. **Q:** Who *was* Elizabeth Blackwell?

   A: She was the first woman physician in the United States.

2. **Q:** Where she was born?

   A: She was born in England.

3. **Q:** When was she born?

   A: She *was* born in 1821.

4. **Q:** When she did come to the United States?

   A: She did come to the United States in 1833.

5. **Q:** Was it hard for her to become a doctor?

   A: Yes, it *was* were. Most medical schools didn't want women.

6. **Q:** How *were* was her grades in medical school?

   A: She was an outstanding student. Her grades were excellent.

7. **Q:** When *did* she graduate?

   A: In 1849.

8. **Q:** What did Dr. Blackwell fight for?

   A: She did *fought* fight for the admission of women to medical schools.

9. **Q:** Where did she goes in 1869?

   A: She returned to London. She worked and wrote there for many years.

10. **Q:** When *did* she die?

    A: She died in 1910.

EXERCISE 6: Pronunciation

 A | *Read and listen to the Pronunciation Note.*

> **Pronunciation Note**
>
> The words **work** and **walk** are sometimes hard to pronounce correctly. Listen to the difference between the vowel sound / ɜ / in *work* and / ɔ / in *walk*. Also remember the / kt / ending in words like **work**ed and **walk**ed is one sound.

B | *Listen and repeat the words.*

   work   works   worked   walk   walks   walked

C | *Listen to the sentences and repeat.*

1. I walked fast.
2. I worked fast.
3. Do you walk after school?
4. Do you work after school?
5. Who works with you?
6. Who walks with you?

EXERCISE 7: Listening

A | *Two people are watching TV. Listen to their conversation. Then circle the letter of the correct answer to the question.*

What kind of a TV show are they watching?
   a. a quiz show   **b.** a talk show

B | *Listen again. Complete the questions. Write the answers.*

1. **Q:** Who _____*painted*_____ *The Night Watch*?   **A:** Rembrandt.

2. **Q:** In what century _____?   **A:** The _____ century.

3. **Q:** Where _____?   **A:** In _____.

4. **Q:** What is _____?   **A:** Rembrandt van Rijn.

5. **Q:** Who _____ Yoko Ono?   **A:** _____

6. **Q:** What _____ of John

   Lennon's _____?   **A:** _____

7. **Q:** Where _____?   **A:** _____

8. **Q:** When _____ their last

   appearance together?   **A:** _____

EXERCISE 8: A Quiz Show

SMALL GROUPS: Prepare a quiz show. On a separate piece of paper, write questions in the past. Choose a host or hostess from your group. Choose classmates in other groups to be contestants.

> **EXAMPLES:** Who starred in the *Twilight* movies?
> What was the *Titanic*?
> Who wrote *One Hundred Years of Solitude*?

EXERCISE 9: What Were You Like As a Child?

PAIRS: Ask your partner what he or she was like as a child. Use boxes A and B for ideas.

> **EXAMPLE:** **A:** When you were a child, were you talkative?
> **B:** Yes. Once my teacher wrote a note to my mother, "Bernie never stops talking. He's smart, but he needs to give other children a turn." What about you? What were you like? Did you study hard?
> **A:** No, I didn't. I began to study hard in high school.

A: Were you _____ ?	**B: Did you _____ ?**
athletic / uninterested in sports	study hard
naughty / well behaved	listen to your parents
stubborn / easygoing	watch a lot of TV
talkative / quiet / shy	play a lot of computer games
cheerful / moody	like music / art / dance

EXERCISE 10: Information Gap: Guess the Musician

Work in pairs (A and B). Student A, follow the instructions on this page. Student B, turn to page 246 and follow the instructions there.

1. Read about the life of the musician Ray Charles. Do not tell your partner his name. Your partner will ask you questions about the person and guess. Answer your partner's questions.

> He was born in Albany, Georgia, in 1930. His family was very poor. He became blind at the age of seven. He learned to read Braille and play music at the St. Augustine School for the Deaf and the Blind in Florida. His mother died when he was a teenager. He left school at 15 and began his career as a musician. He moved to Seattle and started his rise to fame. He started out as a jazz and blues pianist and singer, but over more than 50 years he built a career that combined many types of music. In 2004, he died in Beverly Hills, California. He was 73 years old.

2. Now you will ask your partner questions about a different musician. First, write questions with the words given and the simple past.

1. When / he / born *When was he born?* _____

2. Where / he / born _____
   <small>was</small>

3. What / he / teach himself to play_____
   <small>did</small>

4. Where / he / begin his career _____
   <small>did</small>

5. Who / discover him _____
   <small>did</small>

6. Where / be / he from 1958 to 1960_____
   <small>was</small>

7. What / he / appear in after that _____
   <small>did</small>

8. When / die _____
   <small>did</small>

3. Ask your partner the questions from Part 2 and then guess who the musician is.

EXERCISE 11: Writing

A | *Write a short biography of a musician. Use the simple past. Read your biography to a partner.*

B | *Check your work. Use the Editing Checklist.*

Editing Checklist
Did you . . . ?   ☐ use the simple past correctly   ☐ check your spelling

1. You will ask your partner questions about a musician. First, write questions about the person. Use the words given and the simple past.

   1. Where / be / born _Where was he born?_____

   2. When / he born _____

   3. What / happened to him at the age of seven _____

   4. Where / he / go to school _____

   5. What / he / learn at school _____

   6. Where / he / move _____

   7. How many years / he / be / in the music business _____

   8. When / he / die _____

2. Ask your partner the questions from Part 1 and then guess who the musician is.

3. Now read about the life of the musician Elvis Presley. Do not tell your partner his name. Your partner will ask you questions about the person and guess. Answer your partner's questions.

   > He was a popular singer. He was born in Tupelo, Mississippi, in 1935. He began singing in a local church, and he taught himself to play the guitar. Sam Phillips, the president of Sun Records, discovered him in 1953. By 1956 he was the most popular performer in the United States. Soon after that he became popular all over the world. His music combined country and western music with rhythm and blues. He spent two years, from 1958 to 1960, in the army. He appeared in several movies, but none were very successful. He died in 1977. He is known as the King of Rock and Roll.

Review

Check your answers on page UR-4.

Do you need to review anything?

A | *Complete the sentences with the verbs in parentheses. Use the correct form and the simple past.*

1. Craig Newmark _____ on December 6, 1952.
   (be born)
2. He _____ in New Jersey.
   (grow up)
3. He _____ Morristown High School.
   (attend)
4. He _____ to college in Ohio.
   (go)
5. In 1995 he _____ an email list.
   (start)
6. It _____ a Web-based service in 1996.
   (become)
7. It _____, and today almost everyone knows about Craigslist®.
   (expand)

B | *Write questions with the words in parentheses. Use the simple past.*

1. _____
   (when / she / go to college)

3. _____
   (where / he study)

2. _____
   (who / they / meet)

4. _____
   (how long / they live in Canada)

C | *Complete the questions with **be** or **do**. Use the correct form and the simple past.*

1. _____ you late yesterday?

2. _____ they work last night?

3. _____ he at the park with his son?

4. _____ she marry him?

5. _____ he move?

D | *Correct the paragraph. There are four mistakes.*

Steve Paul Jobs did start college in 1970, but he no did finish it. In 1976 Jobs and his friend begin to make their own computers. They worked in the Jobs' garage. That was the beginning of Apple® Computers. Their company become a big success. Apple® changed the field of computers, and by the age of 30, Jobs was a multimillionaire.

STEP 1 GRAMMAR IN CONTEXT

Before You Read

Look at the photos. Why do people choose a particular career? For example, why do people become fashion designers, makeup artists, or models? Would you like these jobs? Or others?

Read

To get the right job and be successful, you need to know yourself. Read these people's comments and the jobs that match their needs.

1. **I like to learn** new things. **I hope to continue** learning throughout my career.

doctor	software developer
scientist	teacher

2. **I enjoy working** with my hands.

auto mechanic	chef
carpenter	farmer

3. I don't like routine work. **I expect to do** something different every day. I don't like things to be predictable.

actress   musician
fire fighter   police officer

4. I'm very competitive. **I hate losing.** People say I have a type A personality.

attorney   politician
investment banker   professional athlete

5. I love the outdoors. **I can't stand wearing** a suit. **I avoid wearing** formal clothes.

anthropologist   gardener
farmer   park ranger

6. **I enjoy interacting** with people. **I love helping** them with their problems.

hotel manager   psychologist
physical therapist   social worker

After You Read

A | Practice *PAIRS: Now read the comments aloud. Take turns reading the comments.*

B | Vocabulary *Circle the letter of the best meaning for the words in* **blue.**

1. He's not good at math. He **avoids** working with numbers.

   a. tries not to   b. is afraid of

2. He **can't stand** speaking with angry customers.

   a. is good at   b. hates

3. He always does the same thing. He's **predictable**.

   a. not surprising; expected   b. suprising

4. Everyone likes her. She has a pleasant **personality**.

   a. way of behaving   b. way of smiling

5. She needs **formal** clothes for her brother's graduation and her sister's wedding.

   a. dresses   b. dress clothes

6. He hates losing. He's **competitive**.

   a. wants to play sports   b. wants to win

C | Comprehension *Read the descriptions. Circle the letter of the career that **doesn't** belong.*

1. You expect to make a lot of money. You always want to win.

   a. lawyer   b. investment banker   c. social worker

2. You often need to wear a suit.

   a. banker   b. farmer   c. lawyer

3. You're a "people person." You enjoy interacting with others.

   a. teacher   b. physical therapist   c. computer programmer

4. Your work routine changes every day.

   a. chef   b. artist   c. actress

5. You don't wear formal clothes at work.

   a. teacher   b. carpenter   c. politician

GERUNDS AND INFINITIVES

Subject	Verb	Gerund (Verb + -ing)
I	enjoy	dancing.

Subject	Verb	Infinitive
She	wants	to sing.

Subject	Verb	Infinitive or Gerund
They	like	driving.
		to drive.

Verb + Gerund	Verb + Infinitive		Verb + Infinitive or Gerund
avoid	agree	refuse	hate
enjoy	decide	want	like
finish	expect		continue
keep	hope		love
keep on	intend		prefer
regret	need		try
think about	plan		*en*

GRAMMAR NOTES

1	A **gerund** is a noun that is formed by the **base form of a verb + -ing**. Some verbs, such as *enjoy*, *finish*, and *keep*, can be followed by a gerund.	• I **enjoy singing**. • We **finished studying** at 8:00. • She **keeps asking** about the job.
2	An **infinitive** is *to* + **the base form of the verb**. Some verbs, such as *want* and *need*, can be followed by an infinitive.	• I **want to work**. • She **needs to write** a résumé. • He **wants** to change jobs.
3	Some verbs, such as *like* and *hate*, can be followed by a gerund (*-ing* form) or an infinitive (*to* + base form).	• I **like writing**. • I **like to write**.

STEP 3 FOCUSED PRACTICE

EXERCISE 1: Discover the Grammar

Write **I (verb + infinitive)** or **G (verb + gerund)** for each statement.

_G_ **1.** I enjoy working with people.   ____ **5.** I avoid wearing a suit.

____ **2.** He needs to get a job.   ____ **6.** He refused to work late.

____ **3.** She prefers to work at night.   ____ **7.** They hope to move in July.

____ **4.** I prefer working in the daytime.   ____ **8.** They finished eating at 10:00.

EXERCISE 2: Infinitives
(Grammar Note 2)

Complete the sentences with the words from the box. Use infinitives.

complete	~~find~~	leave	move	send	work

1. John's looking for a job. He hopes _____to find_____ a job in this city.

2. He likes this city. He doesn't want _____to____move____ away.

3. He sees his friends every weekend. He refuses ____to____work____ on weekends.

4. He plans _____to____send____ out some letters of application this afternoon.

5. In two years he intends _____to____leave____ his job and go to business school.

6. He hopes __to___complete____ his M.B.A. in four years.

EXERCISE 3: Gerunds
(Grammar Note 1)

Complete the sentences with the words from the box. Use gerunds.

apply	do	go	leave	~~take~~	work

1. He finished _____taking_____ final exams last week.

2. He is thinking about _____applying_____ for a part-time job for the summer.

3. He enjoys _____doing_____ sales work.

4. He doesn't like _____working_____ with his hands.

5. He regretted _____leaving_____ his part-time job, but he needed time to study.

6. He avoided _____going_____ out with friends for a month before his final exams.

252 UNIT 22

EXERCISE 4: Gerunds and Infinitives

(Grammar Notes 1–3)

Complete the conversation. Use gerunds or infinitives with the verbs in parentheses.
One verb can be used with both a gerund or an infinitive.

ELENA: Do you enjoy _____acting_____?
1. (act)

JULIAN: Yes. I love _____.
2. (act)

ELENA: Is it hard to find work as an actor?

JULIAN: Very hard. Many people want _____ actors. You need
3. (become)

_____ talent, patience, and luck.
4. (have)

ELENA: Do you ever want _____ careers? Do you ever regret
5. (change)

_____ so much time
6. (spend)

looking for work?

JULIAN: No. I refuse _____
7. (give up)

my dream. I keep

_____ for new parts.
8. (try out)

I think I'm a great actor, and

I plan _____ the
9. (show)

world!

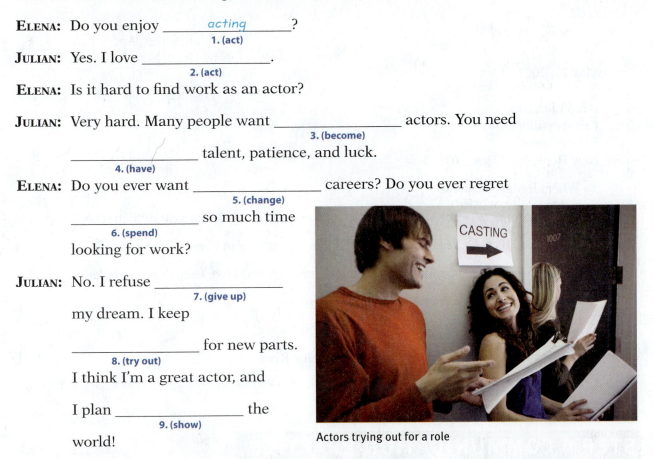

Actors trying out for a role

EXERCISE 5: Gerunds and Infinitives

(Grammar Notes 1–2)

Complete the sentences with the words from the box. Use infinitives and gerunds.

get	look	meet	study	tell	~~work~~

1. Do you enjoy _____working_____ with children?

2. Do you plan _____ an advanced degree?

3. He hoped _____ with the president of the company. Instead he met with

the vice president.

4. I regret _____ him about my problem with my previous employer.

5. He keeps _____ at his watch. I hope he isn't bored.

6. Many people decide _____ law after watching courtroom dramas.

EXERCISE 6: Editing

Correct the letter. There are seven mistakes. The first mistake is already corrected.
Find and correct six more.

35 Main Street, Apt. 6
New Hope, New Jersey 07675

May 27, 2012

Head Librarian
Kennedy Library
7 West Street
New Hope, New Jersey 07675

To Whom It May Concern:

           to
I want apply for a part-time job at Kennedy Library. I am in my senior year of high school.

I expect attend State College next year, and I plan to majoring in library science. I enjoy to

read and to work with the public. I'm good at computers, and I like keep things in order.

I've enclosed a résumé. I hope hearing from you soon.

Sincerely,

Joe Reed

STEP 4 COMMUNICATION PRACTICE

EXERCISE 7: Pronunciation

A | *Read and listen to the Pronunciation Note.*

Pronunciation Note
Of is usually pronounced with the unstressed sound **/ əv /** . When *of* comes after a consonant sound, we link the consonant with *of*. **EXAMPLE:** out of ice cream

B | *Listen and repeat.*

1. out of town
2. out of everything
3. out of juice
4. out of eggs
5. out of order

C | *PAIRS: Answer the questions. Use the phrases in Part B.*

1. **A:** Do we have any orange or grape juice?

   B: No, we're _____ .

2. **A:** Does the copy machine work?

   B: No, it's _____ .

3. **A:** Is he in town?

   B: No he's _____ .

4. **A:** Do we have any eggs?

   B: No, we're _____ .

5. **A:** Where are you going?

   B: Shopping for food. We're _____ .

EXERCISE 8: Listening

A | *Listen to a conversation between two friends. When do the friends meet?*
   a. every week
   b. for the first time in years

B | *Listen again. Write* **T** (**True**) *or* **F** (**False**) *for each statement. Change the false statements to make them true.*

_____ 1. Ken plans to go back to school for more training.

_____ 2. Cindy got tired of working for a big company.

_____ 3. Cindy plans to write a book.

_____ 4. Cindy enjoys planning conventions.

_____ 5. Cindy likes to work with animals.

_____ 6. Ken wants to have lunch with Cindy on Saturday.

EXERCISE 9: Discussion: Likes

PAIRS: For each category, write something that you enjoy doing. Then tell your partner. Use infinitives and gerunds. Your partner then agrees or tells about something he or she prefers.

EXAMPLE: **A:** I like playing golf.
   B: I do too. OR I prefer to play tennis.

1. sports: _____*golf*_____   3. books: _____   5. desserts: _____

2. movies: _____   4. music: _____   6. cars: _____

EXERCISE 10: Game: What Do I Do?

SMALL GROUPS: Each group thinks of an occupation and gives the other groups hints.
Use only the verbs in the chart on page 251.

EXAMPLE: MOHAMMED: You want to help people.
TATIANA: You need to study for many years.
HECTOR: (Student from another group): Are you thinking about a doctor?
MOHAMMED: Yes, we are.

EXERCISE 11: Problem Solving: Finding the Right Job

PAIRS: Ask your partner the questions. Talk about possible jobs.

- Do you enjoy working with people?
- Do you want to make a difference in the world?
- Do you want to be rich?
- Do you dislike traveling?
- Do you want to be famous?
- Do you want a safe job (one that you can keep when times are bad)?
- Do you want to help others?
- Do you like to "do your own thing"?

EXERCISE 12: Writing

A | *Write about your future career goals. Use gerunds and infinitives.*

EXAMPLE: I enjoy window shopping and studying all the latest fashions. I also love to draw. I hope to combine my two passions and become a fashion designer. I plan to study art and fashion in college this year. I hope to get an internship with a design company in the summer. I expect to graduate in four years. In 10 years I hope to have my own fashion design business.

B | *Check your work. Use the Editing Checklist.*

Editing Checklist

Did you . . . ?
☐ use infinitives and gerunds correctly
☐ check your spelling

A | *Underline the correct words to complete the sentences.*

1. Do you regret **to start / starting** a business?

2. I hope **to sell / selling** my business next year.

3. She decided **to return / returning** to school.

4. She hopes **to become / becoming** a pilot.

5. She enjoys **to fly / flying** and **to see / seeing** the world.

6. Her parents plan **to help / helping** her reach her goal.

B | *Complete the sentences with the words in parentheses. Use the correct form.*

1. She doesn't want _____to work_____ evenings.
   (work)

2. Her boss refuses _____to_____ her hours.
   (change)

3. She's thinking about _____to_____ her job and _____going_____ back to
   (quit)   **(go)**
   school.

4. She wants _____to_____ computer science.
   (study)

5. She enjoys _____doing_____ Web design.
   (do)

C | *Correct the paragraph. There are eight mistakes.*

Carol volunteers at a hospital. She enjoys to take care of patients. Some patients
refuse ᵗᵒ do exercise, but Carol keeps to push them. Carol intends study physical therapy
in college. She needs ᵗᵒ ᵗᵃᵏᵉ taking a lot of science courses. She expects to went to college
next fall. She hopes ᵗᵒ get a degree in physical therapy in five years. She prefers t̶o̶
working with teenagers, but she will work with adults too.

23 Simple Present, Present Progressive, and Simple Past

CREATIVITY

STEP 1 GRAMMAR IN CONTEXT

Before You Read

A | *GROUPS: What can you do with the items below? Write as many ideas as you can. Be as creative as possible.*

aluminum foil   **hairdryer**   **straws**   **Ziploc® bag**

EXAMPLE: You can wrap your hair with aluminum foil to make it curly.

B | *Share your ideas with the class. Now vote. Which ideas were the most interesting?*

Read

Read the online article about creativity.

ARTS	SCIENCE	POLITICS	TECHNOLOGY	SEARCH:

What **does** it **mean** to be creative? To be creative **means** to see things in a new way. New inventions often **come** from old ideas. **Do** you **know** a new invention that **came** from an older one?

Glue **is** a very old invention, from 250,000 B.C., but Krazy Glue® **is** a new kind of glue. It **is** extremely strong. In fact, it **can glue** your fingers together. Dr. Harry Coover **invented** this kind of glue in 1942. He **wanted** to use it for airplanes, but it **didn't work**. Later, in 1962, scientists **realized** they could use the glue in surgery.[1] They **used** it to save lives in wars. Nowadays doctors **are** still **using** a kind of Krazy Glue® during surgery.

How **do** new inventions **come about**? Sometimes, a new invention **is** the result of two old ideas combined. The motorcycle, for example, **is** a combination of a car and bicycle. New inventions can also **happen** over time, in steps. One creative idea **comes** after another, and the invention **changes**— adjustments **take** place—and the invention **improves**. We **see** this in today's computers and phones, which **are changing** all of the time.

Picturephone, 1965

New ideas **do not** always **meet** with public approval at first. Often it **takes** time for people to accept new ways of thinking. In France, in the late 1800s, painters **came up with** a style of painting called Impressionism. At first people **disliked** this art and **rejected** the style, but later they **accepted** and **admired** it. And in this century, the public first **rejected**, and then **began** to accept ebooks.

[1] **surgery:** medical treatment in which a doctor cuts open the body to fix or remove something inside

These days we **are learning** more about creativity through a recent invention. The MRI[2] **takes** pictures of the body which **are** more powerful and accurate than X-rays. Scientists **are** now **using** MRIs to study the human brain. MRIs **show** them what **happens** in the brain when a person **is thinking** creative thoughts. So in the future, we may have a deeper understanding of the creative process. One day scientists may even invent a pill for creativity. Would you try such a pill?

[2] **MRI:** magnetic resonance imaging

After You Read

A | Practice *PAIRS: Now read the article aloud. Take turns reading each paragraph.*

B | Vocabulary *Complete the sentences with the words from the box.*

accepted	came up with	comes after	invented	rejected

1. Who _____ came up _____ with the idea for Krazy Glue®?

2. What number _____ come after _____ 9,999?

3. At first, they _____ rejected _____ his suggestion, but later they agreed to it.

4. We _____ accepted _____ his invitation to the party.

5. Thomas Edison _____ invented _____ the lightbulb.

C | Comprehension *Read the statements. Write **T** (**True**) or **F** (**False**).*

_____ **1.** To be creative means that you are an artist.

_____ **2.** Glue is not a new invention.

_____ **3.** Krazy Glue® is not used by doctors any more.

_____ **4.** Sometimes a new invention is a combination of two older ones.

_____ **5.** The art movement Impressionism ended around 1800.

_____ **6.** It took people time to like Impressionism.

_____ **7.** Scientists are using MRIs to understand the human brain and creativity.

SIMPLE PRESENT

Affirmative Statements				Negative Statements		
Subject	**Verb**	**Time Marker**		**Subject**	**Verb**	**Time Marker**
I	**paint**			I	**don't paint**	
He	**paints**	sometimes.		He	**doesn't paint**	often.
They	**paint**			They	**don't paint**	

PRESENT PROGRESSIVE

Affirmative Statements				Negative Statements		
Subject	**Verb**	**Time Marker**		**Subject**	**Verb**	**Time Marker**
I	**'m painting**			I	**'m not painting**	
He	**'s painting**	now.		He	**'s not painting** / **isn't painting**	now.
They	**'re painting**			They	**'re not painting** / **aren't painting**	

SIMPLE PAST

Affirmative Statements				Negative Statements		
Subject	**Verb**	**Time Marker**		**Subject**	**Verb**	**Time Marker**
I				I		
He	**painted**	last week.		He	**didn't paint**	last week.
They				They		

GRAMMAR NOTES

1	REMEMBER: Use the **simple present** to tell about **things that happen again and again** or to **tell facts**. Use the simple present with **non-action verbs** even when something is happening now.	• He **goes** to work every day. • Some doctors **use** glue during surgery. • I **like** your idea.
2	REMEMBER: Use the **present progressive** to talk about **an action that is happening now or nowadays**.	• He **is looking** at your MRI now. • Scientists **are studying** the brain these days.
3	REMEMBER: Use the **simple past** to tell about **things that are finished**.	• He **had** a good idea. • At first people **rejected** his work.

STEP 3 FOCUSED PRACTICE

EXERCISE 1: Discover the Grammar

Read the conversation. Underline the present progressive verbs once. Underline the simple present verbs twice. Circle the simple past verbs.

A: What are you doing?

B: I'm looking at a plan of my apartment. It's really tiny. Now with a baby we need more space. I'm trying to redo it.

A: Check out Gary Chang of Hong Kong. He's an architect. He lives in a 333-square-foot apartment, but he divided his small apartment into 24 rooms.

B: Are you kidding?

A: I'm not kidding. I read about it online. And I even saw it on YouTube.™

EXERCISE 2: Simple Present and Simple Past

(Grammar Notes 1, 3)

Complete the conversation with the verbs in parentheses. Use the correct form.

A: When _____*did*_____ you _____*get*_____ a cat?
　　　　　　　1.　　　　　　　　**2. (get)**

B: I _____*got*_____ Yume a month ago.
　　　　3. (get)

A: She _____*was is so*_____ cute! But you _____*travel*_____
　　　　　　4. (be)　　　　　　　　**5. (travel)**

a lot for your job. What _____*do*_____ you
　　　　　　　　　　　　　　　　6.

_____*do*_____ when you're away? Who
　　7. (do)

_____*is taking*_____ care of her and _____*feeding*_____ her?
　　8. (take)　　　　　　　　　　　**9. (feed)**

B: Nobody.

A: What _____*do*_____ you _____*mean*_____?
　　　　　　10.　　　　　　　**11. (mean)**

B: Take a better look. She's a robotic cat. She

_____ and _____ sounds like a cat, but she's a robot.
　　12. (move)　　　　　　**13. (make)**

A: That's amazing. Where _____*did*_____ you _____ her?
　　　　　　　　　　　　　　　14.　　　　　　　**15. (get)**

B: She's from Japan. I _____ her online.
　　　　　　　　　　16. (buy)

EXERCISE 3: Simple Present, Present Progressive, and Simple Past (Grammar Notes 1–3)

Complete the paragraph with the verbs in parentheses. Use the correct form.

Where _____*do*_____ new ideas _____*come*_____ from? Sometimes they
　　　　1.　　　　　　　　　　　**2. (come)**

_____ from the world of <u>science fiction</u>. 科/공상/소설
　3. (come)

Mary and Bill _____ on a train now. They _____ their laptop
　　　　　　　4. (be)　　　　　　　　　　　　　**5. (use)**

computers on their way to work. Mary and Bill _____ unusual. Millions of
　　　　　　　　　　　　　　　　　　　6. (be / not)

people _____ laptops and _____ them on their way to work.
　　　7. (have)　　　　　　　　　　**8. (use)**

The laptop computer _____ in the 1970s. However, in 1977 James Hogan
　　　　　　　　9. (exist / not)

_____ about one in *Inherit the Stars*. In this science fiction book, Hogan
　10. (write)

_____ a small computer that fit into a briefcase.
　11. (describe)

Now Mary and Bill _____ their office building. The office doors
　　　　　　　　　　12. (enter)

_____ automatically. In 1899 doors _____ automatically. But
　13. (open)　　　　　　　　　　　　　　**14. (not / open)**

H. G. Wells _____ about such doors in his novel *When the Sleeper Wakes*.
　　　　　15. (write)

These are just two examples in which science fiction showed us the future.

EXERCISE 4: Editing

Correct the paragraph. There are seven mistakes. The first mistake is already corrected.
Find and correct six more.

>   Jay Leno is a comedian. He also ~~love~~ *loves* to collect cars. One of his cars needs not gas. It's a
>
> Baker electric car. Baker invent an electric car in 1909. In the early 1900s, electric cars was
>
> popular in the United States. Then Henry Ford did produce inexpensive cars that used gas.
>
> People stopped buying electric cars. But nowadays people is trying to keep the air clean.
>
> So electric cars are become popular once again.

STEP 4 COMMUNICATION PRACTICE

EXERCISE 5: Listening

A | *Listen to a talk about X-rays. Then circle the correct letter.*

Doctors, dentists, and _____ use X-rays.

   a. airline companies   **b.** baggage companies   **c.** airplane manufacturers

B | *Listen again. Read the questions. Circle the correct letter.*

1. Where was Wilhelm Roentgen from?

   (a.) Germany   **b.** Austria

2. When did he discover X-rays?

   a. 1859   **b.** 1895

3. Whose hand did he first X-ray?

   a. his hand   **b.** his wife's hand

4. How did people learn about X-rays?

   a. from Roentgen   **b.** from newspapers

5. What did Roentgen win?

   a. the Nobel Prize   **b.** the Pulitzer Prize

6. What did Roentgen's friends tell him to call X-rays?

   a. X-rays   **b.** Roentgen rays

EXERCISE 6: Pronunciation

 A | *Read and listen to the Pronunciation Note.*

> **Pronunciation Note**
>
> **Compound nouns** are two nouns we put together as one. They can be two words or one word. We **stress** the **first noun**.
>
> EXAMPLES: credit card
>
> notebook

B | *Listen and repeat these compound nouns.*

1. bike trip
2. office building
3. houseboat
4. motorbike
5. library book
6. wedding ring

C | *PAIRS: Student A, choose a sentence. Student B, say the compound noun Student A is thinking of. Remember to stress the first noun. Take turns.*

EXAMPLE: **A:** I'm thinking of a trip by bicycle.
  B: A bike trip.

1. I'm thinking of a building with offices.
2. I'm thinking of a bicycle with a motor.
3. I'm thinking of book you can borrow from the library.
4. I'm thinking of a ring you wear when you are married.

EXERCISE 7: Information Gap

Work in pairs (A and B). **Student A,** *follow the instructions on this page.* **Student B,** *turn to page 266. Follow the instructions on that page.*

1. Ask your partner questions to complete your chart.

EXAMPLE: **Student A:** Who invented the ATM?
  Student B: Don Wetzel invented the ATM.
  Student A: When did he invent it?
  Student B: In 1968.
  Student A: Where is he from?
  Student B: He's from the United States.

Invention	Inventor	Year	Country
ATM	Don Wetzel	1968	United States
credit card			
dishwasher			
eyeglasses			
fork			
paper money			
subway			
YouTube™			

2. Now your partner will ask you questions. Answer the questions with information from the chart.

Answers to Student B's Questions

Invention	Inventor	Year	Country
bicycle	Baron Karl von Drais de Sauerbrun	1818	Germany
disposable diapers	Marion Donovan	1950	U.S.
mirror (glass)	the Venetians	c. 1200	Italy
paper	Ts'ai Lun	c. 105	China
pencil	Conrad Gessner	1565	Switzerland
satellite	Soviet Space program	1957	Russia
thermometer	Galileo	1592	Italy
World Wide Web	Tim Berners-Lee	1989	U.K.

3. GROUPS: Talk about the inventions. Are they still good? Are there newer and better inventions?

EXERCISE 8: Writing

A | *Imagine you are living in the future. Choose the year. Write about life in that year. Write about something you're doing now and something you did. Include the simple present, present progressive, and simple past.*

EXAMPLES: It's 3010. As usual the weather is sunny and 65 degrees. It never rains or snows. Sometimes people complain. They say, "We want some bad weather."

I live in France, but I go to school in Spain. Right now I'm flying to school in my new aeromobile. It's a lot of fun. I'm flying across the border and looking at the beautiful mountains below.

Last month two exciting things happened. On the first of the month, scientists announced a cure for the cold. Finally. On the 15th of last month, my great granddad celebrated his 150th birthday. The whole family met, and we had a party for him in his new home on the bottom of the ocean.

B | *Check your work. Use the Editing Checklist.*

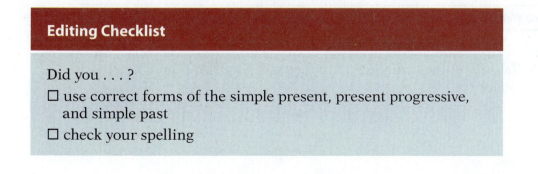

Editing Checklist

Did you . . . ?
☐ use correct forms of the simple present, present progressive, and simple past
☐ check your spelling

INFORMATION GAP FOR STUDENT B

1. Your partner will ask you questions. Answer the questions with information from the chart.

Answers to Student A's Questions

Invention	Inventor	Year	Country
ATM	Don Wetzel	1968	U.S.
credit card	Frank McNamara, Ralph Schneider	1950	U.S.
dishwasher	Josephine Cochrane	1886	U.S.
eyeglasses	Salvino degli Armati or Alessandro di Spina	1280s	Italy
fork	—	2000 B.C.E.	China
paper money	—	late 900s	China
subway	Sir John Fowler	1863	U.K.
YouTube	Steven Chen, Chad Hurley, and Jawed Karim	2005	U.S.

2. Now ask your partner questions to complete your chart.

EXAMPLE: **Student B:** Who invented the bicycle?
Student A: Baron Karl von Drais de Sauerbrun.
Student B: When did he invent it?
Student A: In 1818.
Student B: Where was he from?
Student A: Germany.

Invention	Inventor	Year	Country
bicycle	Baron Karl von Drais de Sauerbrun	1818	Germany
disposable diapers			
mirror (glass)			
paper			
pencil			
satellite			
thermometer			
World Wide Web			

3. GROUPS: Talk about the inventions. Are they still good? Are there newer and better inventions?

Check your answers on page UR-5.

Do you need to review anything?

A | *Complete the sentences with the verbs in parentheses. Use the simple present, present progressive, or simple past.*

1. My brother _____ a sculpture class now.
   (take)
2. Each week the students _____ sculptures out of recycled materials.
   (make)
3. Last month he _____ a sculpture out of soda cans.
   (make)
4. He really _____ the class.
   (like)

B | *Complete the paragraph with the verbs in parentheses. Use the simple present, present progressive, or simple past.*

Whitcomb Judson _____ a zipper in 1893. His zipper
                    1. (invent)

_____, and nobody _____ it. Later the B. F. Goodrich
2. (work / not)   3. (want)

company _____ interested in a zipper for rain shoes, and Judson's zippers
            4. (become)

_____ to sell. Today we still _____ zippers. Right now factory
5. (start)   6. (use)

workers _____ zippers in clothes, bags, shoes, and many other things.
            7. (sew)

C | *Complete the questions with the words in parentheses. Use the correct form.*

1. _____
                    (Where / you / go / last weekend)
2. _____
                    (How / you / get there)
3. _____
                    (What / you / see / at the museum)
4. _____
                    (How / be / the museum)
5. _____
                    (you / often/ go there)

D | *Correct the sentences. There are four mistakes.*

1. Last night I did watch a movie about fish.

2. The fish were beautiful, and I enjoy the movie.

3. My brother is watching the movie now, but he don't like it.

4. He is only liking action films.

PART VII

From Grammar to Writing

ORGANIZATION: TIME SEQUENCE MARKERS

1 | *Look at these sentences. Which words show the time?*

  1. He studies at home in the evening.

  2. At present I live on Bleeker Street.

2 | *Study the information about time sequence markers.*

> You can organize your writing by using **time sequence markers**. Some common markers for the time of day are **in the morning**, **in the afternoon**, **in the evening**, and **at night**.
>
> **EXAMPLE:**
> Monique works **in the morning**.
>
> Some common markers for the past, present, and future are **in the past**, **at present**, and **in the future.**
> **EXAMPLE:**
> **At present**, I'm a student.

3 | *Read this story about a country doctor. Underline the time sequence markers. Then write about a day in the life of someone you know well.*

> Michelle Hirch-Phothong is a country doctor. Her day begins at 6:30 in the morning. At seven o'clock she is at the hospital. She visits her patients and discusses their problems with the nurses and other doctors. Michelle enjoys talking to her patients. She listens carefully and never rushes.
>
> In the afternoon Michelle works at a clinic. The clinic is busy, and patients are often worried about their health. Michelle and the other doctors try to help them.
>
> At six o'clock in the evening Michelle leaves the clinic. She goes home and relaxes. Every evening at seven o'clock Michelle goes to Bangkok in the Boondocks. That's my restaurant, and Michelle is my wife. Michelle and I usually enjoy a delicious Thai dinner alone.
>
> Sometimes, however, people come to the restaurant and tell Michelle their medical problems. I say, "Tell them to go to the clinic." But Michelle never sends them home without listening to their problems and offering advice. Michelle is a wonderful doctor.

4 | *Exchange papers with a partner. Did your partner follow the directions? Correct any mistakes in grammar and spelling.*

5 | *Talk to your partner. Discuss the mistakes you made. Then rewrite your own paper and make any necessary changes.*

PART

VIII

THE FUTURE

STEP 1 GRAMMAR IN CONTEXT

Before You Read

PAIRS: Do you ever read or write letters to the editor of a newspaper? Tell your partner about a letter you remember.

EXAMPLE: This city is going to increase the cost of transportation. Last week there was a letter against the increase. I agree with the writer.

Read

Read the letters from students to the editor of their school newspaper.

www.dailycolumbus.com/letters_to_the_editor

DAILY COLUMBUS
The website of Columbus College

| Home | Campus | City | Sports | Classifieds |

LETTERS TO THE EDITOR

To the Editor:

Last week President Clark talked about plans for a new fitness center[1] for our college. The center sounds great. It**'s going to have** a beautiful gym, a track for running, an Olympic size pool, saunas, steam rooms, a basketball court, exercise machines, and weight-lifting equipment.[2] But this fitness center **is going to cost** a lot of money.

Where is the money **going to come** from? You guessed it. Most of the money **is going to come** from us. Our tuition **is going to increase**. That's why I'm against the plan. With a tuition increase, more students **are going to need** to work while they go to school. We**'re not going to have** time to enjoy the fitness center. We**'re not going to have** time to study.

Why is President Clark doing this? He only wants a fitness center because other schools have them. He thinks more students **are going to come** to our school if we have a fancy fitness center. But we're here for a good education, not to enjoy a state-of-the-art fitness center.

—*Joe Molina*

To the Editor:

A week ago President Clark announced plans for a new fitness center for our college. I love the idea. It**'s going to give** us a chance to relax and unwind[3] before and after classes. College is not just a time to sit in a library and study. It's a time for us to make our bodies *and* our minds stronger.

When the gym is built, **I'm going to go** there every day. Yes. We**'re going to pay** for it. There **is going to be** a tuition hike.[4] But in my opinion, it's worth it. It**'s going to improve** our lives.

Last month a study showed that most students gain 10 pounds in their freshman year. I'll bet that**'s not going to happen** once we have our new fitness center.

—*Alison Meadows*

[1] *fitness center:* a place to exercise
[2] *equipment:* machines
[3] *unwind:* to relax and feel no stress
[4] *hike:* an increase

After You Read

A | Practice *PAIRS: Read the Letters to the Editor again aloud. Take turns reading each paragraph.*

B | Vocabulary *Circle the letter of the best meaning for the words in blue.*

1. Is the **tuition** at your school the same as it was last year?

   a. work **b.** money for school

2. Our teacher **announced** that there will be a school party next Thursday.

   a. said **b.** answered

3. They **increased** the number of students from 22 to 25 per class.

   a. raised **b.** changed

4. The train is two dollars more than the bus. **Is it worth it?**

   a. How much is the train? **b.** Is there value in paying extra for the train?

5. I am **against** the idea of raising taxes.

   a. not for **b.** worried about

6. **In my opinion** students need a fitness center.

   a. I know **b.** I think

C | Comprehension *Read the sentences. Is the statement for or against the fitness center? Write the letter in the correct box.*

a. "It's going to cost a lot of money."
b. "It's going to be a place to relax and unwind."
c. "It's going to keep students in good shape."
d. "More students are going to need to work during the school year."
e. "Tuition is going to increase."
f. "It's going to attract more students."

For the Fitness Center	Against the Fitness Center
	a

BE GOING TO FOR THE FUTURE

Affirmative Statements			
Subject + Be	**Going to**	**Base Form of Verb**	
I'm He's We're You're* They're	going to	study	tonight.
It's		rain	

Negative Statements			
Subject + Be	**Not**	**Going to**	**Base Form of Verb**
I'm He's We're You're They're	not	going to	sleep.
It's			rain.

*You're can be both singular and plural subjects.

Yes / No Questions					
Be	**Subject**	**Going to**	**Base Form of Verb**	
Am	I			
Are	you	going to	drive	tomorrow?
Is	he			

Short Answers	
Affirmative	**Negative**
Yes, you are.	No, you're not.
Yes, I am.	No, I'm not.
Yes, he is.	No, he's not.

Wh- Questions					
Wh- Word	**Be**	**Subject**	**Going to**	**Base Form of Verb**	
What	is	she		do?	
Where	are	they	going to	go?	there?
How	am	I		get	

Short Answers
Meet her friend.
To the library.
By bus.

GRAMMAR NOTES

1 There are different ways to express **the future**.

USAGE NOTE: In speaking, *be going to* is more common than *will*.

- We **are going to buy** a car.
- We **are buying** a car next month.
- We **will buy** a car.

2 One way to express the future is with a form of *be* + *going to* + **the base form of the verb**.

Use **contractions** of *be* in speaking and informal writing.

Remember to use a form of *be* before *going to*. Remember to use the base form of the verb after *going to*.

- He **is going to start** at 9:00.
- They **are going to start** at 9:00.

- He**'s going to start** at 9:00.
- They**'re going to start** at 9:00.

NOT: He ~~going to~~ start at 9:00.
NOT: He's going to ~~starts~~ at 9:00.

3	Use *be going to* + base form • **to state facts about the future** • **to make predictions** • **to talk about plans**	• The politicians **are going to meet** in Rome. • There **is going to be** a change in the climate. • I can't go to the restaurant. I**'m going to take** my friend to the airport.
4	Use *probably* with *be going to* to say that **you think something will happen, but you are not sure.**	• We're **probably** going to start at 9:00. • It's **probably** going to rain.
5	**Future time markers** usually come at the beginning or the end of a sentence. Some common future time markers are: *tomorrow*, *next week*, *next month*, *this weekend*, and *in 2100*.	• They are going to start construction **next week**. • **Next week** they are going to start construction.
6	Sometimes we use **the present progressive + a future time marker** to talk about the future. This is especially true with the verb *go* and verbs such as *drive* or *fly*. We do not use the present progressive with non-action verbs to talk about the future.	• We**'re going** there **next week**. • He**'s driving** to the country **this weekend**. • He**'s going to need** a new car next year. Not: He's needing a new car next year.

STEP 3 FOCUSED PRACTICE

EXERCISE 1: Discover the Grammar

A | *Read the sentences. Underline all examples of* **be going to** *and the base form of the verb that follows.*

1. Last week Mayor Jonas talked about building a sports stadium. It's <u>going to seat</u> 300,000 people.

2. They're going to build a garage for the stadium. It's going to have spaces for 5,000 cars.

3. The mayor is giving a speech on Wednesday here at our school. She's going to talk about raising money for the stadium.

4. They're going to build stores around the stadium. The stores are going to provide jobs for a lot of people.

5. Some people don't want the city to build a new stadium. They're against it because the city is going to destroy some historic buildings when they build the stadium.

B | *Look at Part A. Circle the sentence that uses present progressive for the future.*

EXERCISE 2: *Be going to* for the Future

(Grammar Notes 2–4)

Complete the sentences with **be going to** and the verbs in parentheses.

A: The city needs money.

B: What _____*is*_____ the mayor _____*going to do*_____ about it?
              1.   **2. (do)**

A: He _____ taxes.
           3. (increase)

B: _____ he _____ city workers?
        4.   **5. (lay off)**

A: No. Two thousand city workers _____. The city
                                             6. (retire)

_____ new police or teachers.
     7. (hire / not)

B: That's not good. Crime _____.
                                  8. (probably / increase)

A: I agree.

B: And children _____ a good education.
                     9. (probably get / not)

A: I _____ a letter to the mayor.
         10. (write)

B: What _____ you _____?
           11.   **12. (say)**

A: I _____ him to bring more business to the city.
        13. (tell)

B: How _____ he _____ that?
           14.   **15. (do)**

A: Tourism. That's the answer.

EXERCISE 3: *Be going to* for the Future: *Wh-* Questions

(Grammar Notes 2–5)

Read the news announcement. Write questions with **be going to** and the words in parentheses on the next page. Then answer the questions. Use short answers.

NEW HIGH SCHOOL ON OAK STREET

The city plans to start building a new high school on Oak Street next March at a cost of $45 million. The builder expects to finish the school in three years. The school will have space for 3,000 students.

1. (What / city / build)

   A: _What's the city going to build?_

   B: _A new high school._

2. (Where / it / be)

   A: _____

   B: _____

3. (When / the builders / start)

   A: _____

   B: _____

4. (How much / it / cost)

   A: _____

   B: _____

5. (How long / it / take)

   A: _____

   B: _____

EXERCISE 4: *Be going to* for the Future
(Grammar Notes 1–3)

The West Street Association is against the construction of a new building on West Street.
Complete their letter to the editor with the affirmative or negative form of **be going to.**

To the Editor:

Mr. Romp wants to build a 20-story building on West Street. The West Street Association is

against the plan. It _'s going to change_ the area. All the buildings on West
        1. (change)

Street are only four or five stories high. A very tall building _____
                                                                    2. (look)

good. The new building _____ garage spaces
                          3. (have)

for 50 cars, but there _____ 200 apartments.
                          4. (be)

There _____ enough parking spaces. There
         5. (probably / be)

_____ a lot more traffic in the area and
   6. (be)

_____ terrible. Let's stop construction of the Romp Tower!
   7. (look)

EXERCISE 5: Simple Past, Simple Present, *Be going to*   (Grammar Notes 1–4)

Complete the conversations with the verbs in parentheses. Use the simple past, the
simple present, or **be going to** for the future.

CONVERSATION A

INEZ: _____Did_____ you _____listen_____ to the weather report?
                1.   2. (listen)

ROBERTO: Yes. It _____ sunny and warm today and tomorrow.
                        3. (be)

INEZ: Good. There _____ a town meeting outdoors in East Park
                          4. (be)

tomorrow.

CONVERSATION B

DANIEL: The mayor _____ to close Maple Street to cars next month. He
                          1. (want)

_____ it a place for people to walk. No cars will be allowed.
     2. (make)

ALISA: How _____ you _____ about it?
                  3.   4. (know)

DANIEL: The mayor _____ it last night on his weekly radio show.
                          5. (announce)

ALISA: I _____ it's a great idea.
             6. (think)

DANIEL: Well, storeowners aren't happy. They say they _____ business.
                                                                7. (lose)

ALISA: What else _____ the mayor _____ last night?
                        8.   9. (say)

DANIEL: In the next five years he _____ this city into a center for the arts.
                                          10. (turn)

ALISA: How _____ he _____ that?
                  11.   12. (do)

DANIEL: He _____ cheap housing for artists. He _____ a
              13. (offer)   14. (build)

concert hall, and he _____ artwork in the park.
                            15. (put)

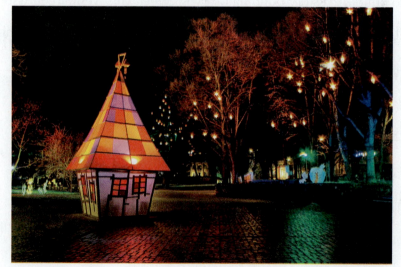

EXERCISE 6: Present Progressive for the Future

(Grammar Note 6)

*Look at the mayor's schedule for next Monday and Tuesday. Write questions with the given words. Use the **present progressive for the future**. Then write short answers.*

Monday   October 12

10:00 A.M. Mayors' Meeting

12:00 P.M. Lunch with community leaders

4:30 P.M. Meeting with California Energy Council

7:00 P.M. Meeting with Police Commissioner Ron Byrd

11:30 P.M. American Airlines—Flight #41 from Los Angeles to Washington D.C. Dulles Airport

Tuesday   October 13

7:48 A.M. Arrive Dulles Airport

1:00 P.M. State University—speech

3:00 P.M. Senior Center Opening

5:00 P.M. Dinner for police chief—Grand Hotel

1. Who / he / have lunch with on Monday?

   Q: *Who is he having lunch with on Monday?*

   A: *He's having lunch with community leaders.*

2. What / he / do / Monday afternoon?

   Q: _____

   A: _____

3. Who / he / meet / at 7:00 P.M. on Monday?

   Q: _____

   A: _____

4. What time / he / fly home from Los Angeles?

   Q: _____

   A: _____

(continued on next page)

5. Where / he / speak/ in Washington, D.C.?

Q: _____

A: _____

6. When / he speak to the senior citizens?

Q: _____

A: _____

7. Where he / go / to a dinner for the police chief?

Q: _____

A: _____

EXERCISE 7: Editing

Correct the newsletter article. There are five mistakes. The first mistake is already corrected. Find and correct four more.

VILLAGE GREEN APARTMENTS

Dear Residents:

Last week the mayor talked about building a sports stadium in our neighborhood. I think it's a terrible idea. It's going ^to^ cost taxpayers millions of dollars. It going to mean traffic jams. Parking is being difficult, and it's going to bringing noise to the area.

Next Monday at 7:00 P.M. the mayor is goes to answer questions at the public library. Please come out and speak out against the new stadium.

Sincerely,
Dale Ortiz
President, Residents' Association

EXERCISE 8: Pronunciation

A | *Read and listen to the Pronunciation Note.*

> **Pronunciation Note**
>
> In informal speaking, **going to** is often pronounced **"gonna"** when it comes before a verb.
>
> **EXAMPLE:** We're "gonna" win this race. (**going to** + **verb**)
>
> Do not pronounce *going to* as "gonna" when *going* comes before the preposition **to** + **a place**.
>
> **EXAMPLE:** We're going to the movies. (**going to** + **place**)

B | *Listen to the sentences. Check (✓) when you hear* **going to** *and when you hear* **"gonna."**

going to	"gonna"
1.	
2.	
3.	
4.	
5.	
6.	
7.	

C | *Listen and repeat the sentences.*

1. He's going to a concert.
2. They're going to be late.
3. It's going to rain.
4. We're going to the library.
5. I'm going to think about it.

EXERCISE 9: Listening

A | *Listen to a conversation about a new building. Circle the correct letter.*

Why does the man want to buy the newspaper?

a. He wrote a letter and wants to see if his letter is in the paper.

b. He wants to see if the paper is for the new building.

B | *Listen again. Answer the questions.*

1. What are two reasons for building the new apartment building?

    a. _____

    b. _____

2. What are two reasons against building it?

    a. _____

    b. _____

3. Is the man for or against the new building? _____

EXERCISE 10: Conversation: Changes in Your Life

PAIRS: Tell about an upcoming change in your life or the life of someone you know well. For example, a move or a new job. Your partner asks questions about the change. Then talk about a good and a bad thing about the change. Take turns.

> **EXAMPLE:** **A:** My sister is moving away from the city.
> **B:** Why is she moving?
> **A:** She needs a larger home. She has two children. She's going to have more space, but she and her husband are going to have a long commute to work.

EXERCISE 11: Writing

A | *GROUPS: Read the changes in the chart for Columbus College and the city of Columbus. Choose one school change and one city change. Discuss reasons why you are for or against the change.*

School Changes	City Changes
50% of courses will be online.	No cars on Main Street on weekends
No tests, just written reports	Higher taxes on clothes and entertainment to pay for better schools
No smoking on college campus	Restaurants need to show calorie and fat content of all food on menus.

> **EXAMPLE:** Fifty percent of classes will be online courses.
> **A:** I think that's a terrible idea. Online courses will be boring.
> **B:** I disagree. In my opinion, we're going to have great online discussions.

B | *Write an email letter to the editor. Explain why you are for or against one of these changes. Explain what the change is going to mean. Use* be going to *for the future.*

EXAMPLE:

letters_to_the_editor

Dear Editor:

Last week the college president spoke about a law to ban cars on Main Street on weekends. I think that's a great idea. The street is going to be safer for students. The air is going to be cleaner. It's going to be quieter. The change is going to make the campus area a better place to walk, shop, and dine.

Sincerely,

Daniel Rivera

C | *Check your work. Use the Editing Checklist.*

Editing Checklist

Did you . . . ?
☐ use correct forms of ***be going to*** for the future
☐ check your spelling

A | Complete the sentences with **be going to** and the words in parentheses. Use the future. Use contractions when possible.

The city _____ a waterfront park. It _____ millions of dollars.
            1. (build)   **2. (cost)**

It _____ an amusement park. There _____ a few restaurants.
     3. (have)   **4. (be)**

Construction _____ until next summer.
            5. (begin / not)

B | Complete the sentences with **be going to** and the words in parentheses. Use the future and the affirmative or negative form. Use contractions when possible.

1. Everyone is happy. Taxes _____. No one likes to pay taxes.
                                           (increase)

2. It's raining hard. We _____ soccer in the park.
                            (play)

3. John is in the hospital. We _____ him. Do you want to come?
                                    (visit)

4. It's Mary's last year. She _____ in December and move away.
                                  (retire)

5. I'm tired and it's late. I _____ any more work.
                         (do)

C | Look at Eun Young's schedule. Write questions with the words in parentheses. Use the present progressive for the future. Write short answers.

MONDAY: dentist 5:30	TUESDAY: meet Yu Chen Pappa Pizza 6:30

1. (When / she / go to the dentist)

    Q: _____   A: _____

2. (Where / she / meet / Yu Chen)

    Q: _____   A: _____

3. (she / meet / Yu Chen / on Monday)

    Q: _____   A: _____

D | Correct the paragraph. There are four mistakes.

    This city going to change under our new mayor. People's going to ride bikes, and they're gonna use public transportation. They're no going to drive big cars. There are probably going to be higher tolls on bridges and more bike paths on the roads.

STEP 1 GRAMMAR IN CONTEXT

Before You Read

What do you think will be different by the year 2025? 2050? By 2100?

> EXAMPLE: I think people will travel to the past and the future.

Read

Future Science Magazine *asked scientists to make predictions for the year 2050. How will we look? How will we travel? How long will we live? Read their predictions.*

www.futuresciencemag.com

FUTURE SCIENCE
What's in Store[1] for Us in 2050?

1. More people **will be** vegetarians. They **won't eat** any meat or fish.
2. People **will look** bigger than people today.
3. People **will read** each other's thoughts.
4. They **will take** memory pills.
5. Cars **will run on** solar[2] energy.
6. Private planes **will be** common.
7. Travel to the moon **will be** common.
8. Robots **will cook** our meals. We **won't spend** a lot of time in the kitchen.
9. On average, people **will weigh** 11 pounds (5 kilograms) more, and they **will be** about 5 inches (12.5 centimeters) taller.
10. People **will live** to be 100 years old on average, and the majority of people **will be** over 60.
11. People **won't need** so many tissues. There **will be** a cure for the common cold.
12. Paper money and coins[3] **will disappear**. People **will use** credit cards for all their purchases.

---

[1]***be in store:*** to be about to happen to someone
[2]***solar:*** from the sun
[3]***coins:*** metal money such as quarters or dimes

After You Read

A | **Practice** *PAIRS: Read the predictions again aloud. Take turns reading each prediction.*

B | **Vocabulary** *Complete the sentences with the words from the box.*

common	disappear	meal	spend time	vegetarian

1. He never eats meat. He's a _____.

2. In the future, travel to the moon will be _____.

3. Did the moon _____ behind a cloud?

4. What's your favorite _____ of the day?

5. We like to _____ in the laboratory.

C | **Comprehension** *Read the questions. Circle the letter of the correct answers based on the article in* Future Science Magazine. *There may be more than one correct answer.*

1. How will people look?

   a. taller   **b.** shorter   **c.** smaller

2. Where will people travel?

   a. to the moon   **b.** to Mars   **c.** to the past

3. What will increase?

   a. the number of vegetarians   **b.** the average life span   **c.** the number of colds

4. What will be common in 2050?

   a. coins   **b.** private planes   **c.** travel to the moon

WILL FOR THE FUTURE

Affirmative Statements			
Subject	***Will* / *'ll***	**Base Form of Verb**	**Time Marker**
I			
You*			
He			
She	**will**	**leave**	tomorrow.
It	**'ll**		
We			
They			

Negative Statements			
Subject	***Will Not* / *Won't***	**Base Form of Verb**	**Time Marker**
I			
You*			
He			
She	**will not**	**leave**	tonight.
It	**won't**		
We			
They			

*You is both singular and plural.

Yes / No Questions			
Will	**Subject**	**Base Form of Verb**	**Time Marker**
	I		
	you		
	he		
Will	she	**arrive**	tonight?
	it		
	we		
	they		

Short Answers					
Affirmative			**Negative**		
	you			you	
	I			I	
	he			he	
Yes,	she	**will**.	No,	she	**won't**.
	it			it	
	we			we	
	they			they	

Future Time Markers	
today	
tonight	
tomorrow	
this	morning
	afternoon
	evening
tomorrow	morning
	afternoon
	evening
	night
Saturday	night

Future Time Markers with *Next* and *In*		
next		week
		month
		year
		Monday
		weekend
in		2020
		the 22nd century
		20 years
		two weeks
		a few days

GRAMMAR NOTES

1	Use *will* + **the base form of the verb** to talk about things that will take place in the future.	• The class **will begin** on November 2. • We **will meet** tomorrow at 10:00 A.M. • The plane **will arrive** at 6:00 P.M. NOT: The plane will ~~to arrive~~ at 6:00 P.M. NOT: The plane will ~~arrives~~ at 6:00 P.M.
	BE CAREFUL! Use the base form of the verb after *will* or *won't*. Remember, the base form does not change.	
2	Use **contractions** of *will* **with pronouns** in speaking and informal writing.	• **We'll** be there before 3:00.
	BE CAREFUL! Do not use contractions in affirmative short answers.	**A:** Will they be there? **B:** Yes, they will. NOT: Yes, ~~they'll~~.
3	Use *will* to make **predictions**.	• In 2050 there **will be** more megacities. Those cities **are going to be** very crowded.
	USAGE NOTE: In writing, we often use *will* in one sentence and *be going to* in the next sentence.	
4	Use *will* to make a **promise** or **give assurance**.	• **I'll be** back in five minutes. • I **won't do** that again.
5	Use *will* to **ask for** or **offer** something.	**A: Will** you **help** me? **B:** Don't worry. I**'ll help**.
6	***Won't*** is the contraction of ***will*** + ***not***. It has two meanings. Use *won't* to mean the **negative future**. Use *won't* to mean "**refuse(s) to**."	• He **won't be** in school tomorrow. • The child **won't eat** carrots.
7	To say that something is not definite, use ***probably*** with *will* for the future.	• People will **probably** take more vacations.
8	Some **time markers** are used only for the future. Other time markers can be used for the past or the future.	FUTURE • She won't be home **tomorrow**. FUTURE • She'll be home **this afternoon**. PAST • She was at the library **this afternoon**.

EXERCISE 1: Discover the Grammar

Read the sentences. How is **will** *used? Match the sentences with the descriptions.*

__b__	**1.** I won't do it. I think it's wrong.	**a.** predicts something
____	**2.** Will you show me how to use that computer?	**b.** refuses to do something
____	**3.** I'll be back by 9:00.	**c.** promises to do something
____	**4.** There won't be any meeting on February 8.	**d.** asks for something
____	**5.** By 2020 people will fly to the moon for fun.	**e.** tells about something that is not going to happen

EXERCISE 2: *Will* for the Future

(Grammar Notes 1–7)

Complete the conversations with **will** *or* **won't** *and the verbs in parentheses.*

1. A: Mom, when _____*will*_____ dinner _____*be*_____ ready?
 (be)

 B: Robot Bob says it _____ ready in 22 minutes.
 (be)

2. A: Do you really think scientists _____ a cure for the cold?
 (find)

 B: I hope so. It _____ a lot of money. People _____ work
 (save) **(miss)**
 so often.

3. A: Dr. Smith, my great grandmother _____ her memory pills. She says
 (take)
 they taste bad. _____ you _____ her some that taste
 (give)
 good?

 B: Don't worry. I _____ her some that taste like candy.
 (give)

4. A: When do you think we _____ astronauts to the planet Mars?
 (send)

 B: No one knows. Right now we're spending less money on space exploration. So it
 _____ longer than we thought.
 (probably / take)

5. A: Where _____ the wedding _____?
 (take place)

 B: The wedding _____ on the moon.
 (be)

 A: And where _____ you _____ for your honeymoon?
 (go)

 B: We _____ to Mars.
 (probably / go)

EXERCISE 3: *Will* for the Future

(Grammar Notes 1–7)

*Complete the conversation with **will** and the verbs in parentheses.*

A: So, Laura, when _____*will*_____ you _____*finish*_____ the article about the future?
       ㅤㅤㅤㅤㅤㅤ**1.**ㅤㅤㅤㅤㅤㅤㅤㅤㅤㅤ**2. (finish)**

B: It _____ ready until 4:00 P.M., but I think you _____ it.
       ㅤㅤㅤ**3. (not / be)**ㅤㅤㅤㅤㅤㅤㅤㅤㅤㅤㅤㅤㅤㅤㅤㅤㅤ**4. (like)**

A: You interviewed Dr. Reicher, right?

B: Yes, I did. He says computers _____ us stay healthy.
       ㅤㅤㅤㅤㅤㅤㅤㅤㅤㅤㅤㅤㅤㅤ**5. (help)**

A: Oh, yeah? How's that?

B: In the future, we _____ computers inside our bodies. They
       ㅤㅤㅤㅤㅤㅤㅤㅤㅤㅤ**6. (have)**

       _____ constantly _____ things such as our blood sugar and
       ㅤㅤㅤ**7.**ㅤㅤㅤㅤㅤㅤㅤㅤㅤㅤㅤ**8. (check)**

       blood pressure.

A: _____ diabetes and heart disease _____?
       ㅤㅤ**9.**ㅤㅤㅤㅤㅤㅤㅤㅤㅤㅤㅤㅤㅤㅤㅤㅤ**10. (disappear)**

B: No, but people _____ from those diseases so often, and people
       ㅤㅤㅤㅤㅤ**11. (probably / die / not)**

       _____ longer.
       ㅤ**12. (live)**

A: And when _____ this _____?
       ㅤㅤㅤㅤㅤㅤㅤㅤ**13.**ㅤㅤㅤㅤㅤㅤㅤ**14. (happen)**

B: By 2030.

A: That's really not so far away.

EXERCISE 4: *Will* for the Future

(Grammar Notes 2–3, 8)

*Look at the chart of predictions. Write questions about Fogville with the words in parentheses. Use **will** for the future. Answer the questions.*

Predictions for Fogville in 2050			
The cost of housing	↓	Crime	→
The cost of health care	↓	The percent of people under 25	↑
Taxes	↓	The percent of people over 65	→

Key		
Increase	=	↑
Stay the same	=	→
Decrease	=	↓

1. **A:** _Will the cost of housing increase?_____
   ㅤㅤㅤㅤㅤㅤㅤㅤ**(the cost of housing / increase)**

   B: _No, it won't. The cost of housing will decrease._____

2. **A:** _____
   ㅤㅤㅤㅤㅤㅤㅤㅤ**(the cost of health care / stay the same)**

   B: _____

3. A: _____
                          (taxes / stay the same)

   B: _____

4. A: _____
                        (the percent of people under 25 / decrease)

   B: _____

5. A: _____
                        (the percent of people over 65 / decrease)

   B: _____

EXERCISE 5: Review of Present, Past, Future

(Grammar Notes 3–4, 6–8)

Complete the conversation. Use the verbs in parentheses. Use the simple present, the simple past, or the future with **will.** *Use contractions where possible.*

A: _____*Did*_____ you _____*hear*_____ the lecture last week?
        1.   **2. (hear)**

B: No, what _____ it about?
            3. (be)

A: The future. According to Professor Johns, by the year 2100 there _____
                                               4. (be)

cities in the ocean, we _____ trips to the moon, and we _____
                   5. (take)   **6. (learn)**

everything from computers.

B: By 2100? We _____ all _____ gone by then. _____
                7.   **8. (be)**   **9. (like)**

the people _____ his lecture?
            10.

A: Yes, they did. They always do. He _____ how to make any subject
                                    11. (know)

fascinating.

EXERCISE 6: Editing

Correct the conversation. There are six mistakes. The first mistake is already corrected.
Find and correct five more.

A: What did he say?

B: He said there ₌ be an increase in the population. Many young people will moves to the
                  will

area. Taxes will increases. The value of homes will also to increase.

A: How about crime? Will it increases?

B: No, it doesn't.

A: Well, it sounds like a great place to live.

STEP 4 COMMUNICATION PRACTICE

EXERCISE 7: Pronunciation

 A | *Read and listen to the Pronunciation Note.*

> **Pronunciation Note**
>
> In conversation we often **link** the **subject pronoun** (*I, you, he, she, it, we,* OR *they*) and *will*. The final vowel sound of *will* often sounds like **/ əl /**.
>
> **EXAMPLES:** I'll she'll it'll we'll

B | *Listen and repeat the contractions.*

I'll   you'll   he'll   she'll   it'll   we'll   they'll

C | *Now listen and repeat the sentences.*

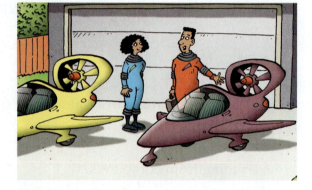

1. You'll fly to the moon.
2. He'll visit you on the moon.
3. They'll be there too.
4. She'll help you fly the spaceship.
5. I'll be with you shortly.
6. It'll cost a lot of money.
7. We'll see them the following year.

EXERCISE 8: Listening

A | *Listen to a conversation between a TV news reporter and two people. Read the question. Circle the correct letter.*

Why is the man talking to the two people?

    a. They made a lot of money.   **b.** They won a lot of money.

B | *Listen again. Answer the questions.*

1. What will the woman do with her money?

    a. _____

    b. _____

2. What will the man do with his money?

_____

3. What does the man mean when he says, "They'll get over it."

_____

EXERCISE 9: Class Survey

SMALL GROUPS: Look at the predictions in the Future Science article on page 283. Do you agree? What are your predictions? Discuss your answers. Report to the class.

EXAMPLE: We all think paper money will disappear. People will use credit cards or check cards to pay for everything. Coins are heavy, and bills are not clean. These cards are the way of the future.

EXERCISE 10: Survey: In the Future

A | Complete the information.

1. Write the name of something that is very popular today.

_____

2. Write the name of a country and a time in the future.

_____

B | Complete the questions below with your answers from Part A. Then survey five classmates. Ask them the questions.

1. Will _____ still be popular in _____?

2. Will _____ be a popular tourist destination in _____?

C | Report your results to the class.

EXAMPLE: I asked five people this question: "Will DVDs still be popular in 10 years?" Four out of six students said, "No."

EXERCISE 11: Making Predictions

A | Make predictions about these fields for the year 2050. Tape them on the wall.

environment   health   jobs   medicine   sports   technology

EXAMPLE: Nobody will be hungry.

B | Number all the predictions. Go around and read each prediction. Choose four predictions. Tell if you agree or disagree with them.

EXERCISE 12: Writing

A | GROUPS: Talk about how life will be in the future. Use these topics:

education   fashion   food   homes   tourism   travel

EXAMPLE: A: I think people will wear paper clothes.
B: I disagree. People will worry about the environment. They won't wear throwaway clothes.
C: I think people will wear special clothes in the summer. They will be light, but they will protect them from the sun.
D: And in the winter they will wear clothes that are light in weight, but very warm.

B | *Choose a year. Choose a topic from Part A. Write about how things will be different.*
*Use **will** for the future and **be going to** for the future.*

EXAMPLE: TRAVEL IN 2050
In 2050 people will have new ways to travel. First of all, people will have their own wings. They're going to use them to fly distances of 50 miles or less. The wings won't take up much space, so people won't have to "park" their wings. People will also travel with flying cars. These cars will go up to 200 miles an hour. People are going to use their flying cars to travel 200 to 400 miles. There will be regular planes and jets, and there will be spaceships for trips to other planets.

C | *Check your work. Use the Editing Checklist.*

Editing Checklist
Did you . . . ? ☐ use ***will*** for the future correctly ☐ use ***be going to*** for the future correctly ☐ check your spelling

A | *Write questions with* **will** *and the words in parentheses.*

1. _____
   (Where / people / travel / in 20 years)

2. _____
   (people / fly / to the moon)

3. _____
   (How / they / get around)

4. _____
   (the climate / change)

5. _____
   (people / look / different)

B | *Circle the correct word to complete the sentences.*

1. He doesn't like hats. He **will / won't** wear them.

2. I'm busy tomorrow morning. I **will / won't** be at work until noon.

3. He's good at computers. He probably **will / won't** be able to fix your computer.

4. The sale ends today, but there **will / won't** be a sale next month.

5. I need more time. I **will / won't** be ready for at least a half an hour.

C | *Write questions with* **will.** *Use the same ideas in all sentences.*

1. Yesterday was hot. Today is hot. _____ it _____ tomorrow too?

2. Last week he had a test. This week he has a test. _____ he _____ next week too?

3. Last September there was a storm. This September there was a storm.

   _____ there _____ next September too?

4. Yesterday it rained. Today it rained. _____ it _____ tomorrow too?

5. He worked late yesterday. He worked late today. _____ he _____ tomorrow too?

D | *Correct the paragraph. There are five mistakes.*

   I usually bring my lunch to work, but tomorrow I no will bring it because it's my birthday. My co-workers will takes me out to a restaurant. We'll to order a few different dishes, and we'll share them. They'll singing "Happy Birthday," and they'll give me a small gift. I'm sure it will is a lot of fun.

26 *May* or *Might* for Possibility
WEATHER

STEP 1 GRAMMAR IN CONTEXT

Before You Read

Answer the questions.

1. How do you know what the weather will be? (*I watch TV, check my phone or computer, listen to the radio, read the newspaper*)
2. How often do you think the weather report is wrong? (*rarely, sometimes, often, almost always*)

Read

Read the conversation and TV weather report.

MOTHER:	Shh. The weather report is coming on.[1]
ANNOUNCER:	It's Sunday, May 15. The time is 9:00 A.M. And now here's the weather forecast with Luis Malina.
METEOROLOGIST:	Good morning, everyone. If you plan to be outdoors today or Monday, wear a warm jacket and bring an umbrella. The weather will continue to be unseasonable.[2] Today will be cold and windy. And heavy rain will begin

[1] **coming on:** starting
[2] **unseasonable:** unusual for the time of year

tonight or tomorrow. For your morning commute, there **may be** flooding on the highways.

So, if you can, take public transportation. And don't put away those umbrellas too soon because we'll have more rain on Tuesday and Wednesday. By Thursday the weather **may become** milder with only a 20 percent chance of showers.[3] We **might** even **see** some sun. But until then, my friends, my best advice is stay indoors with a good book or movie.

ALEX: I guess that means no soccer tomorrow.

MOTHER: Don't be too sure. You **may** still **have** a game. The meteorologist[4] is often wrong. Remember last Friday. He predicted a beautiful day, but it was awful. And last week he said we **might have** a major[5] storm. It turned out to be sunny and dry.

ALEX: Maybe.

MOTHER: I just hope you don't play in the rain.

ALEX: We **might**. The last time it rained we played the entire game. Playing in the mud was great! And we won!

---

[3] **chance of showers:** a short period of heavy rain
[4] **meteorologist:** weather reporter
[5] **major:** big

After You Read

A | Practice *GROUPS OF THREE: Now read the conversation aloud.*

B | Vocabulary *Complete the sentences with the words from the box.*

| commute | entire | flooding | highways | mild | predicted | storm |

1. They canceled the game because they expected rain the _____ day.

2. He lives outside the city. His _____ to work is an hour and a half each way.

3. There is always _____ on that street when it rains. The city needs to fix the problem.

4. The meteorologist _____ beautiful weather for the next three days.

5. There is bad traffic on all the major _____. I think we should wait to go home.

6. The _____ is getting worse. They may close the airport.

7. I want to live someplace where the weather is sunny and _____.

C | Comprehension *Circle the correct weather for each day, according to the forecast.*

Sunday	
sunny and warm	cold and windy

Monday	
light rain	heavy rain

Tuesday	
rainy	sunny

Wednesday	
sunny	rainy

Thursday	
sunny—no chance of rain	sunny—20% chance of rain

STEP 2 GRAMMAR PRESENTATION

MAY OR MIGHT FOR POSSIBILITY

Affirmative Statements			
Subject	**May / Might**	**Base Form of Verb**	
I You* He She We They	**may might**	**play**	soccer.
It	**may might**	**rain**	tonight.

Negative Statements				
Subject	**May / Might**	**Not**	**Base Form of Verb**	
I You* He She We They	**may might**	**not**	**play**	soccer.
It	**may might**	**not**	**rain**	tonight.

*You is both singular and plural.

GRAMMAR NOTES

1	Use *may* or *might* to express **possibility** about the present or the future.	**A:** Where's John? **B:** I don't know. He **may be** on vacation. **A:** What are you going to do this weekend? **B:** We **might go** to a movie.
	May and *might* have almost the same meaning, but *may* means something is a little more possible than *might*.	• It **might** rain. *(It's possible.)* • It **may** rain. *(It's more possible.)* • It**'ll probably** rain. *(It's likely.)* • It **will** rain. *(It's definite.)*

2	*May* and *might* are **followed** by the **base form of the verb**.	• He **might go** to the movies.
		  Not: He might ~~goes~~ to the movies.
		  Not: He might ~~to go~~ to the movies.

	There are no contractions for *may* or *might*.	He might not go to the movies. Not: He ~~mightn't~~ go to the movies.
3	**USAGE NOTE:** We usually use *will* or *be going to*, not *may* or *might*, to **ask *yes / no* questions about the future**.	**A: Will** you **go** to the party? **B:** I might. OR I may. **A: Are** you **going to see** that movie tonight? **B:** We might. OR We may. Not: ~~May~~ you go to the party?
4	We use *I think I might* for possibility. We use *I'm sure* + **subject** + *will* for certainty.	• **I think I might** have the flu. • **I'm sure I will** be there. Not: I'm sure I ~~might~~ buy that book.
	We use *I think I will* for something that is likely.	• **I think I'll call** the doctor.
5	*May* and *might* are modals. *Maybe* is an adverb. It means "there's a possibility."	**Maybe I'll go** to the party. = **I might go** to the party. OR **I may go** to the party.
	Maybe I will has a similar meaning to *I might* or *I may*.	**A:** Are you going to the game? **B: Maybe.** = **I may**. OR **I might**.
6	We use *it might* or *it may* to talk about the weather.	• **It might** rain tonight. • **It may** snow tomorrow.

EXERCISE 1: Discover the Grammar

Match the sentences. Write the correct letter.

__d__ **1.** It's definitely going to rain.   **a.** It probably won't rain.

____ **2.** There's an 80 percent chance of rain.   **b.** It'll probably rain.

____ **3.** There's about a 50 percent chance of rain.   **c.** It won't rain.

____ **4.** There's a 10 percent chance of rain.   **d.** It will rain.

____ **5.** It's definitely not going to rain.   **e.** It may rain.

EXERCISE 2: Affirmative of *May* or *Might*

(Grammar Notes 1–2, 4)

Complete the conversations with **may** *or* **might** *and the verbs from the box. Use the affirmative or negative form.*

be	cancel	have	leave	~~rain~~	take

1. A: Take your umbrella. I think it _____ *might rain* _____ this afternoon.

   B: Really? The forecast was for sun.

2. A: Start dinner without me. It _____ me a long time to get

      home. The rain is causing flooding on the highway.

   B: That's OK. We'll wait.

3. A: Sandy looks upset.

   B: She is. She _____ her trip. Her sister is in the hospital.

4. A: Why are you so worried?

   B: The kids are camping tonight, and the forecast is for unusually cold weather. They

      _____ enough clothes.

5. A: Where's John? The meeting will start in a few minutes.

   B: He _____ late. All flights are delayed because of the wind.

6. A: How are you feeling now?

   B: Terrible. I _____ the office early.

EXERCISE 3: *May/ Might / Will / Will probably*

(Grammar Notes 1–3)

Read today's weather forecast. Complete the sentences with the correct words in parentheses.

Today

Cloudy with periods of rain
High of 50°

Winds SSE
at 30 to 40 mph

60 percent
chance of rain

1. It _____ *will be* _____ a very windy day.
   (will be / won't be)

2. It _____, but it _____ all
   (will probably rain / probably won't rain)   **(may not rain / won't rain)**
   day.

3. The temperature _____ 60 degrees.
   (may reach / probably won't reach)

4. _____ they _____ the ball
   (Will cancel / Might cancel)
   game for this afternoon?

5. They _____ the game if the rain is heavy.
   (might cancel / won't cancel)

EXERCISE 4: *Maybe* and *May / Might*

(Grammar Note 5)

*Replace **maybe** with **may** or **might**. In some cases you may need to add a subject or a subject and a verb.*

1. **A:** Do you have an extra umbrella?

   B: I'm not sure. ~~Maybe I have one~~ *I may have one* in that closet.

2. **A:** Where are the baby's shoes?

   B: Maybe they are in the top drawer.

3. **A:** Are they going to cancel the barbecue?

   B: Maybe. The forecast is for heavy rain.

4. **A:** Where will you meet if it rains?

   B: Maybe we'll meet at the mall.

5. **A:** Will she bring her daughter in the rain?

   B: Maybe.

EXERCISE 5: Editing

Correct the conversations. There are six mistakes. The first mistake is already corrected. Find and correct five more.

1. **A:** Where's Bill?

   B: ~~I'm sure~~ *I think* he might be on vacation in Florida.

   A: He may needs his winter jacket. It's 40 degrees there today.

2. **A:** We maybe go to the park. Do you want to join us?

   B: No thanks. It's very windy. Why don't you do something indoors?

3. **A:** May you take the highway?

   B: Yes, I may. It's usually faster than the city streets.

4. **A:** Are you going to finish your paper on climate change today?

   B: I want to, but I mightn't have enough time.

5. **A:** What's the weather report?

   B: It's sunny now, but it may to rain this afternoon.

STEP 4 COMMUNICATION PRACTICE

EXERCISE 6: Pronunciation

A | *Read and listen to the Pronunciation Note.*

> **Pronunciation Note**
>
> For numbers that end in **-ty** such as *thirty, forty, fifty,* etc., we stress the **first syllable** of the word. For numbers that end in **-teen**, we usually stress the **second syllable**.

B | *Listen and circle the word you hear.*

1. 16   60

2. 13   30

3. 19   90

4. 15   50

5. 18   80

C | *Now listen and complete the conversations. Write the words you hear. Then practice the conversation with a partner.*

Tornadoes have wind speed from 40 to 300 miles an hour.

1. **A:** This tornado has winds of _____

    miles an hour.

   B: Did you say 115 or 150?

   A: _____.

2. **A:** It's _____ degrees.

   B: Was that 60 or 16?

   A: _____.

3. **A:** There are _____ inches of snow.

   B: Was that 14 or 40?

   A: _____.

4. **A:** It's _____ degrees below zero.

   B: Did you say 13 or 30?

   A: _____.

EXERCISE 7: Listening

A | *A couple is taking a trip to Oregon. Listen to their conversation. What is the conversation about? Circle the correct letter.*

   a. The things the man is taking with him on the trip

   b. The things the man is going to do on the trip

B | *Listen again. What reason does the man give for packing these things in his suitcase?*

1. boots _They may go mountain climbing._____

2. a raincoat _____

3. two hats _____

4. two books _____

5. a sports jacket _____

EXERCISE 8: Discussion

PAIRS: Take turns asking about your partner's plans for tonight. Use **may, might,** *and*
will probably *in your answers. Use the ideas in the list or your own. Explain your answer.*

- stay indoors
- listen to the weather report
- go running
- watch a movie
- study English
- eat out
- cook dinner

EXAMPLE: **A:** Are you going to stay indoors?
           B: I think so. I'll probably stay home and watch a movie tonight. How about you?
           A: I might eat out. I may try that new Korean restaurant. My friend says it's very
                   good.

EXERCISE 9: Writing

A | *You are a reporter for UpToDateWeather.com. Write a weather report for the next*
three days for your region. Look at pages 294–295 for ideas. Use **may** *and* **might**
where possible.

EXAMPLE: Good evening. This is Hye Won Paik with the three-day forecast. Tomorrow you will
            want to take out your running shoes. We're going to have perfect weather. It's going
            to be sunny and warm. On Wednesday, it will still be warm, but we may see some
            clouds. Then on Thursday, temperatures will drop, and we might have a shower in
            the evening.

B | *Check your work. Use the Editing Checklist.*

Editing Checklist
Did you . . . ? ☐ use *may* and *might* correctly ☐ check your spelling

UNIT 26 Review

Check your answers on page UR-5.

Do you need to review anything?

A | *Circle the correct words to complete the sentences.*

1. She may **to go / go** to the library.

2. He may **buy / buys** a new car.

3. It **mightn't / might not** rain tonight.

4. They **maybe / may** return the TV.

5. **Will / Might** you go to the party?

B | *Complete the sentences with* **may** *or* **might** *and the verbs from the box. Use the affirmative or negative form.*

get	need	see	snow	stay

1. Take your boots. It _____ this afternoon.

2. Start dinner without me. I _____ home from work until 10:00 P.M.

3. Karina is upset. The doctor says she _____ surgery.

4. Here's a gift. I _____ you before your birthday.

5. Traffic is heavy now. I _____ here for a while.

C | *Rewrite the sentences. Replace* **Maybe** *with* **may** *or* **might** *and the correct word order.*

1. Maybe there's a restroom in the library. _____

2. Maybe he's the director. _____

3. Maybe the plane is late. _____

4. Maybe they are cousins. _____

5. Maybe it's his coat. _____

D | *Correct the sentences. There are five mistakes.*

1. He might goes on vacation next week.

2. He may works late tomorrow.

3. They might to visit him tomorrow. Are you free?

4. I might not help him. I might to help her instead.

5. She maybe take a yoga class.

From Grammar to Writing
TIME CLAUSES WITH *When*

1 | *Study this information about time clauses.*

1. I was six years old. I loved to play with dolls.

_____

2. I graduate next year. I will work for a bank.

_____

2 | *Combine the sentences using* **when***. Look at the chart below for help.*

1	We can combine two sentences that tell about time by using a **time clause** and a **main clause**. *When I was six* is a **time clause**. It is not a sentence and can never stand alone. It needs a main clause.	• I was six. I started school. 　　TIME CLAUSE　　MAIN CLAUSE • **When** I was six, I started school.
2	When we use **present time clauses**, the verbs in both the time clause and the main clause are written in the **present**.	PRESENT TIME CLAUSE　　MAIN CLAUSE • When I **get** home, I **have** dinner.
3	When we use **past time clauses**, the verbs in both the time clause and the main clause are written in the **past**.	PAST TIME CLAUSE　　MAIN CLAUSE • When I **got** home, I **had** dinner.
4	When we use a **future time clause**, the future time clause uses the **simple present**. The main clause uses the **future**.	FUTURE TIME CLAUSE　　MAIN CLAUSE • When I **get** home, I **will have** dinner. (First I'll get home. Then I'll have dinner.)
5	You can begin a sentence with the time clause or the main clause. When the time clause begins the sentence, put a **comma** before the main clause. There is no comma when the main clause begins the sentence.	PRESENT TIME CLAUSE　　MAIN CLAUSE • When I get home**,** I will have dinner. 　MAIN CLAUSE　　PRESENT TIME CLAUSE • I will have dinner when I get home.

3 ⏐ *Rewrite this paragraph using three time clauses.*

My Dream

I was a child. I loved to play "make-believe" games. Sometimes I was a cowboy, and sometimes I was a prince. I became a teenager. I got a job at a video store. I saw many movies. I also made a couple of videos, and I acted in all the school plays. Now I'm studying film and acting at school. I will finish college next year. I will move to Hollywood. I hope to become a movie star.

4 ⏐ *Write a paragraph about yourself at different times of your life. Include a part about your future.*

5 ⏐ *Exchange papers with a partner. Did your partner follow the directions? Correct any mistakes in grammar and spelling.*

6 ⏐ *Talk to your partner. Discuss the mistakes you made. Then rewrite your own paper and make any necessary changes.*

PART
IX

COUNT / NON-COUNT NOUNS;
MUCH / MANY; QUANTIFIERS

27 Count and Non-Count Nouns, Quantifiers, Articles

RESTAURANTS AND FOOD

STEP 1 GRAMMAR IN CONTEXT

Before You Read

*What do you usually look for in a restaurant? Check (✓) three things that are important to you. Put an **X** next to three things that are not important.*

_____ unusual food   _____ a quiet place

_____ polite service   _____ a lively place

_____ fast service   _____ low prices

_____ a beautiful atmosphere   _____ food I like

_____ an unusual atmosphere   _____ big portions

Read

Read the online restaurant reviews.

www.kassandrasfoodreview.com

Kassandra's Food Reviews

Al Hambra ★★★★

Rich **spices** are the **draw**[1] at **Al Hambra**. The **flavor** of **ginger**, **garlic**, **cumin**, and **lemon** make the **chicken** in a **tagine (ceramic pot)** our favorite **choice**. Another great **choice** for the main **course** is the **lamb** with **ginger**. Note: There isn't **much beef** on the **menu**, and there isn't **any pork**. However, there are **many choices** of fresh **fish**, **chicken**, and **lamb**. All the **appetizers** are great. We especially like an **appetizer** called *zaalouk*. This is a **salad** made of **eggplant** and **tomato**. For **dessert** we recommend **the** almond **cookies**. There aren't **many tables** at Al Hambra, so be sure to make a **reservation** well in advance.

[1]*draw:* attraction

Topkapi ★★★

Topkapi serves Turkish **food** in a colorful **atmosphere**. The **mirrors**, **lights**, and yellow and red **colors** give this **restaurant a** warm, inviting **look**. The **food** is delicious. Try the vegetable **combo**[2] to begin. The pita **bread** with **hummus**, **yogurt**, and **tahini** is excellent. For the main **course** I suggest the lamb **kebab** with rice and salad. The best **dessert** is the **baklava**. This is **a** sweet **pastry** made with **pistachios** or **walnuts**. Enjoy your **baklava** with Turkish **coffee**. But beware, Turkish **coffee** is very strong.

Note: You may need to wait **a few minutes** even with a **reservation**, but the **atmosphere**, **food**, and **service** are worth the **wait**.

[2]**combo:** combination

After You Read

A | Practice *PAIRS: Now read the restaurant reviews aloud.*

B | Vocabulary *Complete the sentences with the words from the box.*

atmosphere	delicious	main course	menu	reservation	service

1. The food was _____. We will definitely go back to that restaurant.

2. Everything on the _____ is fresh and tasty. Order whatever you like.

3. I ordered steak for my _____. My friend ordered a pasta dish.

4. All the servers are polite and helpful. The _____ was excellent.

5. The restaurant has soft lights, slow music, and beautiful flowers everywhere. The

   _____ is romantic.

6. Be sure to make a _____ in advance. That restaurant is always crowded.

C | Comprehension *Read the descriptions of the restaurants. Write* **AH (Al Hambra)** *or* **T (Topkapi)** *for each statement.*

_____ **1.** People come here for the spices.

_____ **2.** There is no pork on the menu.

_____ **3.** They serve chicken cooked in a ceramic pot.

_____ **4.** The reviewer recommends the lamb kebab.

_____ **5.** The best dessert is the baklava.

COUNT AND NON-COUNT NOUNS; QUANTIFIERS, ARTICLES

Affirmative Statements

Singular Count Nouns		
	Article or *One*	Singular Noun
She wants	a	banana.
	an	apple.
	one	banana. apple.

Plural Count Nouns		
	Number or Quantifier	Plural Noun
He owns	seven	restaurants.
	a few	
	some	
	a lot of	
	many	

Non-count Nouns		
	Quantifier	Non-count Noun
Carol needs	a little	help.
	some	coffee.
	a lot of	

Negative Statements

Singular Count Nouns		
	Article or *One*	Singular Noun
I didn't buy	a	pear.
	an	apple.
	one	pear. apple.

Plural Count Nouns		
	Number or Quantifier	Plural Noun
I didn't buy	two	pears.
	any	
	many	
	a lot of	

Non-count Nouns		
	Quantifier	Non-count Noun
I didn't buy	any	milk.
	much	
	a lot of	

The Definite Article *The*		
Count Noun	Plural Count Noun	Non-count Noun
I need **the menu**.	She has **the napkins**.	He has **the butter**.

GRAMMAR NOTES

1	*A*, *an*, and *the* are **articles**. An article comes before a noun. It can also come before an adjective + noun.	• **The** pears are delicious. • **a** pear / **a** juicy pear • **an** avocado
2	There are two kinds of nouns: **count nouns** and **non-count nouns**. **Count nouns** are ones that we can count. We cannot count **non-count nouns**.	• **Count:** a pear, an apple • **Non-count:** milk, water, salt

3	Use **a**, **an**, or **one** before a singular count noun. Use **a** before a **consonant sound**. Use **an** before a **vowel sound**.	• **a salad**, **an onion**, **one olive** • **a c**upcake • **an a**vocado
	BE CAREFUL! Do not put *a*, *an*, or a number before a non-count noun. Do not add *-s* or *-es* to a non-count noun.	• There's **salt** on the table. Not: There's ~~a salt~~ on the table. Not: There's ~~salts~~ on the table.
4	**A** and **an** are **indefinite** articles. **The** is a **definite** article.	• (You're hungry. You are looking for a restaurant. You see one and say, "There's **a restaurant**.")
	We use *a* or *an* to talk about a person or thing for the first time, or when it is not clear which person or thing you mean.	I want to go to a **Thai restaurant**, but I don't know a good one.
	We use *the* when it is clear which person or thing you mean.	• We ate chicken and rice. **The chicken** was good, but **the rice** was bad.
5	You can use the **definite article** *the* before singular count nouns, plural nouns, and non-count nouns.	• **The restaurant** is open. • **The menus** are there. • **The soup** is delicious.
6	Use **some** before plural count nouns and non-count nouns in affirmative statements.	• He wrote **some invitations.** • He drank **some juice**.
	Use **any** before plural count nouns and non-count nouns in negative statements.	• He didn't mail **any invitations**. • He didn't drink **any soda**.
	We usually use **any** in *yes / no* questions.	YES / NO QUESTIONS • Did you buy **any** milk? • Did you buy **any** bananas?
	We can also use **some** in *yes / no* questions when we offer something or ask for something.	AN OFFER • Would you like **some** juice? A REQUEST • Can I have **some** more coffee?
7	Use **a few** for small amounts and **many** for large amounts with count nouns. Use **a little** for small amounts and **much** for large amounts with non-count nouns.	• I ate **a few peanuts**. • I ate **many grapes**. • I used **a little salt**. • I didn't use **much pepper**.
	BE CAREFUL! *Much* is not usually used in affirmative statements. We usually use *a lot of* instead.	• I drank **a lot of water**. Not: I drank ~~much water~~.

(continued on next page)

8	Some nouns can be <u>both</u> **count** and **non-count nouns**.	COUNT NOUN • He bought three **cakes** for the party.
		NON-COUNT NOUN • He ate some **cake**.
	USAGE NOTE: In informal speaking, some non-count nouns are used as count nouns.	• I'd like **two coffees** and **two sodas**. *(I'd like two cups of coffee and two cans of soda.)*

REFERENCE NOTES

See Appendix 5 on page A–5 for spelling and pronunciation rules for plural nouns.
See Appendix 12 on page A–12 for a list of common non-count nouns.

STEP 3 FOCUSED PRACTICE

EXERCISE 1: Discover the Grammar

A | *Read the sentences. Circle the noun in each sentence. Then check (✓) whether the noun is used as a singular count noun, a plural count noun, or a non-count noun.*

	Singular Count Noun	Plural Count Noun	Non-count Noun
1. We ate a little (chicken).	☐	☐	☑
2. I need some information.	☐	☐	☐
3. There's a menu over there.	☐	☐	☐
4. There aren't many customers.	☐	☐	☐
5. We ate some bread.	☐	☐	☐
6. We need one more napkin.	☐	☐	☐
7. There was one server there.	☐	☐	☐
8. It's about 6 miles (10 kilometers) from here.	☐	☐	☐
9. The coffee is expensive.	☐	☐	☐
10. There aren't any rolls.	☐	☐	☐
11. There isn't any food left.	☐	☐	☐
12. The people here are very kind.	☐	☐	☐

B | Read the situations. Circle the correct letter.

1. You're in a restaurant. You need a napkin. Your friend sees one and says,

   _____.

   a. "Here's a napkin."   **b.** "Here's the napkin."

2. You ask about a person's job. Someone says, _____.

   a. "He's the lawyer."   **b.** "He's a lawyer."

3. It's your child's 10th birthday. You ask her what she wants for her party. She says,

   _____.

   a. "Please bake a cake."   **b.** "Please bake some cake."

4. You're at a restaurant. You say, _____.

   a. "Please pass some salts."   **b.** "Please pass the salt."

EXERCISE 2: *A, An, The*   (Grammar Notes 3–4)

Complete the conversation with **a**, **an**, *or* **the**.

A: Where's _____the_____ party?
     1.

B: At Rectangles Restaurant.

A: Are _____ Garcias coming?
            2.

B: Yes, they are.

A: He's _____ chef, right?
            3.

B: Yes, he is. His wife is _____ chef
                    4.

   too.

A: I hope they like _____ food at Rectangles.
                 5.

B: I'm sure they'll like _____ atmosphere and _____ service.
                      6.   7.

A: Where do they work?

B: She works at _____ Spanish restaurant, and he works at _____
               8.   9.

   Peruvian one.

A: Where are their restaurants?

B: _____ Spanish restaurant is in downtown Manhattan. _____ Peruvian
       10.   11.

   restaurant is on Queens Boulevard in Rego Park in New York.

EXERCISE 3: A, An, The

(Grammar Notes 3–5)

Correct this paragraph. Add **a**, **an**, or **the**. There are 10 more missing articles.

> Kel Warner is ^a college student. He's English major. He has great part-time job. He writes
>
> for school paper. He's food critic. Kel goes to all restaurants in his town and writes about
>
> them. He can take friend to restaurants, and school newspaper pays bill. Kel really has
>
> wonderful job.

EXERCISE 4: Some, Any

(Grammar Note 6)

Complete the conversation with **some** or **any**.

MAN: Could you bring _____some_____ more bread, please?
　　　　　　　　　　　　1.

SERVER: Certainly. . . . Here you go. Anything else?

MAN: _____ water, please. With ice.
　　　　　2.

SERVER: Would you like _____ water too, ma'am?
　　　　　　　　　　　　　3.

WOMAN: No thanks, I don't feel like having _____ water. Hmm, maybe . . . how
　　　　　　　　　　　　　　　　　4.

　　about a glass of ginger ale?

SERVER: Sure.

WOMAN: Also, could we have _____ more butter?
　　　　　　　　　　　　5.

SERVER: Of course.

MAN: Do you have _____ fish dishes? I don't eat meat, and I don't see
　　　　　　　　　　6.
　　_____ fish on the menu.
　　7.

SERVER: I'm sorry—we don't have fish, but we have _____ delicious vegetarian
　　　　　　　　　　　　　　　　　8.

　　dishes.

EXERCISE 5: Many, Much

(Grammar Note 7)

Complete the sentences with **many** or **much**.

1. Boston's South End has _____many_____ good restaurants.

2. You can find _____ delicious dishes from different parts of the world

   including Brazil, France, Italy, Ethiopia, the Middle East, and Korea.

3. There isn't _____ parking on Saturday night, so it's better to use public transportation.

4. If you don't have _____ time, try Falafel King. The service is fast, and the food is tasty.

5. If you don't have _____ money, try the Bakery Café. There are _____ delicious choices at reasonable prices.

6. _____ of the best restaurants are on Tremont Street. _____ people call that street "restaurant row."

EXERCISE 6: *Many, Much*

(Grammar Note 7)

Complete the conversations. Use **much** or **many** and the words from the box.

choices	people	time
information	restaurants	~~traffic~~

1. **A:** How long did it take you to get to the South End?

   B: There wasn't _____ *much traffic* _____, but it still took us an hour to get there.

2. **A:** It was a holiday. Were _____ open?

   B: Yes, we had a lot of choices.

3. **A:** Was your boyfriend with you?

   B: Yes, but he didn't have _____. He had to leave at 9:00, and we only got to Tremont Street at 8:15.

4. **A:** How _____ were you with?

   B: There were six of us. We chose a small Italian restaurant.

5. **A:** How was the food?

   B: Delicious, but there weren't _____.

6. **A:** Did you find out about the area from your hotel concierge?

   B: No, he didn't have _____. I got everything from the Internet.

EXERCISE 7: *A few, A little, Much,* or *Many*

(Grammar Note 6)

Complete the sentences with **a few, a little, much,** or **many.**

1. We need to get some more apples. We only have _____*a few*_____ left.

2. There's _____ pea soup in the refrigerator. I didn't finish it all.

3. There's just _____ milk. We need to stop for more.

4. I want to buy _____ onions for an onion soup.

5. We don't have _____ cheese. Let's add that to the list.

6. We don't have _____ rolls. I'll stop at the bakery and buy some more.

7. Hurry. There isn't _____ time. The supermarket will close in half an hour.

EXERCISE 8: Editing

Correct the paragraph. There are nine mistakes. The first one is already corrected. Find and correct eight more.

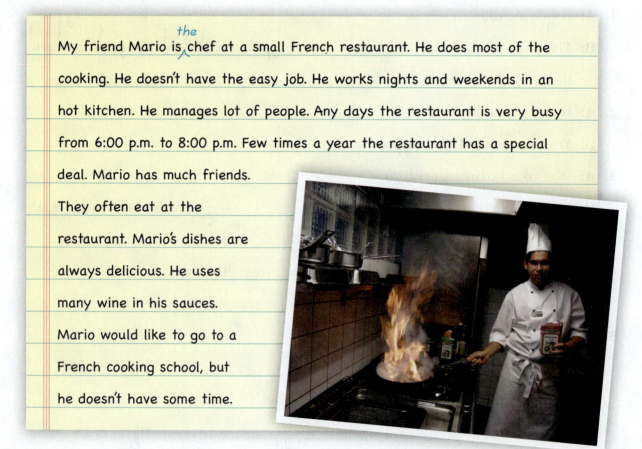

My friend Mario is ^the chef at a small French restaurant. He does most of the cooking. He doesn't have the easy job. He works nights and weekends in an hot kitchen. He manages lot of people. Any days the restaurant is very busy from 6:00 p.m. to 8:00 p.m. Few times a year the restaurant has a special deal. Mario has much friends. They often eat at the restaurant. Mario's dishes are always delicious. He uses many wine in his sauces. Mario would like to go to a French cooking school, but he doesn't have some time.

EXERCISE 9: Pronunciation

A | *Read and listen to the Pronunciation Note.*

Pronunciation Note
The indefinite article **a** is usually unstressed and sounds like /ə/.
EXAMPLE: a little sugar

B | *Listen and repeat the phrases.*

a delicious dish   **a little butter**   **a little salt**

a few eggs   **a little cheese**

a few minutes   **a little pepper**

C | *Now listen and complete the recipe. Then listen again and repeat each sentence.*

1. Put _____ in a frying pan.

2. Heat the pan and add _____ and _____.

3. Scramble the eggs for _____.

4. Add _____ and _____.

5. Enjoy _____ of scrambled eggs.

EXERCISE 10: Listening

A | *Listen to a conversation. Miguel helps Theresa prepare for a party. Circle the food Miguel buys.*

cheese	**ice**	**nuts**	**soda**
chips	**ice cream**	**salsa**	**tuna**

B | *Listen again. Answer the questions.*

1. What's the problem?

   _____

2. Why is Miguel upset?

   _____

EXERCISE 11: Presentation

A | *Imagine that you are a TV chef. Think of an appetizer, a main course, and a dessert. Write notes on the steps for your presentation. Remember to include articles and quantifiers.*

B | *Now tell about the meal you will prepare. The class asks questions about the meal.*

EXAMPLE: Good afternoon and welcome to Pietro's Cooking Class. Today I will prepare a meal fit for a king. I'll begin with the salad. It's easy to make. The salad will have a lot of lettuce, a few pieces of carrot, a few walnuts, and some mango. I'll add a little creamy Italian dressing. Next I'll show how to make some carrot soup. Then for the main course I'll prepare lamb shish kebab with rice and some mixed vegetables.

EXAMPLE: STUDENT A: What will you make for dessert?
STUDENT B: For dessert, I will prepare an orange almond cake.

EXERCISE 12: A Restaurant

A | *Think of a restaurant you know. Complete the sentences with true statements about the restaurant. Use the suggestions from the box or your own ideas.*

big selection	fast service	lower prices	organic ingredients
cool design	free parking	music	tables outside
desserts	garden	new drinks	vegetarian choices

Name of restaurant: _____

There's a(n) _____

There aren't any _____

There aren't many _____

There isn't any _____

There isn't much _____

It doesn't have any _____

B | *SMALL GROUPS: Tell your group about the restaurant.*

EXAMPLE: The name of my restaurant is Tiramisu Restaurant.
There's a beautiful garden in the back of Tiramisu Restaurant.
There aren't any rooms for private parties.

EXERCISE 13: Writing

A | *Write a review of the restaurant you described in Exercise 12 or any other restaurant, coffee shop, or cafeteria. Rate the restaurant and give the address and phone number. Tell about the food, the atmosphere, and the prices.*

EXAMPLE:

Rating scale

★★★★ = excellent
★★★ = good
★★ = fair
★ = poor

★★ Fairfax University Cafeteria
40 Union Square, Middletown, NJ 07748
555-459-0909

You're hungry. You don't have much time. You don't have much money. Where can you grab some food? Try the cafeteria at Fairfax University. It's a self-service restaurant. There are a lot of choices and a lot of tables. There's never a long wait. The quality varies, so be careful what you order. The vegetables and spaghetti are overcooked, but the sandwiches are excellent. The bread is always fresh, and the fillings are delicious. Check out Fairfax University Cafeteria for a tasty bite.

B | *Check your work. Use the Editing Checklist.*

Editing Checklist

Did you . . . ?
☐ use count and non-count nouns correctly
☐ use indefinite and definite articles correctly
☐ use quantifiers correctly
☐ check your spelling

UNIT 27 Review

Check your answers on page UR-6.

Do you need to review anything?

A | *Circle the correct words to complete the sentences.*

1. The baby spilled his milk. I need **a little / a few** napkins.

2. Please pass **a / the** salt.

3. Will you buy **a / an** avocado for the salad?

4. We didn't find **any / some** avocados at the store.

B | *Complete the sentences with* **a few, a little, many** *or* **much.**

1. There weren't _____ people at the party, only 10 or 12.

2. These days I don't have _____ free time. I work and study.

3. I only had _____ money with me. I couldn't pay for everyone.

4. We spent _____ days at the beach. It was great.

C | *Complete the sentences with* **a, an,** *or* **the.**

We bought grandpa _____ watch and _____ tie. I hope he
            1.   **2.**
liked _____ watch. He didn't like _____ tie. Next year we'll take
       3.   **4.**
him to _____ restaurant. He always likes _____ good meal.
         5.   **6.**

D | *Correct the conversations. There are six mistakes.*

1. **A:** What are you looking for?

   B: I need a little stamps. I wrote any postcards, and I want to mail them.

2. **A:** There isn't some yogurt in the refrigerator. There's only half a container.

   B: There isn't much eggs either. We need to go shopping, but we don't have many

   time.

28 How much / How many, Quantifiers, Enough, Adverbs of Frequency

DESSERTS, COOKING, AND BAKING

STEP 1 GRAMMAR IN CONTEXT

Before You Read

PAIRS: Ask your partner these questions.
- Do you have a favorite dessert? What is it?
- Where is it from?
- Do you know the recipe?
- How often do you eat it?

Read

Read the conversation. Each month Robert Fertita's English class has a party. A student brings a typical dessert from his or her country and tells the class about it.

WASANA: Carlos, try some of my dessert. It's very popular in Thailand. It's a mango and rice dessert.

CARLOS: No thanks, Wasana. I'm not that hungry.

WASANA: Just try **a little.** I think you'll like it.

CARLOS: OK, but just **a little**. That's **enough**. . . . Hmm. It's not bad.

WASANA: What do you mean, not bad. It's delicious.

CARLOS: Actually, it is pretty good. It's just that color . . . I don't **usually** eat purple rice. **How often** do you have it?

WASANA: My mom **often** makes it when mangoes are in season.

CARLOS: What's in it?

WASANA: Well, there's white rice and black rice, coconut milk, sugar, salt, and mangoes. It's not so hard to prepare.

CARLOS: Maybe I'll try to make it. **How much rice** do you use?

WASANA: A cup of white rice and a cup of black rice. The black rice gives it that dark color.

CARLOS: **How much coconut milk**?

WASANA: Two cups.

CARLOS: And **how many mangoes**?

(continued on next page)

WASANA: Three.

CARLOS: I have an idea, Wasana. How about if I buy the ingredients, and I watch you prepare the dessert? Then I'll really know how to make it.

WASANA: OK. But then you have to show me how to make those delicious cookies from your country.

CARLOS: You mean the ones with the *dulce de leche* filling?

WASANA: Yes. They were wonderful.

CARLOS: Um. I er . . . I just went to the grocery store and bought them. They sell them all over my neighborhood.

After You Read

A | Practice *PAIRS: Now read the conversation aloud.*

B | Vocabulary *Complete the sentences with the words from the box.*

ingredients	in season	neighborhood	prepare	pretty good	taste

1. This lemon chicken has an amazing _____.

2. Peaches are not _____ right now, so I bought apples.

3. It takes a long time to _____ that dish.

4. There are two good fruit and vegetable stores in my _____.

5. This cake is _____, but I prefer the ice cream.

6. Do you know the _____ of this cake? I want to make it.

C | Comprehension *Make the false statements true based on the conversation.*

1. Wasana doesn't want Carlos to try her dessert.

2. Wasana's dessert is popular in Turkey.

3. Carlos likes the look of Wasana's dessert.

4. Wasana's dessert has two kinds of fruit.

5. Carlos brought fruit from his country.

HOW MUCH / HOW MANY, QUANTIFIERS, ENOUGH

Questions with *How Much*			Answers
How Much	**Non-count Noun**		**Quantifier**
How much	milk	do you need? did she buy?	**A lot.** (A lot of milk.) **Two quarts.** (Two quarts of milk.) **A carton.** (A carton of milk.) **A glass.** (A glass of milk.) **A cup.** (A cup of milk.) **A little.** (A little milk.)

Questions with *How Many*			Answers
How Many	**Plural Count Noun**		**Quantifier**
How many	apples	do we need? did he buy?	**A lot.** (A lot of apples.) **One bag.** (One bag of apples.) **Two pounds.** (Two pounds of apples.) **One or two.** (One or two apples.) **A few.** (A few apples.)

Statements with *Enough*			
		Enough	**Noun (Plural Count or Non-count)**
We	have / don't have	enough	vegetables. meat.

Questions with *Enough*			
		Enough	**Noun (Plural Count or Non-count)**
Do you / Does he	have	enough	vegetables? milk?

QUESTIONS ABOUT FREQUENCY

Questions with *How Often*				Answers
How often	**do**	I you we they	**bake?** **cook?**	Three times a day. Every (Sunday). Once a week. Rarely. Once in a while. Never.
	does	he she		
		it	**break?**	

ADVERBS AND EXPRESSIONS OF FREQUENCY

Adverbs of Frequency			
Subject	Adverb	Verb	
I		cook	
He She It	usually almost never	cooks	on Tuesdays.
We You* They		cook	

Adverbs of Frequency with *Be*			
Subject	*Be*	Adverb	
I	am		
He She It	is	usually almost never	busy.
We You* They	are		

You is both singular and plural.

Adverbs of Frequency	
always	100%
almost always	
frequently	
usually / often	
sometimes	50%
rarely / seldom	
almost never	
never	0%

Expressions of Frequency	
Emiko cooks	every day. twice (a day). three times (a month). several times (a year). once in a while.

GRAMMAR NOTES

1	Use **how much** or **how many** to ask about quantity. Use **how much** with non-count nouns. Use **how many** with count nouns. Use **a little** with non-count nouns. Use **a few** with count nouns.	**A: How much** juice do you have? **B: A little.** OR I have **a little juice**. **A: How many** lemons do you need? **B: A few.** OR We need **a few** lemons.
2	It is not necessary to repeat the noun after *how much* or *how many* if the noun was named before or if the noun is understood.	**A: How much** does it cost? *(How much money is it?)* **B:** Ten dollars. **A:** I bought some cupcakes. **B: How many did you buy**? *(How many cupcakes did you buy?)*
3	You can **count non-count nouns** by using **measure words** or **containers**. Measure words include *a quart, a liter, an ounce, a kilogram, a teaspoon,* and *a tablespoon*. Containers include *a cup, a glass, a can, a jar,* and *a box*.	• Please get me **one quart of milk**. • He drank **two glasses of water**.

4	***Enough*** means the amount you need. Use *enough* before plural count nouns and non-count nouns. ***Not enough*** means less than the amount you need. Use *not enough* before plural count nouns and non-count nouns.	• We have **enough eggs**. *(We need six eggs, and we have six eggs.)* • We have **enough juice**. • There **aren't enough apples**. • There **isn't enough milk**.
5	***How often*** asks questions about **frequency**. *How often* is usually used with the simple present or simple past. It is rarely used with the present progressive.	• **How often** do you bake? NOT: How often ~~are you baking?~~
6	**Adverbs** and **expressions of frequency** tell **how often** we do something. Adverbs and expressions of frequency are often used with the simple present. They rarely occur with the present progressive.	• Tim **always** shops at the Farmer's Market. • Marta goes to class **every day**. • They **usually** open the market at 9:00. NOT: They ~~are usually opening~~ the market at 9:00.
7	Adverbs of frequency usually come **after the verb *be***. They usually come **before other verbs** in the simple present. ***Sometimes***, ***usually***, and ***often*** can also come at the beginning of a sentence. **BE CAREFUL!** Don't begin a sentence with ***never*** or ***always***. **BE CAREFUL!** Don't use negative adverbs of frequency (*rarely*, *seldom*, *almost never*) in negative sentences.	• Yoko **is usually** on time. She **isn't usually** late. • She **rarely eats** dessert. • She **doesn't often eat** dessert. • He **sometimes goes** to the bakery. • **Sometimes** he **goes** to the bakery. • I **never** cook. NOT: ~~Never~~ I cook. NOT: I ~~rarely don't~~ cook.
8	**Expressions of frequency** are time markers. They usually come at the beginning or at the end of a sentence.	• He eats an orange **every day**. • **Every week** she goes to the bakery.

REFERENCE NOTES

See Unit 35 page 411 for a discussion of *enough* after an adjective.
See Appendix 12, page A-12 for a list of quantity expressions.

EXERCISE 1: Discover the Grammar

A | *Underline the noun in each phrase. Then check (✓) the category.*

	Singular Count Noun	Plural Count Noun	Non-count Noun
how much <u>milk</u>			✓
how many eggs			
a lot of raisins			
enough sugar			
a little juice			
a lemon			

B | *Underline the adverbs of frequency. Circle the expressions of frequency.*

1. He almost <u>always</u> cooks.

2. She usually bakes.

3. Once in a while he bakes.

4. Every weekend they go to a café.

5. They often meet friends there.

6. It is frequently crowded.

EXERCISE 2: *How much / How many / How often*

(Grammar Notes 1–2, 4)

Complete the conversations with **How much, How many,** *or* **How often.** *Complete the answers with* **much, many,** *or* **often.**

1. **A:** _____How many_____ meals do you prepare in a week?

   B: Not _____. I eat breakfast and lunch at school.

2. **A:** _____ does he eat out?

   B: Not _____. He likes to eat at home.

3. **A:** On average _____ time does it take you to prepare dinner?

   B: Not _____. Only about 15 or 20 minutes.

4. **A:** _____ times a week do you shop for food?

   B: Not _____. We usually shop once or twice a week.

5. **A:** _____ do they spend on food each week?

   B: Not _____. They shop when there are sales.

6. **A:** _____ do you bake?

   B: Not _____. There's a great bakery in our neighborhood.

EXERCISE 3: Word Order: Adverbs and Expressions of Frequency   *(Grammar Notes 5–7)*

Write sentences with the words in parentheses.

1. (chocolate / Hugo / and / Every afternoon / has coffee / a piece of)

   Every afternoon Hugo has coffee and a piece of chocolate.

2. (hot / is / always / The coffee)

   _____

3. (almost always / dark / is / The chocolate)

   _____

4. (never / It / white chocolate / is)

   _____

5. (Hugo / never drinks / in the evening / coffee)

   _____

6. (hot chocolate / drinks / usually / He)

   _____

7. (drinks / Sometimes / he / ginger tea)

   _____

EXERCISE 4: *Enough*   *(Grammar Note 4)*

Complete the sentences with **enough** *and the words from the box.*

chairs	cupcakes	drinks	ice	plates	room	~~time~~

1. We can't bake a cake. There isn't _____ *enough time* _____. People will be here soon.

2. People get thirsty. Are there _____?

3. Is there _____ for the drinks? The drinks aren't cold.

4. You can't put those cupcakes on that table. There isn't _____.

5. There aren't _____ for everyone. Why don't you cut them in half?

6. People won't want to stand. Are there _____?

7. People will want to put their dessert on something. Are there _____?

EXERCISE 5: Containers

(Grammar Note 3)

Complete the conversation with the words in parentheses. Write the correct words.

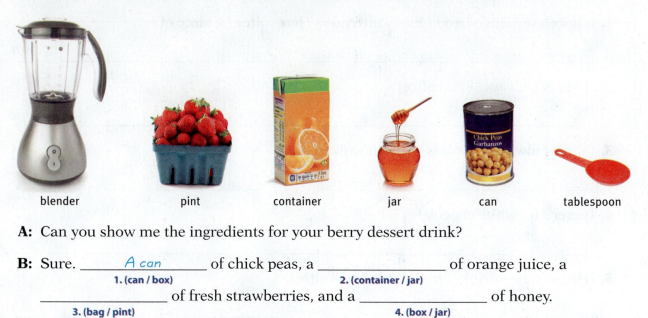

blender   pint   container   jar   can   tablespoon

A: Can you show me the ingredients for your berry dessert drink?

B: Sure. _____ A can _____ of chick peas, a _____ of orange juice, a
         1. (can / box)   **2. (container / jar)**

_____ of fresh strawberries, and a _____ of honey.
  3. (bag / pint)   **4. (box / jar)**

A: And how do you make this drink?

B: I put the _____ of chick peas, 1½ _____ of orange juice,
                5. (can / box)   **6. (cups / bags)**

2 _____ of strawberries, and 2 or 3 _____ of honey in a
  7. (cups / cans)   **8. (tablespoons / cans)**

blender. When it's smooth, I add six ice cubes. Then I blend it again. Delicious!

EXERCISE 6: Editing

Correct the conversations. There are seven mistakes. The first mistake is already
corrected. Find and correct six more.

1. **A:** How ~~much~~ *many* cookies are there in the box?

   B: Only one. Mary ate the rest.

2. **A:** How often do you bake?

   B: Always I bake on the weekend.

3. **A:** Do we have cake enough for everyone?

   B: Yes, we do.

4. **A:** How many flour do you need?

   B: Two cups.

5. **A:** How many egg are there in the cake? And how much sugars?

   B: Four eggs and three cup of sugar.

EXERCISE 7: Pronunciation

🎧 **A** | *Read and listen to the Pronunciation Note.*

> **Pronunciation Note**
>
> Sometimes when people get hurt they say, "Ow." That's the **/ aʊ /** sound in words such as **how** or **flour**.

🎧 **B** | *Listen and underline the / aʊ / sound in the sentences.*

1. Now, add the eggs.

2. How much brown sugar do you need?

3. You need about two cups of sugar.

4. How many pounds of flour did you buy?

5. Take the cupcakes out of the oven.

6. How many ounces of milk does this need?

🎧 **C** | *Listen again and repeat the sentences.*

EXERCISE 8: Listening

🎧 **A** | *Listen to a conversation. Write T (True) or F (False) for each statement.*

_____ 1. Robert is giving Laura a recipe.

_____ 2. Laura thinks Robert's red velvet cupcakes are good.

_____ 3. Robert doesn't want to give Laura the recipe.

_____ 4. Laura writes down the recipe.

🎧 **B** | *Listen again and check (✓) the ingredients in the recipe.*

✓ flour	_____ butter	_____ red food color
_____ cocoa powder	_____ eggs	_____ vanilla extract
_____ baking soda	_____ sour cream	_____ cream
_____ salt	_____ milk	_____ sugar

EXERCISE 9: Survey

Survey five students. Report the results to the class. Ask "How often do you
_____*?" with the activities in the list.*

bake   **cook**   **do dishes**   **eat dessert**   **eat out**   **go to a bakery**

EXAMPLE: Mi Young frequently eats dessert. But she rarely bakes or cooks. So she often eats out.
Sometimes she eats at a bakery.

EXERCISE 10: Information Gap

Work in pairs. **Student A,** *follow the instructions on this page.* **Student B,** *turn to page 332*
and follow the instructions there.

1. Look at the list of ingredients. Ask your partner questions to find out how much you
   need of each ingredient to make chocolate chip cookies. Write the amounts.

Chocolate Chip Cookies
7 ounces chocolate chips
_____ flour
_____ teaspoons baking powder
1 cup chopped walnuts
_____ butter
_____ sugar
_____ brown sugar
_____ eggs, slightly beaten
1 teaspoon vanilla extract

EXAMPLE: STUDENT A: How much flour do you use for the chocolate chip cookies?
STUDENT B: Two and half cups.

2. Now look at the list of ingredients for apple pie. Answer your partner's questions.

Apple Pie

The Crust
2 cups flour
1 teaspoon salt
2/3 cup shortening
5 tablespoons cold water

The Filling
1/3 cup sugar
1/4 cup flour
1/2 teaspoon ground cinnamon
1/2 teaspoon ground nutmeg
a pinch of salt
8 medium-size apples
2 tablespoons butter

EXAMPLE: STUDENT B: How much flour do you use in the apple pie crust?
STUDENT A: Two cups of flour.

EXERCISE 11: Group Presentation

GROUPS: You are preparing dessert for 50 people. Decide what you will serve and how much. Be specific and include different kinds of desserts. Each student talks about one or two of the desserts. Suggestions: nuts, cheese, fruit, dessert drinks, cakes, cookies, mocha ice cream, and flan.

EXAMPLE:

STUDENT A: I'm going to buy a variety of nuts. I'm going to get a pound of salty cashews and a pound of unsalted peanuts. I'm also going to buy some almonds and raisins. I like the combination of a salty and sweet dessert.

STUDENT B: I'm going to bake 30 red velvet cupcakes. I'm going to frost half of them and leave half of them without frosting.

STUDENT C: I'm going to buy fresh fruit. I'm going to buy pears, grapes, and strawberries.

EXERCISE 12: Writing

A | *Describe the desserts your group bought for the party in Exercise 11. Use quantity expressions where possible.*

EXAMPLE: We prepared desserts for 50 people. We served nuts, cakes, cookies, fresh fruit, cheese, and crackers. We brought 3 pounds of mixed nuts. Sonia baked a chocolate cake and Ana made three dozen chocolate chip cookies. Mohammed brought fresh fruit. He brought 2 pounds of pears, apples, and two pineapples. Pierre brought a lot of different kinds of cheese and crackers.

B | *Check your work. Use the Editing Checklist.*

Editing Checklist

Did you . . . ?
☐ use quantity expressions correctly
☐ check your spelling

1. Look at the list of ingredients for chocolate chip cookies. Answer your partner's questions.

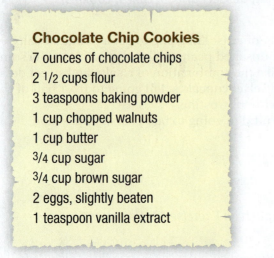

Chocolate Chip Cookies

7 ounces of chocolate chips

2 1/2 cups flour

3 teaspoons baking powder

1 cup chopped walnuts

1 cup butter

3/4 cup sugar

3/4 cup brown sugar

2 eggs, slightly beaten

1 teaspoon vanilla extract

EXAMPLE: STUDENT A: How much flour do you use for the chocolate chip cookies?
STUDENT B: Two and a half cups.

2. Now look at the list of ingredients. Then ask your partner questions to find out how much you need of each ingredient to make apple pie. Write the amounts.

Apple Pie

The Crust

_____ flour

1 teaspoon salt

2/3 cup shortening

_____ cold water

The Filling

_____ sugar

_____ flour

1/2 teaspoon ground cinnamon

1/2 teaspoon ground nutmeg

a pinch of salt

_____ medium-size apples

_____ butter

EXAMPLE: STUDENT B: How much flour do you use in the apple pie crust?
STUDENT A: Two cups of flour.

A | *Complete the sentences with* **How many** *or* **How much**.

1. _____ people went to the party?

2. _____ noise was there?

3. _____ servers did they hire?

4. _____ bread did he eat?

5. _____ desserts did they bring?

B | *Write questions with the words in parentheses. Begin with* **How many, How much,** *or* **How often**.

1. _____
(you / go to the movies)

2. _____
(close friends / you have)

3. _____
(time / you spend online)

4. _____
(people / live in your home)

5. _____
(you / check email)

C | *Write sentences with the words in parentheses.*

1. _____
(usually / I / a few times a week / bake)

2. _____
(in the house / They / have / food / never / enough)

3. _____
(soccer / we / Every weekend / play / in the park)

4. _____
(a / He / glass / spilled / of grape juice)

5. _____
(salt / She / a little / added / to the soup)

D | *Correct the sentences. There are five mistakes.*

1. Never I eat breakfast at home.

2. She once in a while bakes.

3. Do you have milk enough?

4. How much tomatoes did they buy?

5. I rarely don't cook.

Unit 28 Review: *How much / How many*, Quantifiers, *Enough*, Adverbs of Frequency   **333**

STEP 1 GRAMMAR IN CONTEXT

Before You Read

Does your city or town have any of these problems? Check (✓) them.

- ❑ too much noise or traffic
- ❑ not enough jobs
- ❑ too few parking spaces
- ❑ too much crime
- ❑ too few parks
- ❑ too hot or too cold

Read

Read the online article about three U.S. cities. Which of these cities would you want to live in most?

DREAM LOCATIONS

Home | Lifestyle | Photos

Miami Beach

Some call my town *The American Riviera*. Others say it's the *Latin Hollywood*. For me, it's the best place to live. We have sunny weather, beautiful sandy beaches, and graceful palm trees. From January to March the sky is mostly blue, and the temperature is in the 70s almost every day. There are a lot of water activities, and the night life is great. It is a cosmopolitan area with people from all over the world. But the climate isn't perfect.

In the summer months the weather is **too hot** and **humid**, and storms are common. Public transportation isn't very good. There are **too few busses**, and there isn't a subway, so there's **too much traffic**. It's hard to find a good job. Unemployment is high, and most salaries are low. Some say they pay you here in sunshine. But if you have a job, and you like warm weather, sandy beaches, and a rich nightlife, Miami Beach is a great place to live.

Times Square, New York City

Kenai Peninsula, Alaska

Some say this city is the capital of the world. It has a rich cultural life and offers lots of things to do. There are great theaters, restaurants, museums, sports stadiums, and a wonderful nightlife. There are job opportunities, good health care, and a truly multicultural atmosphere with people from all over the world. It's called the city that never sleeps.

But housing is much **too expensive**. You pay a fortune to live in an apartment the size of a closet. The schools are often **too crowded**. There is a good subway system, but there is **too much traffic**. Still, this is a city of opportunity, and I'd rather live here with 8 million other New Yorkers than any other place on earth.

I find most cities **too busy**, **too dirty** with **too much traffic**, **pollution**, and **crime**. They also have **too many people**, and **too few animals**. That's why I love my town of Kenai in the Kenai Peninsula of Alaska. Here the air is clean, and you can hike and fish and see the stars at night. Of course, it's **too cold** for some people, and there's **too little sunlight** for others. But I'm happy here in this small town far away from the hubbub[1] of big city life.

[1]*hubbub:* confusion

After You Read

A | Practice *PAIRS: Read the article again aloud. Take turns reading each section.*

B | Vocabulary *Complete the sentences with the words from the box.*

climate	crime	free time	housing	pollution	unemployment

1. The _____ here is awful. Summers are too hot, and winters are too cold.

2. The _____ from the factories is causing health problems among children in the area.

3. That's a very safe area. There is almost no _____.

4. The government is building _____ for the poor of the city.

5. We're working too much. We have no _____.

6. _____ is low here, so he expects to find a good job soon.

Too much / Too many, Too + Adjective   **335**

C | Comprehension *Read the statements. Write **MB** (Miami Beach), **NYC** (New York City), or* **K** (Kenai), *based on the reading. Some statements are true for more than one place.*

_____ 1. There's a lot of traffic.

_____ 2. It has a great nightlife.

_____ 3. It's great for hiking.

_____ 4. There are many wild animals.

_____ 5. Housing is very expensive.

_____ 6. The transportation system is poor.

_____ 7. People here feel close to nature.

_____ 8. This city has a lot of opportunities.

STEP 2 GRAMMAR PRESENTATION

TOO MUCH / TOO MANY / TOO + ADJECTIVE

	Too Many / Too Few	**Plural Count Noun**
There are	**too many**	**cars**.
	too few	**parking spaces**.

	Too Much / Too Little	**Non-count Noun**		*Too*	**Adjective**
There is	**too much**	**noise**.	It's	**too**	**hot**.
	too little	**light**.			**cold**.

GRAMMAR NOTES

1

Too many and ***too much*** mean "more than the right amount." These words usually have a negative meaning. Use *too many* before plural count nouns. Use *too much* before non-count nouns.

Too few is the opposite of *too many*.
Too little is the opposite of *too much*.
Both *too few* and *too little* mean "not enough." These words usually have a negative meaning. Use *too few* with count nouns. Use *too little* with non-count nouns.

- **Too many** students registered for that course. *(There was room for 10 students. Fifteen people registered.)*
- It costs **too much** money. *(We can't afford it.)*

- There were **too few** books. *(There were books for five people, but seven people needed books.)*
- There was **too little** time. *(We couldn't finish.)*

2

Use ***too*** + **adjective** to say that something has a negative result.

- The water is **too cold**. *(We can't swim here.)*

REFERENCE NOTE

See Unit 35, page 411 for more about *too* + adjective and *very*.

EXERCISE 1: Discover the Grammar

Underline the adjectives that follow **too**. *Circle the nouns that follow* **too much, too many, too few,** *and* **too little.**

1. Housing is too <u>expensive</u> there. Let's not move there.

2. They're building a new school. This school is too crowded.

3. The commute to work was too long. It took two hours each way.

4. There are too many cars on the highway. Let's take a different route.

5. I have too little information about that neighborhood. I don't want to rent a place without more information.

6. There's too much crime in that area.

7. There are too few jobs in that city. People are moving away.

EXERCISE 2: *Too much / Too many*

(Grammar Note 1)

Complete the sentences with **too many** *or* **too much** *and the words from the box.*

crime	noise	pollution	rats	storms	~~unemployment~~

1. Jobs are hard to find. There's _____*too much unemployment*_____ in this town.

2. The climate isn't good. There are

   _____.

3. The streets aren't safe. There's

   _____.

4. It's often hard to breathe here.

   There's _____.

5. There's _____

   in that neighborhood. We won't be able to sleep at night.

6. There are _____ in that area. They should do something to

   get rid of them.

EXERCISE 3: *Too* + Adjective

(Grammar Note 2)

Add **too** *before the adjective in each sentence.*

1.   *too*
   Homes are ⌃ expensive in that area. That's why people can't afford to live there.

2. We don't want to move there. The commute is long. It's two hours to downtown.

3. The train is crowded at this time. Let's take a later train.

4. That house is small for you. There are six people in your family. How will you manage?

5. It's not small for us. We love the location. We can manage.

6. I don't like that area. Winters are long.

EXERCISE 4: *Too few / Too little*

(Grammar Note 1)

Complete the conversations. Use **There is, There are,** *or* **There was,** *and* **too few** *or* **too little** *and the ideas in parentheses.*

1. **A:** What's the problem?

   B: _____*There are too few doctors*_____ in that hospital. The hospital
   (not enough doctors)
   administration needs to hire more doctors or people's health will suffer.

2. **A:** Why is the grass brown?

   B: _____ this past summer.
   (not enough rain)

3. **A:** Why are so many people moving?

   B: _____ in this area.
   (not enough jobs)

4. **A:** Why are all those people moving so far out?

   B: _____ in the center of town.
   (not enough affordable housing)

5. **A:** _____ this area.
   (not enough schools)
   B: That's true, but the city is planning to build two new schools.

6. **A:** _____ around here.
   (not enough parks)
   B: I agree. The city planners need to build more parks.

EXERCISE 5: *Too much / Too many / Too few / Too little / Too* (Grammar Notes 1–2)

Complete the conversations with **too**, **too many**, **too much**, **too few**, *or* **too little**.

1. **A:** What's wrong with Middletown?

   B: The climate. It gets _____ *too much* _____ rain and humidity. It's damp most of the year.

2. **A:** Why don't you want to move to Rockford?

   B: The climate there is OK, but the health care is terrible. There are _____ doctors and hospitals.

3. **A:** How about moving to Newtown?

   B: It's boring. There are _____ things to do.

4. **A:** How was the new restaurant on Spring Street?

   B: It was _____ dark. I wasn't able to read the menu or see my food. There was _____ light.

5. **A:** Do you go to that beach?

   B: Not in the summer. There are _____ people at that time of year. It's _____ crowded.

6. **A:** Did you take the job?

   B: No. The salary was _____ low, and there were _____ holidays and sick days.

7. **A:** Am I _____ late for the talk about the environment?

   B: Yes, it began an hour ago.

8. **A:** Which car did you buy, the Cruiser or the Mercedes?

   B: Neither. The Mercedes was _____ expensive, and the Cruiser had _____ problems.

EXERCISE 6: Editing

Correct the conversations. There are seven mistakes. The first mistake is already corrected. Find and correct six more.

1. **A:** I'd like to move to the suburbs. The city is ^too^ noisy for me.

   B: Not me. I think the suburbs are quiet.

2. **A:** What's wrong with that company?

   B: There are too many managers and too little workers.

3. **A:** Did you buy that apartment?

   B: No. It was too money for too few space.

4. **A:** Don't go by bus. It will take too many time. Take the train. It's a lot faster.

   B: Yes, but it's too much expensive. The bus is half the price.

STEP 4 COMMUNICATION PRACTICE

EXERCISE 7: Pronunciation

A | *Read and listen to the Pronunciation Note.*

> **Pronunciation Note**
>
> - To pronounce / t / as in **time**, touch the upper gum ridge with your tongue.
> - To pronounce / θ / as in **three** or / ð / as in **this**, place your tongue tip between your upper and lower front teeth.
> - The / t / and / θ / sounds are not voiced. The vocal cords do not vibrate.
> - The / ð / sound is voiced. The vocal cords vibrate.

B | *Listen. Then place your hand on your throat and repeat the words.*

/ t / not voiced	/ θ / not voiced	/ ð / voiced
ten		then
tear		there
tease		these
tree	three	
taught	thought	
tin	thin	

C | *Listen and underline the* / **t** / *sound. Underline the* / **θ** / *sound twice. Circle the* / **ð** / *sound.*

1. I thought Ted taught about the environment.

2. There are three trees in front of their house.

3. Is it true that the technician went through the house in only thirty minutes?

D | *Listen again and repeat each sentence.*

EXERCISE 8: Listening

A | *A couple looked at three apartments. Listen to their conversation with a real estate salesperson. Which apartment did the couple like the most? Circle the correct letter.*

    a. the first one   **b.** the second one   **c.** the third one

B | *Listen again and complete the chart.*

	What They Liked	What They Didn't Like
First apartment		
Second apartment		
Third apartment		

EXERCISE 9: Role Play

Act out a situation with a partner. Use **too, too much, too many, too few,** *or* **too little,** *in your conversation.*

Situation 1:

A salesperson is trying to convince a customer to rent a tiny apartment that is far from everything.

Situation 2:

Two friends live in the same big city. One friend wants to move away from the city. The other wants to stay.

    EXAMPLE: **A:** I want to move to Australia for a few years.
                     B: Don't move! It's too far away!

EXERCISE 10: Describe Your City

SMALL GROUPS: Write four good things and four bad things about the city or town you are in. Use **too, too much, too many, too few,** *and* **too little.**

    EXAMPLE: **Good**   **Bad**
                           There's a wonderful concert hall here.   There are too few parking spaces.
                           There isn't much pollution here.   There are too few bicycle paths.

EXERCISE 11: Writing

A | *Write an email to a newspaper. Complain about one aspect of life in your city. Use two of the following:* **too, too much, too many, too few,** *or* **too little.**

EXAMPLE: Young people are the future of this city, but there are too few jobs for them here. Too many young people have nothing to do. The city needs to help them find jobs. In the past, the city spent too much money on roads and highways and too little on job training. Many young people don't have good workplace skills. The city needs to offer job training and practical skills. The city should offer courses in how to write a resumé, take an interview, and get and keep a job. This newspaper complained that too many young people are getting into trouble. With good jobs, young people will stay out of trouble.

B | *Check your work. Use the Editing Checklist.*

Editing Checklist

Did you . . . ?
- ☐ use **too many**, **too much**, **too little**, **too few**, and **too** correctly
- ☐ check your spelling

A | Add **too, too much,** or **too many** to each sentence. Use a ^ symbol.

1. That movie was long. I didn't enjoy it.

2. We have homework. We can't go to the movies today.

3. I bought milk. Who's going to drink it?

4. There are trucks on that road. Let's take another route.

5. It takes time to get there by bus. Let's take the train.

B | Complete the sentences with **too, too much, too many, too little,** or **too few.**

1. That desert town is _____ hot, and it gets _____ rain.

2. Unemployment is high in that area. There are _____ jobs.

3. That town is not safe. There is _____ crime.

4. This area has _____ dishonest politicians.

C | Rewrite the sentences with **too little** or **too few.**

1. There's not enough rain. _____

2. There aren't enough subways. _____

3. There's not enough sunlight. _____

4. There aren't enough traffic lights. _____

5. There isn't enough water. _____

D | Correct the paragraph. There are five mistakes.

The climate here is terrible. It gets too much hot in the summer and too cold in the winter. There's too many snow and ice. Winters are to long. There are too little comfortable days with mild temperatures and blue skies. Also, there's too many air pollution from all the traffic on the streets. I want to move.

PART IX

From Grammar to Writing
A BUSINESS LETTER

1 | *PAIRS: When we write a business letter, we follow a certain style. We use this style for all letters that are not to friends or relatives. Look at the business letter and answer the questions.*

1. Where does your address belong?

   _____

   _____

2. Where does the date belong?

   _____

   _____

3. Where does the name and the address of the person you are writing to belong?

   _____

   _____

4. How do you address the person you are writing to?

   _____

   _____

5. What do you do in the first sentence?

   _____

6. What does the last line of the letter say?

   _____

7. How do you end the letter?

   _____

8. What do you write last?

   _____

Rua Rio de Janeiro 12 **1**
São Paulo, Brasil

March 12, _____ **2**

Lee Spencer, Director **3**
International English Language Institute
Hunter College
New York, New York 10021

Dear Mr. Spencer: **4**

I am interested in attending Hunter College's **5**
International English Language Institute in the fall.

Would you please send me an application and a
catalog of your courses?

Thank you for your prompt attention to this request. **6**

Sincerely yours, **7**

João Lima **8**
João Lima

---

2 | *Read the rules we use to write a business letter.*

1. Write your address at the top left of the page.

2. Write the date below your address.

3. Skip at least two lines. Write the name and address of the person you are writing to on the left margin below the date.

4. When you write a letter, it's best to write to a person by name. If you don't know the person's name, you may write "Dear Sir / Madam:" or "To Whom It May Concern:"; be sure to use a colon (:) after the name.

5. In your first sentence, explain what you want.

6. In the last line of your letter, you usually thank the person you are writing to.

7. You may end a letter with "Sincerely yours" or "Yours truly."

8. Finally, write your signature, and write your name below your signature.

3 | *Write one of the following business letters. Follow the rules in Part 2.*

1. Ask for a bulletin of courses and an application for a language program.

2. Ask for a list of moderately priced apartments near the college.

4 | *Exchange letters with a partner. Did your partner follow the directions? Correct any mistakes in grammar and spelling.*

5 | *Talk to your partner. Discuss the mistakes you made. Then rewrite your own paper and make any necessary changes.*

PART
X

MODALS: REQUESTS, ADVICE, NECESSITY

Advice: *Should, Ought to, Had better*
DOS AND DON'TS OF THE BUSINESS WORLD

STEP 1 GRAMMAR IN CONTEXT

Before You Read

PAIRS: Look at the photo of Angelina Jolie and Cambodian Prime Minister Hun Sen. In the United States, a firm handshake is important in business. Is it important in other countries too? Discuss with your partner.

Read

Read the online article about doing business in Chile and Egypt.

GLOBAL BUSINESS

BUSINESS NEWS   MONEY MARKETS   POLITICS   SMALL BUSINESS   SEARCH:

Global Business

It's always a good idea for business people to know the customs of people in the place they are doing business. If you don't know the customs, you might insult someone and lose a business deal. Here is some advice for anyone headed for[1] Chile.

First of all, when **should** you **go**? Chileans usually take vacations in January and February so you **should not plan** a business trip during those two months. Many offices will be closed for the summer vacation.

Next, how **should** you greet people at business meetings? When attending a business meeting in Chile, you **ought to greet** and **shake hands** with everyone. Later at business dinners and receptions, men sometimes greet other men with hugs. Women often hug and touch cheeks while kissing the air. You **should not be** surprised to get a hug or kiss from a Chilean you know. During a meal, you **should keep** your hands on the table, not in your lap.

In Chile, an open palm upward with the fingers separated means "stupid." You **should avoid** making this gesture. And beware[2]! Slapping your right fist[3] into your left open palm[4] is very impolite. You**'d better not make** that gesture, or you may insult or anger someone.

---

[1] *headed for:* going to
[2] *beware:* be on guard against
[3] *fist:* a hand with fingers closed tightly together
[4] *palm:* the inside of hand

Now in Egypt, you **should not expect** to do business on Fridays. It is the Muslim day of rest. Also, throughout the Arab world, people use the Islamic calendar (also called Muslim calendar or Hijri calendar) and the Western calendar. To avoid confusion, you **should put** two dates on paperwork—the Hijri (Islamic) date and the Gregorian (Western) date.

If you're invited for a meal, you **should eat** with your right hand. In many countries with large Muslim and Hindu populations, people consider the left hand unclean. In Egypt leaving a little food is a sign that you are full, so you **shouldn't eat** everything on your plate. Also, you**'d better not add** salt to your food or you might insult the cook.

What do you know about sitting in Egypt? You **should** never **sit** with legs crossed or **show** the sole[5] of your shoe. In Arab culture, it is a big insult to show the bottom of the foot.

So remember, before you go to another country to do business, learn about the culture. And remember when you're in that country, try and "do as the Romans do."[6]

In the Middle East, it is not polite to cross legs.

---

[5] **sole:** the bottom of foot or shoe
[6] **"do as the Romans do":** copy the people in the place you are visiting

After You Read

A | Practice *PAIRS: Now read the article aloud. Take turns reading each paragraph.*

B | Vocabulary *Complete the sentences with the words from the box.*

business receptions	confusion	consider	customs	insult

1. Business people should know the _____ of the countries they visit.

2. At Chilean _____, men greet other men with hugs.

3. To avoid _____, put the Western and Islamic date on this paperwork.

4. People in the United States _____ a firm handshake is important.

5. It is an _____ to show the bottom of your foot in the Middle East.

C | Comprehension *Write* **T (True)** *or* **F (False)**.

_____ **1.** Chileans often take vacations in July and August.

_____ **2.** Offices in Chile are often closed in February.

_____ **3.** When businessmen meet in Chile at dinners, they do not hug.

_____ **4.** When you eat a meal in Chile, you should keep your hands in your lap.

_____ **5.** Egyptians do business on Friday, Saturday, and Sunday.

_____ **6.** You should not use your right hand when you eat in Egypt.

_____ **7.** You should not add salt to your food in an Egyptian home.

Advice: *Should, Ought to, Had better* **349**

MODALS

Should, Shouldn't, and Ought to

Affirmative Statements		
Subject	**Should / Ought to**	**Base Form of Verb**
I You He She We They	**should** **ought to**	**go.**
It	**should** **ought to**	**happen.**

Negative Statements		
Subject	**Should not**	**Base Form of Verb**
I You He She We They	**should not** **shouldn't**	**go.**
It	**should not** **shouldn't**	**happen.**

Yes / No Questions			
Should	**Subject**	**Base Form of Verb**	
Should	we he they	**wear**	a suit?

Short Answers					
Affirmative			**Negative**		
Yes,	you he they	**should.**	No,	you he they	**shouldn't.**

Wh- Questions			
Wh- Word	**Should**	**Subject**	**Base Form of Verb**
What	**should**	I	**do?**
When		we	**go?**

Had Better and Had Better Not

Affirmative Statements		
Subject	**Had Better**	**Base Form of Verb**
We You	**had better** **('d better)**	**go.**

Negative Statements		
Subject	**Had Better Not**	**Base Form of Verb**
We You	**had better not** **'d better not**	**go.**

Contractions	
I had better → **I'd better**	we had better → **we'd better**
you had better → **you'd better**	you had better → **you'd better**
he had better → **he'd better**	they had better → **they'd better**
she had better → **she'd better**	

GRAMMAR NOTES

1	Use **should** to **give advice** or **talk about what is right to do**. Use *should* + the base form of the verb.	• He should **bring** them a gift. NOT: He should ~~to bring~~ them a gift. NOT: He should ~~brings~~ them a gift.
	Use **should not** for the negative. Use the contraction **shouldn't** in speaking and informal writing.	• We **should not** bring roses. • We **shouldn't** bring roses.
2	We use *should* to talk about the **present** or **future**.	• You **should** do the report **now**. • You **should** turn in the report **tomorrow**.
3	**Ought to** means the same as *should*.	• You **ought to read** that book about Chile. It's very helpful.
4	*Ought to* is not usually used in questions or negatives. We use *should* instead. **USAGE NOTE:** To sound more polite, use *I think* or *Maybe* before saying, "*you should*" or "*you ought to.*"	• **Should** I **wear** a suit? NOT: ~~Ought I to wear~~ a suit? • **I think you should** bring a small gift. • **Maybe you ought to** ask him first.
5	Use **had better** to **give advice**. *Had better* is stronger than *should*. It implies that something bad might happen if you don't follow the advice.	• You **had better call** before you go to the store. *(It may be closed.)*
	Use *had better* + the base form of the verb.	• He **had better send** an email message.
	The negative of *had better* is **had better not**.	• He **had better not** forget his passport.
	We often use the short form **'d better** in speaking and informal writing.	• We**'d better ask** the doctor.
6	**Had better** is used to talk about the **present** or the **future**. (The *had* in *had better* does not refer to the past.)	• I**'d better** finish my report now. • She**'d better not** miss her flight tomorrow.

EXERCISE 1: Discover the Grammar

Read the questions and answers about using business cards in Japan. Underline **should,** **had better, ought to,** *and the base form of the verb.*

1. Q: When <u>should</u> I <u>present</u> my business card?

A: Right after you shake hands or bow.

2. Q: Should I translate my card into Japanese?

A: Yes. It's a good idea to have English on one side and Japanese on the other.

3. Q: What should I do when I get my colleague's card?

A: Read it carefully. You ought to remember the information on it.

4. Q: Can we start our business before we exchange business cards?

A: You'd better not start your business before you exchange business cards.

EXERCISE 2: *Should*: Affirmative and Negative

(Grammar Notes 1–2)

Some international students are talking about customs in their countries. Complete the sentences with **should** *or* **shouldn't** *and the verb in parentheses.*

1. I was in a school cafeteria in the U.S. A guy had a cold. He blew his nose at the table.

   In Korea you _____*shouldn't blow*_____ your nose at the table. It's very impolite.
   (blow)

2. In China, you _____ people. Many people feel uncomfortable when
   (touch)
   others touch them. Here I notice people touch more often.

3. I think that people in North America don't like silence. Someone always speaks. I

   guess you _____ quiet.
   (be)

4. In some cultures, people can clap hands to call a waiter. You _____

   never _____ that here. I think here you _____ until
   (do)   (wait)
   the waiter looks at you. But sometimes the waiter never looks at you.

5. In North America people often say "We'll have to get together" or "I'll see you later."

   But they don't plan to meet me or see me later. In Poland we don't do that. In my

   opinion, Americans and Canadians _____ that. It's confusing.
   (say)

EXERCISE 3: *Should*: Affirmative and Negative

(Grammar Notes 1–2)

Complete the sentences about doing business in Hungary. Use **should** or **shouldn't** and a verb from the box.

arrive	~~avoid~~	be / not	call	keep	pay	surprise / not

1. You ____should avoid____ taking a business trip to Hungary during July and August and from mid-December to mid-January. These are holiday and vacation periods.

2. You _____ on time in all business matters: You _____ late for appointments.

3. You _____ always _____ bills on time, and you _____ the date you promise for deliveries.

4. You _____ adults by their titles and family names unless they ask you not to.

5. It _____ you to get an invitation to go horseback riding. Horseback riding is a popular sport in Hungary.

EXERCISE 4: *Ought to*

(Grammar Notes 3–4)

Complete the sentences with **ought to** and the verbs from the box.

ask	become	~~bring~~	congratulate	invite	send

1. We're going to the Chens for dinner tomorrow night. We ____ought to bring____ a gift.

2. We had a wonderful time at their home. We _____ them a thank-you note.

3. I _____ Mr. Chen. His son graduated from law school last week.

4. We _____ them to our home when the Johnsons are here. I think they'd get along well.

5. Judy Chen _____ a party planner. She's so good at giving parties.

6. I _____ the Chens about doing business in Taiwan. I'm going there next month.

EXERCISE 5: *Had better*: Affirmative and Negative

(Grammar Notes 5–6)

Complete the sentences with **'d better** or **'d better not**.

1. You _____*'d better not*_____ show the soles of your feet in Thailand or Saudi Arabia. It is a big insult.

2. In Hindu and Islamic cultures, you _____ eat with your left hand. It's not polite.

3. In the United States, direct eye contact is a sign of honesty, but in other countries it is a sign of disrespect. You _____ understand these differences when you are meeting with people from different parts of the world.

4. We _____ hug them. They might feel uncomfortable. It's not their custom.

5. You _____ find out about gift giving in their country. The wrong gift may cause misunderstanding.

EXERCISE 6: *Had better*

(Grammar Notes 5–6)

Rewrite the sentences with **had better** or **had better not** based on the information.

1. Be on time when doing business in Germany.

   You had better be on time when doing business in Germany. _____

2. Don't eat everything on your plate in Cambodia.

   _____

   Leave something to show your host was generous with the food.

3. In China, keep eating while your plate is full to show you like your food.

   _____

4. Do not touch a person's head or show the soles of your feet in Thailand.

   _____

   The head is the most sacred part of the body. The foot is the lowest.

5. Don't keep your hands in your pockets in Turkey. It's a sign of disrespect.

   _____

EXERCISE 7: Editing

A | *Correct the conversations. There are six mistakes. The first mistake is already corrected. Find and correct four more. Add* **should** *or* **shouldn't**.

1. **A:** What ^should^ I wear?

   B: You not wear jeans or shorts.

2. **A:** I think I insulted him.

   B: You apologize.

3. **A:** They were really helpful. I send

   them a thank-you note?

   B: That's a good idea.

4. **A:** I take my shoes off?

   B: Yes, please leave them by the door.

5. **A:** When we leave for the business reception?

   B: At 6:15. The invitation is for 6:30, but we don't want to be the first ones there.

B | *Correct five mistakes in the conversations. Add* **'d better** *or* **'d better not**. *The first mistake is already corrected. Find and correct four more.*

1. **A:** I missed the train this morning.

   B: You ^'d better^ leave earlier tomorrow.

2. **A:** You don't fly today. There's a bad hurricane and all flights are late.

   B: Good idea. I'll change my flight for tomorrow.

3. **A:** Can I call John Baker now?

   B: I don't think so. He's on U.S. time. You call him at noon. You won't wake him then.

4. **A:** Is it OK to pay that bill on Friday?

   B: I don't think so. You pay it today.

5. **A:** I told John about my birthday. He doesn't forget about it.

   B: John forgets everyone's birthday except his own.

EXERCISE 8: Pronunciation

 A | *Read and listen to the Pronunciation Note.*

Pronunciation Note
When we say **shouldn't** followed by a verb, the **/ t /** is not fully heard. **Shouldn't say** sounds like **/ ʃʊdən səɪ /** .

B | *Listen and repeat the sentences.*

1. You shouldn't call him.

2. You shouldn't send an email.

3. You shouldn't come early.

4. You shouldn't wear shorts.

5. You shouldn't bring a gift.

EXERCISE 9: Listening

A | *Listen to a conversation between Max and his friends. Then answer the questions.*

1. Where is Max going? To _____

2. How is he getting there? By _____

3. What are his questions about? _____

B | *Listen again. Complete the questions. Write the friends' answers.*

1. **Max:** Should I bow when _____ ?

   Answer: _____

2. **Max:** Should I remove _____ when _____ ?

   Answer: _____

3. **Max:** Should I learn _____ ?

   Answer: _____

EXERCISE 10: Discussion: Gift Giving

A | *PAIRS: Ask and answer the questions below. Talk about gift giving in your culture.*

1. Are gifts exchanged in business? When are gifts usually given?
2. Is the way you wrap a gift important? How and when do you present a gift? Do you open a gift right away or do you open it later?
3. Are there gifts that you shouldn't give?
4. What are the most common gifts in business?
5. How do you feel about giving gifts?
6. What kind of gifts do you like to receive?

B | *Discuss gift giving as a class.*

EXERCISE 11: Conversation: Body Language

A | *GROUPS: Body language is a way people speak without words. Use body language: Say something with your, head, hand, shoulders, arms, eyes, nose, or lips. Does your group understand you?*

B | *Talk about body language with your group.*

C | *Present the results of your discussion to the class.*

EXERCISE 12: Writing

A | *Imagine someone wants to do business in a culture you know well. Give the person advice. Use* **should, shouldn't, had better,** *or* **had better not.** *Use a topic from the box or your own idea.*

being on time	eating habits	using business cards
dressing appropriately	tipping	using forms of address

EXAMPLE: **Forms of Address in the United States**

How do you address people when you are doing business in the United States? Do you use their first names or their last names? Do you use titles? And if so, what are the correct titles?

In the United States managers of companies sometimes tell people to call them by their first names. You shouldn't think it means that you are close. It is a part of the culture. In a business relationship, you should first call a person by a title (for example: Dr., Ms., or Mr.) and their last name. Wait for that person to tell you how he or she wants to be addressed. Some people want to be on a first-name basis and others don't. There are no set rules.

B | *Check your work. Use the Editing Checklist.*

Editing Checklist

Did you . . . ?
- [ ] use **should**, **shouldn't**, **had better**, or **had better not** correctly
- [ ] check your spelling

A | *Circle the correct words.*

1. You **should to / should** read that book.

2. We **better / had better** call the airline.

3. I **shouldn't not / shouldn't** wear that outfit for a business meeting.

4. We **ought / ought to** buy a small gift.

5. I'd **better no / better not** call her now. She goes to bed early.

B | *Complete the sentences with* **had better** *or* **had better not.**

1. You _____ forget to pay that bill. You don't want to pay a late fee.

2. She _____ buy the gift today. The stores will be closed tomorrow.

3. We _____ wait for them any longer. We'll miss our flight.

4. I _____ go by train. The bus is too slow, and I need to be on time.

C | *Complete the sentences with* **should** *or* **shouldn't.**

1. We _____ take him to the hospital. He seems to be in pain.

2. She _____ work alone. She needs to get help.

3. I _____ talk to a plumber about that problem.

4. You _____ forget your notes. You'll need them.

D | *Correct the sentences. There are seven mistakes.*

1. Where should we meets after work?

2. We better take an umbrella tonight. It's going to rain.

3. Should I to make a reservation now for my flight? I think I outta buy it soon.

4. What I should see during my business trip to Uruguay?

5. Should we leaves Brazil tonight or tomorrow?

6. You ought bring flowers to your hostess to thank her for dinner.

Requests, Desires, and Offers: *Would you, Could you, Can you. . . ?*, *I'd like . . .*

NEIGHBORS

STEP 1 GRAMMAR IN CONTEXT

Before You Read

A favor is something you do for someone to help him or her. Read these requests for favors. Which ones are OK to ask a neighbor? Check (✓) your opinion.

	OK	Depends	Not OK
Would you please get my mail while I'm on vacation?			
Could you help me move to a new apartment?			
Can you drive me to the airport?			
Can you lend me $500?			

Read

Jade posts a problem on a message board. Luz reads it and posts some advice. Read their posts. Do you agree with Luz?

Jade Last month my neighbor Gina said, "Jade, **can you do** me a favor? **Can you drive me** to the airport tonight? I have a nine o'clock flight."

I said, "**Sure**, Gina. **I'd be glad to**. **Would you like** me to pick you up at 7:00?"

Then last week Gina said, "Jade, **could you help** me out? I'm going away again for a few days. **Could you water** my plants and walk my dog while I'm away?" Again I said, "**Sure**."

Well, yesterday I needed a favor. I called Gina and said, "Gina, I'm going to paint my bedroom tomorrow afternoon. **Would you lend** me a hand?" She said, "Oh, Jade. **I'd like to help you**, but I'm going to go shopping." I didn't say anything, but I was angry and hurt. What do you think? Was I wrong to feel that way?

Luz0426 No, you were right. Since Gina asks you for favors, she should do favors too. Maybe Gina is a little bit selfish. Maybe she only thinks about herself. Why don't you tell her how you feel? See what she says. Good luck!

After You Read

A | Practice *PAIRS: Now read the posts aloud. Take turns reading each paragraph.*

B | Vocabulary *Match the words and meanings.*

_____ **1. lend me a hand**   **a.** leave

_____ **2. post a message**   **b.** help me

_____ **3. go away**   **c.** write to an online group

_____ **4. be hurt**   **d.** caring only about yourself

_____ **5. selfish**   **e.** feel bad

C | Comprehension *Complete the chart. Who is each sentence about? Check (✓) the correct column.*

	Gina	Jade
1. She would like a ride to the airport.		
2. She offered to pick her neighbor up at 7:00.		
3. She would like her neighbor to water her plants.		
4. She asked her neighbor to help paint her bedroom.		
5. She would like advice.		

STEP 2 GRAMMAR PRESENTATION

REQUESTS, DESIRES, AND OFFERS

Polite Requests				Short Answers	
Would You / Could You / Can You		**Base Form of Verb**		**Affirmative**	**Negative**
Would you				Sure.	Sorry, I can't. I have to work.
Could you	(please)	**help**	me?	Of course.	I'd like to, but I can't. I have a class.
Can you				OK.	Sorry, I'm busy now.

(continued on next page)

Desires				Contractions
Subject	***Would Like***			
I You* He She We They	**would like**	a larger apartment. to move.		I would = **I'd** you would = **you'd** he would = **he'd** she would = **she'd** we would = **we'd** they would = **they'd**

You is both singular and plural.

Offers				Short Answers	
Would	**Subject**	***Like***		**Affirmative**	**Negative**
Would	you	**like**	some blueberries? to join us?	Yes, thank you. Yes, I would.	No, thanks.

GRAMMAR NOTES

1

Would you, ***Could you***, and ***Can you*** are some common ways to make **requests**.

When we agree to a request, we say, ***Sure***. ***Of course***. ***OK***. or ***I'd be glad to***.

A: **Would you (please)** help me carry these books?
B: **Sure**.

A: **Could you (please)** help me carry these books?
B: **Of course.**

Can you is the most common and most informal.

When we don't agree to a request, we say ***sorry*** and **give a reason**.

A: **Can you (please)** help me?
B: **I'd be glad to.**
OR
Sorry, I can't. I have to work.

2

Would like is a polite way of saying *want*.

USAGE NOTE: Use the contraction in speaking and informal writing.

Would like can be followed by **a noun** or **an infinitive**.

- The judge **would like** to see you now.

- **I'd like** some advice.
- We**'d like** to see you.

  NOUN
- I'd like **a snack**.

  INFINITIVE
- I'd like **to get** a snack.

3

Use ***Would you like*** for offers or invitations.

- **Would you like** some help?
- **Would you like** to dance?

EXERCISE 1: Discover the Grammar

Write **R (Request), O (Offer),** or **D (Desire)** for each sentence.

_R_ **1.** Would you give me a ride?

_____ **2.** We'd like to see you again soon.

_____ **3.** Would you like some more lemonade?

_____ **4.** Could you lend me your car?

_____ **5.** I'd like a shorter workday.

_____ **6.** Can I see your photos?

_____ **7.** Would you like another dumpling?

_____ **8.** Would you call her for me?

EXERCISE 2: Requests, Offers, Desires, and Responses   (Grammar Notes 1–3)

Eun Young and Dae Jung are neighbors. Complete the conversation with the phrases from the box.

Could you please	I'd like to do	I'd love to	Of course	Would you like

EUN YOUNG: Dae Jung, I love to listen to your music, but sometimes I can't get to sleep.

_____ _Could you please_ _____ stop practicing by 11:00 P.M.?
   1.

DAE JUNG: _____ I'm sorry. Sometimes I forget the time
   2.

when I practice.

EUN YOUNG: Thanks.

DAE JUNG: Listen, Eun Young, _____ something for you.
   3.

_____ to have dinner together one day next
   4.

week?

EUN YOUNG: Dinner? Sure. _____.
   5.

EXERCISE 3: Responses to Requests and Offers

(Grammar Note 1)

Read the questions. Circle the correct letter.

1. **A:** Would you help me get up?

   B: _____

   (a.) Sure.   **b.** Yes, thanks.

2. **A:** Could you help me with these bags?

   B: _____

   a. I could.   **b.** Certainly.

3. **A:** Can you get my mail while I'm away?

   B: _____

   a. Sorry, I'm going away too.   **b.** No thanks.

4. **A:** Would you like one of these flyers?

   B: _____

   a. Yes, I want.   **b.** Thanks.

5. **A:** Can you drive me to the supermarket?

   B: _____

   a. I could.   **b.** Of course.

6. **A:** Could you do me a favor and watch my bags? I need to move my car.

   B: _____

   a. I'm sure.   **b.** Sure.

7. **A:** Would you like some of my popcorn?

   B: _____

   a. Thanks.   **b.** Sorry, I don't.

8. **A:** Could you give me some money?

   B: _____

   a. Yes, I would.   **b.** Sorry, I don't have any.

EXERCISE 4: Requests, Offers, Desires

(Grammar Notes 1–3)

Rewrite the underlined sentences. Change imperative statements to requests with **Could you please**, **Would you please**, *or* **Can you please. . . ?** *Change* **want** *to* **would like**.

ALEXA: The barbecue looks great. Anything we can do to help?

Could you please bring out the drinks?

JAVIER: Sure. ~~Bring out the drinks~~. They're in the cooler.
1.

ALEXA: OK. . . . Here they are. Where should we put them?

JAVIER: Put the lemonade on the table over there. And Roberto, put the juice over here
2.   3.

next to the buns. And there's a salad in the refrigerator. Bring it out.
4.

ALEXA: Sure. I'll get it.

JAVIER: I think the meat is ready. What do you want—chicken or hamburgers?
5.

ALEXA: Some chicken, please.

JAVIER: What about you Roberto? Do you want chicken too?
6.

ROBERTO: No, I want a burger.
7.

JAVIER: Here you go.

ALEXA: Javier, this chicken is delicious. I want the recipe.
8.

JAVIER: It's easy to make. I soak it in a honey mustard sauce. Then I grill it.

EXERCISE 5: Editing

Correct the conversations. There are five mistakes. The first mistake is already corrected. Find and correct four more.

1. **A:** Could you please move my car at 11:00?

    Sorry.
   B: ~~No, I wouldn't~~. I'll be at work at that time.

2. **A:** We like to rent this apartment. Could please you give us an application?

   B: Of course.

3. **A:** Would you like come for dinner?

   B: Yes, thank you. Would my friend come, too?

4. **A:** Would you help me with these boxes?

   B: I would.

EXERCISE 6: Pronunciation

🎧 **A** | *Read and listen to the Pronunciation Note.*

> **Pronunciation Note**
>
> Do not pronounce the letter **l** in the word **would**. *Would* is pronounced like the word *wood* / **wʊd** / . We pronounce *Would you* / **wʊdʒə** / and *Could you* / **kʊdʒə** / with the / **dʒ** / sound.

🎧 **B** | *Listen and repeat.*

1. Would you like some more lemonade?
2. Could you hold the door open?

3. Would you watch the burgers?
4. Could you hand me a napkin?

EXERCISE 7: Listening

🎧 **A** | *Listen to a telephone conversation beween neighbors. Circle the correct letter.*

Elena asks Ms. Lyons to _____.
   a. watch TV with her   **b.** turn off her TV   **c.** lower her TV volume

🎧 **B** | *Listen again and answer the questions. Circle the correct letter.*

1. How does Ms. Lyons respond?
   a. She agrees to Elena's request.
   b. She doesn't understand Elena's request.
   c. She doesn't agree to Elena's request.

2. What does Ms. Lyons think?
   a. Her neighbor isn't polite.
   b. Her TV isn't too loud.
   c. The walls in her building are thin.

3. What is Elena doing at this time?
   a. She's studying in medical school.
   b. She's working as a doctor.
   c. She's studying for a test for medical school.

4. Ms. Lyons may have a problem. What is it?
   a. She doesn't see well.
   b. She doesn't hear well.
   c. She doesn't have a kind neighbor.

EXERCISE 8: Survey

A | *GROUPS OF 4: Look at the requests in the list. Talk about these requests. Is it OK for a neighbor, a casual friend, or a close friend or relative to ask them? Is it sometimes OK? If so, when? Would you make these requests?*

Would you lend me your car?   Could you lend me $50?

Could you fix my computer?   Could you walk my dog for two weeks?

Would you take my picture?   Could you take me to the hospital?

EXAMPLE: **A:** Young Suk, what do you think about the first request, "Would you lend me your car?" Would you make that request?
B: Not for a neighbor, but I might ask a close relative.

B | *Take notes on your group's responses. Then discuss them with the class.*

EXERCISE 9: Making Polite Requests

PAIRS: Read the situations. Take turns making polite requests. Answer the requests.

EXAMPLE: You're in a restaurant with your neighbor. You want some napkins, which are near your neighbor.
A: Maki, can you please pass the napkins?
B: Here you go.

1. You're in a restaurant with your neighbor. The salt and pepper is in front of your friend. You would like the salt and pepper.

2. It's raining hard and you have to go out. You lost your umbrella. You ask a neighbor to lend you an umbrella.

3. You need to move your sofa. Your neighbor is at your home.

4. You want to hang a painting on the wall. You'd like your neighbor to help you.

5. Your neighbor has parties that keep you up at night. You would like the neighbor to make less noise.

6. Your neighbor borrowed a couple of books a month ago. He still has them.

EXERCISE 10: Extending Invitations

PAIRS: Take turns. Extend invitations to your partner. Your partner can accept or refuse. Use the suggestions from the box or your own ideas

EXAMPLE: **A:** Would you like to come over for dinner tonight?
B: Sure. What time? OR I'd like to, but I can't. I have too much homework.

go running   go to a concert   see a movie   study calculus together

EXERCISE 11: Role Play

PAIRS: Role-play the situations. You and your partner are neighbors.

Situations:

- Invite your neighbor to a party.
- Ask your neighbor to help you put in a new air conditioner.
- Invite your neighbor to a concert. You have an extra ticket.
- Ask your neighbor for a ride to a store.

EXAMPLE: ELENA: Hey, Pierre, I'm going to have a party tomorrow night. Would you like to come?
PIERRE: I'd love to. Is it in your apartment?
ELENA: Yes, it is. Please come at around 8:00.
PIERRE: OK. I'll be there.

EXERCISE 12: Writing

A | *Write two short email requests to neighbors. Use the situations or your own ideas. Use **would** or **could**.*

Situation 1

You are on vacation. You gave your neighbor a key to your home. Ask your neighbor to check your home.

Situation 2

Your neighbor has two teenage sons. They play music at all hours of the night. Ask your neighbor to ask them not to play loud music after 10:00 P.M.

Situation 3

It's winter and the landlord is not giving enough heat. Write to several neighbors and ask them to join you in writing letters of complaint to your landlord.

EXAMPLE FOR SITUATION 1:   Hi John,
Boris and I are having a great time in Aruba. I read about a storm back home, and I hope all is well. Could you please check our house? We'll be back in a couple of days.
Irina

B | *Check your work. Use the Editing Checklist.*

Editing Checklist
Did you . . . ? ☐ use **would you**, **could you**, or **can you** correctly ☐ check your spelling

Check your answers on page UR-6.

Do you need to review anything?

A | *Circle the correct word or words.*

1. **Would you please / Would you like** another apple?

2. **Could you pass / Can you please** the salt?

3. **I'd like / I'll like** some more coffee.

4. **We'd like / We like** some more bread, please.

5. **Can you / Can you to** help me?

B | *Read each question. Circle the correct answer.*

1. Would you please help me? **(Yes, thanks. / Of course.)**

2. Could you drive me home? **(Sure. / I could.)**

3. Would you like another cupcake? **(I could. / Thanks.)**

4. Can you lend me your jacket? **(Sorry, I need it. / No, thanks.)**

5. Can you show me how the new printer works? **(I'd be glad to. / I can.)**

C | *Complete the sentences with* **I'd like, Could you please** *or* **Would you like.**

1. _____ open the door?   4. _____ some water?

2. _____ some more coffee.   5. _____ to go to that concert.

3. _____ drive me to school?

D | *Correct the conversations. There are five mistakes.*

1. **A:** Could please you move my car at 11:00?

   B: No, I wouldn't. I'll be at work then.

2. **A:** I like to see you this weekend. Would you like to go to the park?

   B: I could.

3. **A:** Would you like have some more ice cream?

   B: No, thanks. I'm full.

Necessity: *Have to, Don't have to, Must, Mustn't*

RULES AT SCHOOL

STEP 1 GRAMMAR IN CONTEXT

Before You Read

What do you have to do for your English class? Circle the letter of your answers.

a. do homework   **c.** sit in the same seat for each class   **e.** answer questions in class

b. wear a uniform   **d.** take tests   **f.** do class presentations

Read

Read about the requirements for a college history course.

PROFESSOR: Welcome to American History 102. I'm Rich Anderson. This course covers the period from the American Civil War to the present day.[1] There will be a midterm and a final exam. You **have to score** an average of 65 percent or above on both tests to pass this course. In addition there is a term paper.[2] The term paper **must be** at least 10 pages, and you **have to include** a bibliography.[3] The handout I'm passing out will explain the term paper. Now, are there any questions? . . . Yes?

STUDENT A: When is the term paper due?

PROFESSOR: You **have to hand** it **in** by the last day of class. That's December 15. It **must not be** late. You should hand in an outline by the fourth week of the term. You can email the outline. My email address is on the board and on your handout. You **don't have to give** me a hard copy of the outline, but I would like a hard copy of your paper. Any other questions? . . . Yes?

STUDENT B: Last semester, we **didn't have to buy** a textbook. Is there a textbook for this course?

PROFESSOR: Yes. The textbook is called *American History from the Civil War to Today.*

STUDENT B: Who's the author?

PROFESSOR: I am.

STUDENT B: **Do** we **have to buy** the book?

PROFESSOR: Only if you want to pass.

---

[1] **present day:** today (usually used when talking about history)

[2] **term paper:** students' most important written report of the semester

[3] **bibliography:** a list of the books and other sources used to write a paper

A | **Practice** *PAIRS: Now read the conversation aloud.*

B | **Vocabulary** *Complete the sentences with the words from the box.*

average	final	midterm	pass
due	hard copy	outline	percent

1. To _____ this course, you must hand in a paper and do a group

   presentation.

2. There will be two tests this semester. The _____ will be on October 15,

   and the _____ will be on December 15.

3. The _____ of 100, 95, 99, and 90 is 96.

4. What _____ of the students finish this program in one year?

5. Do I need to print a _____ or is **OK** to send it electronically?

6. I can't meet you today. My term paper is _____ tomorrow.

7. I wrote an _____ of each chapter to help me study for the test.

C | **Comprehension** *Check (✓) what students in Professor Anderson's class* **have to do** *and* **don't have to do.**

	Students have to . . .	Students don't have to . . .
1. take a quiz every week		
2. take a midterm and final exam		
3. give an oral report		
4. hand in an outline		
5. read four books for their term paper		
6. buy the textbook		

MODALS: *HAVE TO* / *DON'T HAVE TO*

Affirmative Statements

Subject	*Have to / Has to*	Base Form of Verb	
I We You They	have to	take	a history class.
He She	has to		
It		be	a three-credit class.

Negative Statements

Subject	*Do Not / Does Not*	*Have to*	Base Form of Verb	
I We You They	don't	have to	take	a history class.
He She	doesn't			
It			be	10 pages long.

Yes / No Questions

Do / Does	Subject	*Have to*	Base Form of Verb	
Do	I you we they	have to	study	tonight?
Does	he she			
	it		be	five pages?

Short Answers

	Affirmative				Negative		
Yes,	you I you they	do.		No,	you I you they	don't.	
	he she it	does.			he she it	doesn't.	

MUST AND *MUSTN'T*

Affirmative and Negative Statements

Subject	*Must*	Base Form of Verb	
I You He She It We They	must must not (mustn't)	arrive	early.

Past of *Have to* and *Must*

Subject	*Had to*	Base Form of Verb	
I You He She It We They	had to	leave	early.

GRAMMAR NOTES

1	Use **have to** and **must** to talk about things that are **necessary**. Both *have to* and *must* are followed by the base form of the verb. *Must* is stronger than *have to*.	• I **have to take** a test next week. • Students **must take** a three-credit history course.
	USAGE NOTE: We usually use *have to* in speaking and informal writing.	
	BE CAREFUL! *Have to* is different from the verb *have*.	• I **have** a psychology class. • I **have to read** 50 pages for this class.
	NOTE: The past of *must* and *have to* is **had to**.	• Last week I **had to buy** a lot of textbooks.
2	Use **don't have to** or **doesn't have to** when there is no necessity. You have a **choice**.	• I **don't have to sit** in the same seat every day. I can sit wherever I want. • He **doesn't have to wear** a suit to work. He can wear a shirt and slacks.
3	**Must not** or the contraction **mustn't** means that you are **not allowed** to do something. You don't have a choice. You can't do it.	• You **must not take** scissors on a plane.
4	Do not repeat *must* or *have to* when you use two verbs or verb phrases with one subject.	• You **must take** a test and **write** a paper. • He **has to work** and **study**. Nот: He must take a test and ~~must~~ write a paper. Nот: He has to work and ~~has to~~ study.
5	**BE CAREFUL!** Do not use *to* after *must*.	• He **must write** a report. Nот: He ~~must to write~~ a report.
6	**USAGE NOTE:** We rarely use *mustn't* in conversation except when talking to small children or telling rules. We use **can't** instead.	• Children, you **mustn't** cross the street when the signal is red. • You **can't** park there. Nот: You ~~mustn't~~ park there.

EXERCISE 1: Discover the Grammar

*Read about a special high school for the arts. Underline all forms of **have to, don't have to, must, mustn't,** and the verb that follows. Circle all examples of the verb **have**.*

New York City has a special high school for music, art, dance, and drama. It's called LaGuardia High School. To be accepted, students have to pass an audition. In addition they must have good grades. The school usually has about 9,000 applicants a year. It accepts about 650 students. All prospective students, even the children of the rich and famous, must audition. They must choose to audition for acting, dance, music, or art. Here are some of the requirements for students interested in art:

1. Each student must submit a portfolio of original artwork. The artwork does not have to be a special size, but all art has to be original. Students mustn't bring in photocopies.

2. Each student must complete three drawing exercises. Students have to bring a pencil and a transcript of their last report card. Students don't have to bring drawing materials. The school has all the necessary drawing supplies for the students.

Madonna with her daughter, Lourdes. Lourdes attends LaGuardia High School.

EXERCISE 2: Have to / Don't have to / Must

(Grammar Notes 1–2)

A | Read LaGuardia High School's audition requirements for dance. Complete the sentences. Use **have to** or **don't have to** and the verbs from the box.

bring	perform
bring / not	take

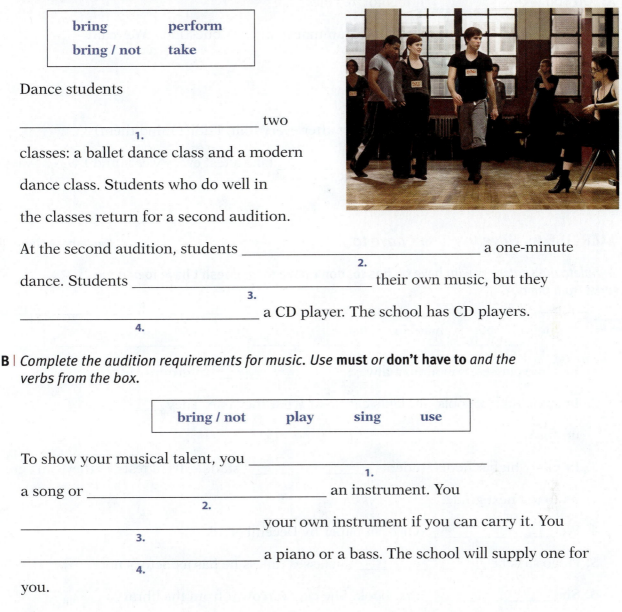

Dance students

_____ two
                    1.

classes: a ballet dance class and a modern

dance class. Students who do well in

the classes return for a second audition.

At the second audition, students _____ a one-minute
                                                            2.

dance. Students _____ their own music, but they
                              3.

_____ a CD player. The school has CD players.
                    4.

B | Complete the audition requirements for music. Use **must** or **don't have to** and the verbs from the box.

bring / not	play	sing	use

To show your musical talent, you _____
                                                      1.

a song or _____ an instrument. You
                        2.

_____ your own instrument if you can carry it. You
            3.

_____ a piano or a bass. The school will supply one for
            4.

you.

EXERCISE 3: Have / Have to / Had to

(Grammar Note 1)

Complete the conversation with **have**, **have to**, or **had to**.

A: Would you like to go to the movies this evening?

B: I can't. I _____*have*_____ a test tomorrow. I _____ study this evening.
                        1.   **2.**

A: What do you _____ study?
                              3.

(continued on next page)

B: Grammar. I _____ review the modals *can*, *could*, *would*, *might*, and *must*.

    4.

We _____ a test every Thursday.

    5.

A: Do you _____ memorize rules?

    6.

B: No. We _____ use the grammar to answer questions. We really

    7.

_____ understand it.

    8.

A: Do you get a lot of tests?

B: Uh-huh. We _____ a quiz after every unit. I don't mind them.

    9.

A: I don't like tests. Last year I _____ take a test every week, and I was always

    10.

worried.

EXERCISE 4: *Have to / Don't have to*

(Grammar Notes 1–2)

Complete the sentences with **have to, has to, don't have to,** *or* **doesn't have to** *and the verbs from the box.*

| attend | buy | hand in | listen | pass | pay | say | wear | ~~work~~ |

1. In some classes you almost always ___*have to work*___ in groups.

2. In some high schools, students can wear what they like. They _____ a uniform.

3. In many high schools students _____ standardized tests or they can't go on to the next grade.

4. We _____ our term paper by December 15.

5. Hugo says he _____ all classes unless he has a doctor's note.

6. She _____ that book. She can borrow it from the library.

7. My psychology class has many students. I _____ to a lecture and take notes. I _____ anything in class. I just have to pass the exams.

8. Jay goes to a college near his home, so he _____ for room and board.

EXERCISE 5: Have to, Must, Must not

(Grammar Notes 1, 3)

Read the signs. Then explain the rule or warning of each. Begin with **You have to,** **You** **must,** *or* **You must not.**

1. No Smoking

You mustn't smoke on the train.

_____

2. I.D. Required

_____

_____

3. Do Not Enter

_____

_____

4. Do not get hairdryer wet

_____

_____

5. Do not drink

_____

_____

6. Do not text when you drive

_____

_____

EXERCISE 6: Editing

Correct the sentences. There are eight mistakes. The first mistake is already corrected.
Find and correct seven more.

1. We ~~has to~~ *have* a lot of new vocabulary words. I can't remember all of them.

2. To learn a new vocabulary word, you must hears it seven times.

3. For me to remember a word, I has to write it down.

4. Avi has a great memory. He just have to hear a word once and he remembers it.

5. Our papers are due next week. I have start working on mine today.

6. We mustn't do any homework today. Tomorrow is a holiday.

7. You mustn't to bring any notes with you to the test.

8. You must to bring a photo ID to the testing center.

STEP 4 COMMUNICATION PRACTICE

EXERCISE 7: Pronunciation

A | *Read and listen to the Pronunciation Note.*

> **Pronunciation Note**
>
> When **have to** or **has to** is followed by a verb, the vowel sound in **to** is unstressed and sounds like / ə / .
>
> **EXAMPLE:** **A:** Why is he selling his house?
> **B:** He has to move.
>
> When **have to** or **has to** is not followed by a verb, there is more stress on **to** and the vowel sounds more like / u / .
>
> **EXAMPLE:** **A:** Do you need to study tonight?
> **B:** Yes, I have to.

B | *Listen and repeat.*

1. **A:** Do you want to go there?

   B: No, but I **have to**.

2. **A:** What does she **have to do**?

   B: She **has to write** a paper today.

3. **A:** When do we **have to pay** the tuition?

   B: We **have to pay** it before class begins.

4. **A:** Do you really **have to work** late tonight?

   B: Yes, I **have to**.

C | *PAIRS: Follow the directions. Then switch roles.*

1. **Partner A:** Tell your partner three things you have to do this week.

2. **Partner B:** Ask your partner, "Do you really have to?"

> EXAMPLE: **A:** This evening I have to study for our test.
> **B:** Do you really have to?
> **A:** Yes, I do. OR No, I don't. I could study tomorrow night.

EXERCISE 8: Listening

A | *Ali is in his second year of college. He is speaking to an advisor about graduate school. Listen to the conversation. What degree is Ali interested in getting?*

_____

B | *Listen again. Write one thing you have to do to get that degree. Write one thing you don't have to do.*

1. _____

2. _____

EXERCISE 9: Discussion

Talk about regulations, management, and teaching methods in schools you know about.
Use **have to, don't have to, must,** *and* **must not.**

> EXAMPLE: My nephew goes to P.S. 28 in Queens. It's a school for children between the ages of four and eight. Children have to be in school by 8:20. They must come on time for school. There's a school uniform, but they don't have to wear it. Children have to work in pairs and groups. They have to participate in class. They have to take a lot of standardized tests. They must not run in the halls or talk when the teacher is talking. The teachers are great, and the school is beautiful. My nephew loves his school. We're happy he goes there.

EXERCISE 10: Survey

A | *In some schools students try to copy their classmates' answers. Ask five classmates how teachers in their schools prevented cheating during tests.*

> EXAMPLE: **A:** We had to cover our papers.

B | *As a class, make a list of things teachers do to prevent cheating. Use* **have to** *or* **must.**

> EXAMPLE: Students have to sit in every other seat.
> Students have to leave cell phones at the front of the class.

EXERCISE 11: Writing

A | *Write about an elementary school in the area where you grew up. Use **have to** and* **must.**

EXAMPLE:

My Elementary School

by Emiko Shinohara

Children in my elementary school in Japan learn to respect the teachers and take care of the classroom. When the teacher enters the room, children must stand. They say, "Thank you for teaching us." Children have to clean the classroom. They wash the desks and clean the boards. In addition, children have to wear a school uniform. Most children like their school uniform and are proud to wear it.

B | *Check your work. Use the Editing Checklist.*

Editing Checklist

Did you . . . ?
☐ use **have to** and ***must*** correctly
☐ check your spelling

Check your answers on page UR-7.
Do you need to review anything?

A | *Circle the correct words to complete the sentences.*

1. You can wear what you want. You **mustn't / don't have to** wear a uniform.

2. It's getting late. We **have to / don't have to** leave.

3. The law says you **must / must not** drive without a license.

4. She can take the test any day this week. She **has to / doesn't have to** take it today.

5. I **have to / mustn't** hand in my term paper tomorrow. I can't go out today.

B | *Complete the sentences with the correct form of* **have, have to, don't have to,** *or* **mustn't.**

1. Children, you _____ cross the street when the light is red.

2. She _____ a lot of homework. She _____ hand in a paper

   and study for a test.

3. The tickets are good any day this week. We _____ use them today.

4. A doctor _____ fill out a medical form before you can use the gym.

C | *Complete the sentences with* **have to** *and a verb from the box. Use the present or past.*

answer	bring / not	give	read	work

1. He _____ two shifts because two co-workers were out sick.

2. We're busy. We _____ two chapters of our history book and

   _____ questions at the end of each chapter. It's due tomorrow.

3. We _____ a presentation in front of the entire school.

4. I _____ my own laptop. They gave me one for my presentation.

D | *Correct the paragraph. There are five mistakes.*

The test starts at 8:10. You must to be in the room at 8:00. You mustn't came late.
You have to has two number two pencils and an eraser. You musts brings proper
identification, such as a photo ID or a passport. You must leave your cell phone in the
front of the room.

PART X

From Grammar to Writing
EXPRESSING AND SUPPORTING AN OPINION

1 | *A fact is something you know to be true; for example, a scientific fact. An opinion is what you believe. Read the sentences. Write* **F** (sentences that express a fact) *or* **O** (sentences that express an opinion).

_____ **1.** I believe that Hollywood actors are not good examples for young people.

_____ **2.** John was in Hollywood last summer.

_____ **3.** The Himalayas are the highest mountains in the world.

_____ **4.** Earth is about 93 million miles from the sun.

_____ **5.** Children shouldn't watch violent movies.

2 | *Study the information about expressing and supporting an opinion.*

1	When you express your opinion, you can use expressions such as: ***In my opinion*** ***I believe*** ***I think*** ***better than*** ***It's better to . . . than to*** ***should / shouldn't***	• **In my opinion**, it's wrong to spank a child. • **I believe** tests are harmful. • **I think** tests are helpful. • Some tests are **better than** others. • **It's better to** give **than to** receive. • Parents **shouldn't** spank their children.
2	After you express your opinion, give reasons to support your opinion.	**OPINION** • In my opinion, it's wrong to spank children. **SUPPORT** • When adults use physical force, children think physical force is OK.

3 | *Read the two paragraphs about Hollywood actors. Circle the sentences that show an opinion. Underline the sentences that support the opinion.*

   I believe that Hollywood actors often set a bad example for young people. Young people look up to them, but these actors show bad values. For example, many stars spend huge amounts of money on homes, cars, and clothes. When young people try to copy their lifestyle, they often buy things they can't afford. Also, most Hollywood actors do not have long-term relationships. They change boyfriends and girlfriends frequently. Finally, many Hollywood actors have cosmetic surgery and go on strict diets, all in order to be more attractive.

In my opinion, some Hollywood stars set a bad example because of their materialism, but others set a good example through their charity. For example, Angelina Jolie and George Clooney are big stars who help others. They give away a lot of their money to help the poor and the sick in different parts of the world. They also encourage others to give to good causes.

4 | *Now write a paragraph on one of the topics. Give your opinion and reasons to support your opinion.*

- Hollywood stars have a right to privacy OR Hollywood stars do not have a right to privacy
- Money can buy happiness OR Money can't buy happiness
- Children shouldn't play violent video games OR Violent video games don't harm children

5 | *Exchange papers with a partner. Did your partner follow the directions? Correct any mistakes in grammar and spelling.*

6 | *Talk to your partner. Discuss the mistakes you made. Then rewrite your own paper and make any necessary changes.*

PART XI

COMPARISONS

The Comparative
COMPARING CITIES

Before You Read

PAIRS: Discuss. Where would you prefer to live? A big city or a small town? Why?

Read

Read the article about two U.S. cities called Portland. Which Portland would you prefer?

A TALE OF TWO PORTLANDS

Portland, Oregon

Portland, Maine

Matt Groening, creator of *The Simpsons*, and Liv Tyler, the popular actress, both come from the city of Portland. However, they come from different states in the U.S.

There are two beautiful U.S. cities named Portland. One is in Maine, and the other is in Oregon. Maine is on the East Coast of the United States, while Oregon is on the West Coast. Both Portlands have ports, but Portland, Oregon, is **farther from** the ocean. At 173 feet above sea level, it is also **higher** in elevation. Both cities are not very big, but they are **bigger than** any other city in their states. Portland, Maine, has a population of about 64,000, whereas Portland, Oregon, is

Liv Tyler played Arwen in three *Lord of the Rings* movies.

much **larger**, with a population of about 540,000. Winter in Oregon is a little **milder than** winter in Maine, but they both have comfortable climates.

Both Portlands offer a nice lifestyle. Portland, Maine, is located on the coast, but the mountains are just 45 minutes away by car. So it's easy to ski in the mountains in the winter or sunbathe on the beaches in the summer. Portland, Oregon, is located on a river. It's a city of different neighborhoods with different personalities. It's much **more diverse**[1] **than** the other Portland. Portland, Maine (founded in 1632), is a lot **older than** Portland, Oregon (founded in 1845).

[1] **diverse:** have people from different backgrounds

A TALE OF TWO PORTLANDS

You may wonder why the two cities have the same name. There's a very good reason. Each of the founders[2] of Portland, Oregon, wanted to name his new city after his hometown. One man came from Boston, Massachusetts. The other came from Portland, Maine. They tossed a coin,[3] and the man from Portland, Maine, won.

[2] **founder:** someone who establishes a business, school, town, etc.
[3] **tossed a coin:** made a decision by throwing a coin (penny, nickel, dime, etc.) in the air and guessing the side it would fall on.

After You Read

A | Practice *PAIRS: Now read the article aloud. Take turns reading sentences.*

B | Vocabulary *Complete the sentences with the words from the box.*

coast	mild	port	ski
diverse	personality	sea level	are located

1. We drove along the _____ and took some great photos of the ocean and the rocks.

2. The ship picked up the passengers at the _____.

3. It was cold yesterday, but today it is _____.

4. We like to _____ in the mountains. We love the snow.

5. The university has a _____ population. Students come from everywhere.

6. She has a warm _____. That's why everyone likes her.

7. That city is high above _____.

8. Washington, Oregon, and California _____ on the West Coast of the United States.

C | Comprehension *Check (✓) the correct Portland.*

	Portland, Maine	Portland, Oregon
1. Which Portland has a bigger population?		
2. Which Portland is older?		
3. Which Portland has more diverse neighborhoods?		
4. Which Portland has warmer winters?		

COMPARATIVES

Adjectives

Comparative Forms of Adjectives				
		Comparative Adjective	*Than*	
Portland, Oregon	is	**bigger** **busier** **more crowded**	**than**	Portland, Maine.

Comparative Forms of Irregular Adjectives				
		Irregular Comparative Adjective	*Than*	
My map	is	**better** **worse**	**than**	yours.
My new office		**farther**		my old one.

Questions with *Which*

Which + Noun					*Which*		
Which	**Noun**	**Verb**	**Comparative Adjective**		*Which*	**Verb**	**Comparative Adjective**
Which	city	is	bigger? more expensive?		**Which**	is	bigger? more expensive?

GRAMMAR NOTES

1	Use the **comparative form of an adjective +** *than* to compare two people, places, or things.	• Alaska is **bigger than** Maine.
2	To form the comparative of most **short (one-syllable) adjectives**, add *-er* to the adjective. Add only *-r* if the adjective ends in *e*. *long—longer* *large—larger* Exceptions: *tired—more tired* *bored—more bored* *fun—more fun*	• The Mississippi River is **longer** than the Hudson River. • For me, the city is **more fun** than the suburbs.

3	To form the comparative of adjectives that end in a **consonant** + **y**, change the **y** to **i** and add **-er**. 　busy—**busier** 　easy—**easier** 　heavy—**heavier**	• These days the stores are **busier** than they were two years ago.
4	To form the comparative of most adjectives of **two** or **more syllables**, add **more** before the adjective. 　expensive—**more expensive** 　intelligent—**more intelligent** Exceptions: 　quiet—**quieter** 　simple—**simpler**	• The train is **more expensive** than the bus. • Is life in the countryside really **simpler** and **quieter**?
5	Use **less** before an adjective to mean the opposite of *more*.	• A car is **more** expensive than a bicycle. • A bicycle is **less** expensive than a car.
6	The adjectives **good**, **bad**, and **far** have irregular comparative forms. 　good—**better** 　bad—**worse** 　far—**farther**	• My new job is **better** than my old one. • The book was bad, but the movie was **worse**. • The bus stop is **farther** than the train station.
7	Use **much** to make comparisons stronger.	• A two-bedroom apartment is **much** more expensive than a one-bedroom apartment. • England is **much** older than New England.
8	**USAGE NOTE:** In formal English, use the subject pronoun after *than*. In informal English, such as casual conversation between friends, you can use the object pronoun after *than*. **BE CAREFUL!** Always compare the same things. **BE CAREFUL!** Do not use two comparative forms together.	SUBJECT PRONOUN • Steve's younger **than she** is. OBJECT PRONOUN • Steve's younger **than her**. • **John's home** is larger than **William's**. OR • **John's home** is larger than **William's home**. NOT: John's home is larger than ~~William~~. NOT: John's home is ~~more~~ larger than William's.
9	Use **which** to ask about a comparison of **people**, **places**, or **things**.	• **Which city** is larger? • **Which** is larger, **Tokyo** or **Seoul**?

REFERENCE NOTE
See Unit 35, page 411 for a discussion of **not as** + **adjective** + **as**.

EXERCISE 1: Discover the Grammar

A | *Read about two cities in Canada. Underline all comparative adjectives.*

Fairmont Le Château Frontenac, Quebec City

Canada has many beautiful cities. Two of my favorites are Quebec City in eastern Canada and Vancouver in Western Canada. Vancouver is right on the Pacific coast, and it's just 7 feet above sea level. Quebec City is farther from the coast and higher than Vancouver. It overlooks the Saint Lawrence River. When I visited Quebec City, I took some great photos of the river from the famous hotel Château Frontenac.

Vancouver

Quebec City has the charm of an old historic city. It is a lot older than Vancouver. Vancouver has an old quarter too, but it's younger than Quebec City's. Vancouver, with its milder climate, is better known for its gardens and parks. Stanley Park in Vancouver is bigger than most urban parks, and people visit it all year round, but I think it's more fun to go in the spring or early summer. That's when the flowers are in bloom.

Vancouver has a larger population than Quebec City and is growing each year. These days many films are made in Vancouver because it is less expensive to make them there than in cities like Los Angeles and New York.

In Vancouver most people speak English, while 95 percent of the people in Quebec City speak French. That is because Quebec City was founded by people from France and still has a continental flavor.

All in all, both cities are great places to visit or live in.

B | *Write the base form of the ten adjectives you underlined in Part A.*

1. _____*far*_____

2. _____

3. _____

4. _____

5. _____

6. _____

7. _____

8. _____

9. _____

10. _____

Fortress, Quebec City

EXERCISE 2: Comparison of Adjectives

(Grammar Notes 1–9)

A | *Complete the conversations with the adjectives in parentheses. Use the comparative form. Add **than** when necessary.*

1. **A:** Which city is _____*more expensive*_____ to live in, Tokyo or Sydney?
   (expensive)

   B: Tokyo is _____ Sydney.
   (expensive)

2. **A:** Which city is _____ in summer, Bangkok or Seoul?
   (hot)

   B: Bangkok summers are _____ summers in Seoul.
   (hot)

3. **A:** Which city has a _____ elevation, Bogota or Mexico City?
   (high)

   B: Bogota is _____ Mexico City.
   (high)

4. **A:** Which river is _____, the Nile or the Amazon?
   (long)

   B: The Nile is _____ the Amazon.
   (long)

5. **A:** Does New York have a _____ subway system
   (good)
   _____ Washington, D.C.?

   B: I don't know. The New York subway goes to more places, but the D.C. Metro is

   _____.
   (clean)

(continued on next page)

6. A: Is winter in Quebec City _____ winter in Vancouver?
(cold)

    B: Yes, it is.

7. A: Is New York a _____ tourist destination
(popular)
_____ San Francisco?

    B: No, they're both very popular tourist destinations.

8. A: Is Miami in summer _____ in winter?
(humid)

    B: Yes, it's much _____ in summer
(humid)
_____ in winter.

9. A: Is Argentina _____ from the South Pole
(far)
_____ Mexico?

    B: No, Argentina is _____ to the South Pole.
(near)

10. A: Was the Hudson River _____ 10 years ago
(polluted)
_____ it is today?

    B: Yes, it was. It is much _____ today.
(clean)

11. A: Which highway has _____ traffic, the West Highway
(heavy)
or the East Highway?

    B: It depends on the time.

B | *Rewrite the sentences. Use **less** and the adjectives in parentheses. Use the comparative form.*

1. Sydney is _____*less expensive*_____ to live in _____*than*_____ Tokyo.
(expensive)

2. Miami is _____ in winter _____ in summer.
(less humid)

3. The Hudson River is _____ today _____ it was
(less polluted)
10 years ago.

4. Is the highway _____ between 7:00 and 8:00 _____ it is
(crowded)
between 8:00 and 9:00?

5. Is the Eiffel Tower _____ than the Egyptian pyramids?
(famous)

EXERCISE 3: Comparison of Adjectives

(Grammar Notes 1–2, 4, 8)

Write sentences comparing the two cities. Use the information in the chart and the words in parentheses.

	Middletown	Lakeville
number of people	100,000	50,000
average household income	$85,000	$63,000
average rent for a two-bedroom apartment	$1,300	$1,000
cost of a cup of coffee	$2.00	$1.00
percent unemployed	7	9
number of hospitals	5	1
average summer temperature	80°F	68°F

1. (average household income / high)

   The average household income in Middletown is higher than the average household income

   in Lakeville.

2. (two-bedroom apartment / expensive)

   _____

   _____

3. (a cup of coffee / less expensive)

   _____

   _____

4. (probably / hard to find work)

   _____

   _____

5. (probably / healthcare / bad)

   _____

   _____

6. (summers / much / warm)

   _____

   _____

EXERCISE 4: Comparison of Adjectives

(Grammar Notes 1–7)

Complete the paragraph with the adjectives in parentheses. Use the comparative form.

You are choosing between two cities to live in, Los Angeles or Glendale. You aren't sure which is a _____*better*_____ choice. Los
1. (good)
Angeles is a much _____ city than
2. (big)
Glendale, and it has all the problems of big cities. Los Angeles is _____ than
3. (polluted)
Glendale, and traffic is _____.
4. (bad)
The streets of downtown Los Angeles are

Rodeo Drive, Los Angeles

_____ too. However, Los Angeles is much _____ than Glendale.
5. (busy) **6. (exciting)**

Bicycle trail, Glendale, California

Los Angeles has a great night life. Glendale is much _____ at night. Both
7. (quiet)
cities have the same great climate. It's hard to compare housing costs. Some parts of Los Angeles are _____ than Glendale
8. (more / expensive)
and other parts are _____. Both
9. (less / expensive)
cities are close, so if you make a mistake, you can always move.

EXERCISE 5: Editing

Correct the sentences. There are seven mistakes. The first one is already corrected. Find and correct six more.

1. Our new apartment is ^*more* comfortable than our old one.

2. Florida is more hotter than Maine.

3. Oregon is far north than California.

4. A motorcycle is more fast than a bicycle.

5. Traffic at 8:00 A.M. is more heavy than traffic at 10:00 A.M.

6. The climate in Portland, Oregon, is mild than the climate in Anchorage, Alaska.

7. The location of Jake's apartment is more convenient than his sister.

EXERCISE 6: Pronunciation

🎧 **A** | *Read and listen to the Pronunciation Note.*

> **Pronunciation Note**
>
> ***Than*** is unstressed and reduced to / ðn / .
>
> **EXAMPLE:** Istanbul is a much larger city than Izmír.

🎧 **B** | *Listen and repeat each sentence.*

1. The Nile River is longer than the Amazon River.
2. The Yangtze River is shorter than the Nile.
3. Quebec City is older than Vancouver.
4. The Pacific Ocean is bigger than the Atlantic Ocean.

EXERCISE 7: Listening

🎧 **A** | *Listen to a conversation between two friends. The woman says, "You can thank our mayor." What is the mayor doing to the city?*

_____

🎧 **B** | *Listen again. Circle the correct word or words to complete each sentence.*

1. The downtown area is **livelier** / **less lively**.

2. The seats on the bus are **more comfortable** / **less comfortable**.

3. It's **easier** / **harder** to take the bus.

4. The air is **cleaner** / **dirtier**.

5. It's **easier** / **harder** to park downtown.

6. West Park is **cleaner and safer** / **dirtier and more dangerous**.

7. East Park is **cleaner and safer** / **dirtier and more dangerous**.

EXERCISE 8: Comparing Train Systems

PAIRS: Look at the information about the London Underground and the Moscow Metro. Together write as many comparative questions as you can. Ask other pairs your questions. Answer their questions. Then compare these subways to others you know.

EXAMPLE: **A:** Is the Underground faster than the Moscow Metro?
B: No, it isn't. It's slower.

	London Underground	**Moscow Metro**
Year opened	1863	1935
Length of tracks	250 miles (400 kilometers)	187.2 miles (301.2 kilometers)
Number of passengers each day	4 million	6.6 million
Hours of operation	5:30 A.M. to 1:15 A.M. (Fri. & Sat. closes at 2:00 A.M.)	5:30 A.M. to 1:00 A.M.
Cost of ride in euros	4 euros for shortest distance	26 rubles = .66 euro
Speed	20.5 mph (33 km / h)	25.82 mph (41.55 km / h)

EXERCISE 9: Discussion: Making Comparisons

PAIRS: Look at the categories in the list. Tell your partner your preferences within each category. Explain why in a sentence with a comparative.

clothes   homes   jobs   travel   vacation places

EXAMPLE: **A:** Do you prefer to travel by bike or by motorcycle?
B: I prefer a motorcycle. It's faster and more exciting. What about you?
A: I prefer a bike. It's safer and better for the environment.

EXERCISE 10: Comparing Cities

Compare cities. Follow the steps.

1. Name a city you know well. (Do not name the city you are in.) Your teacher writes the names everyone suggests on the board.
2. Class: Name adjectives that describe cities, people, and climates. Your teacher writes the adjectives on the board.

EXAMPLES:

Cities	People	Climates
clean	friendly	warm
dangerous	polite	dry
exciting	relaxed	humid

3. Write questions comparing the cities on the board to the city you are in. Use the adjectives on the board or choose your own. Then with a group, ask each other questions comparing the cities.

Examples: (You are now in San Francisco.)
        A: Is Paris cleaner than San Francisco?
        B: I don't think so. I think San Francisco is cleaner than Paris.
        C: Does Sapporo have a warmer climate than San Francisco?
        D: No, it doesn't. Sapporo has a colder climate than San Francisco.

EXERCISE 11: Writing

A | *Compare two ways of travel. Use at least three comparative adjectives.*

Example: Most cities have busses and trains, but in San Francisco some people also travel by trolley, and in Venice people sometimes travel by gondola. Both the trolley and the gondola are more fun than the bus or the train. The gondola is more romantic than the trolley, but the trolley is more exciting, especially when you're traveling down one of San Francisco's steep streets.

B | *Check your work. Use the Editing Checklist.*

Editing Checklist

Did you . . . ?
☐ use comparative adjectives correctly
☐ check your spelling

A | *Circle the correct words to complete the sentences.*

1. She is **more / much** younger than he is.

2. It is colder **then / than** it was yesterday.

3. This singing group is **more popular / popular more** than the other one.

4. The traffic is **more worse / worse** now than it was an hour ago.

5. Which city has a **high / higher** elevation, Bogota or Mexico City?

6. Which city has a **better / more good** transportation system, Quebec or Vancouver?

7. Is your car more comfortable than your **brother / brother's**?

B | *Look at the chart. Make comparisons. Use the words in parentheses.*

	New City	Sun City
Bus fare	$2.00	$3.00
Cup of coffee	$1.20	$1.50
Average home	$200,000	$300,000
Average income	$65,000	$90,000

1. _____
   (bus / expensive)

2. _____
   (cup of coffee / cheap)

3. _____
   (average home / less / expensive)

4. _____
   (average income / high)

C | *Correct the paragraph. There are nine mistakes.*

We moved to the countryside, and we're much more happier. Our home is more larger, and the air is cleaner and polluted less. It less expensive than the city too. Fruits and vegetables are more cheap. The people are friendler too. Of course, our commute is more bad; it's much more long, but we listen to Spanish tapes, and our Spanish is more good.

Adverbs of Manner
Public Speaking

Before You Read

A | *PAIRS: List jobs that require speaking in front of large groups. Compare your list with other pairs' lists.*

B | *How do you feel about giving a speech in front of the following people? Check (✓) your feelings.*

How you feel when you speak in front of . . .			
	your classmates?	your friends and relatives?	your bosses?	250 people you don't know?
calm and confident				
nervous but confident				
nervous and not confident				
nervous and miserable				

Read

Read the blog about public speaking.

Speaking about . . .

Public Speaking by Michelle Jones

👍 Like

Last year my boss asked me to give a presentation. It was a bit of a nightmare. I had never spoken in front of a large group before, so I was nervous. Also, I had to prepare **fast**—I had only two days to get ready. The day of the speech came. There were 40 people sitting in the room waiting for me to speak. My manager was there, and my co-workers. I wanted to run out of the room, so I spoke **quickly**, and I didn't look at anyone. Instead I read from my paper. I was afraid to tell a joke. I wanted to sound smart, so in my speech, I gave a lot of facts. I used big words and long sentences. I received polite applause, but I knew my speech was not appreciated. My friend later told me it was a good speech, but that I didn't speak **loudly** enough.

(*continued on next page*)

The next time I gave a speech, I asked my friend for help. She offered a lot of valuable advice. She helped me to focus on three ideas and to give good examples. In my next speech I spoke **slowly** and **clearly**. I thought **carefully** about everything I wanted to say. I spoke **honestly**, and I gave personal examples. I only said things I really believed. I looked at my audience, and I smiled at the right occasions. This time the applause was long and loud. I connected with the audience, and I felt good. People gave me their time, and I gave them a speech to remember.

After You Read

A | Practice *PAIRS: Read the blog again aloud. Take turns reading the sentences.*

B | Vocabulary *Circle the letter of the best meaning for the words in* **blue**.

1. The **audience** was interested in every word he said.

   a. people who write about a performance   **b.** people who watch a performance

2. When he heard the long **applause**, he felt satisfied.

   a. clapping of hands   **b.** stamping of feet

3. Most of his speech was light and funny, but he spoke **seriously** at the end of his talk.

   a. in a way that says something is wrong   **b.** in a way that says something is important

4. He told us many **facts** about his country.

   a. true things   **b.** interesting things

5. We laughed at his **jokes**.

    a. funny stories   **b.** gestures

6. The people clapped to be **polite**, but they didn't really enjoy his talk.

    a. show good manners   **b.** show anger

7. She **appreciated** my help and thanked me many times.

    a. was nervous about   **b.** was grateful for

C | Comprehension *Check (✓) the advice you got from the public speaking blog.*

____ **1.** Speak quickly.   ____ **5.** Use humor.

____ **2.** Speak slowly.   ____ **6.** Give personal examples.

____ **3.** Use big words.   ____ **7.** Have many ideas, not just three or four.

____ **4.** Look at audience.   ____ **8.** Speak briefly.

STEP 2 GRAMMAR PRESENTATION

ADVERBS OF MANNER

Subject	Verb	Adverb
He	spoke	well.
		badly.
		clearly.

Subject	Verb		Adverb
She	finished	her speech	quickly.

Adverb formed with Adjective + *-ly*		Same Adjective and Adverb Form	
Adjective	**Adverb**	**Adjective**	**Adverb**
bad	badly	early	early
careful	carefully	fast	fast
loud	loudly	late	late
quick	quickly	long	long
quiet	quietly	**Irregular Adverb Form**	
sarcastic	sarcastically	**Adjective**	**Adverb**
slow	slowly	good	well

GRAMMAR NOTES

1	**Adverbs of manner** describe action verbs. They say **how** or the way something happens. The adverb often comes at the end of the sentence.	• She spoke **slowly**. • He walked **fast**.
2	Most adverbs of manner are formed by adding **-ly** to an adjective. **BE CAREFUL!** Some words that end in -ly are adjectives, not adverbs. **Examples:** *lively, lovely, ugly, lonely, friendly* These adjectives have no adverb form.	ADJECTIVE • She's a **careful** driver. ADVERB • She drives **carefully**. ADJECTIVE • She's a **friendly** person. • It's a **lonely** job.
3	Some **adverbs** of manner have the **same form as adjectives**.	ADJECTIVE · ADVERB • She's a **hard** worker. She works **hard**.
4	*Well* is the adverb for the adjective *good*. *Well* is also an adjective that means "in good health." **USAGE NOTE:** In very informal speaking, when people ask, "How are you?" some people respond, "I'm good."	ADJECTIVE • She's a **good** speaker. ADVERB • She speaks **well**. ADJECTIVE • I feel **well**.
5	**Linking verbs** can connect a subject and an adjective. **Linking verbs** are followed by **adjectives**, not adverbs. Common linking verbs are *appear, be, become, feel, look, seem, smell, sound,* and *taste*.	LINKING VERB · ADJECTIVE • The grapes **taste good**. NOT: The grapes taste ~~well~~. • She **seems sad**. • It **sounds beautiful**.

EXERCISE 1: Discover the Grammar

Read the paragraph. Underline the adverbs of manner in the paragraph.

A public speaker should remember three things: to entertain, to instruct, and to inspire. Author Bob Rosner likes to say, "It's ha-ha and ah-ha." When you instruct, speak briefly and clearly. Don't speak too long. And don't speak too fast. Use humor. It helps your audience relax. And remember that great speeches inspire and move an audience. Know your audience and touch their emotions.

EXERCISE 2: Adverbs of Manner

(Grammar Notes 1–4)

Complete each sentence with the adverb form of the adjectives in parentheses.

1. He spoke _____*quickly*_____.
   (quick)
2. Sally writes _____.
   (good)
3. They speak Spanish _____.
   (fluent)
4. He spoke _____.
   (clear)
5. He drove _____.
   (fast)
6. The audience listened _____.
   (careful)
7. Did he drive _____?
   (dangerous)
8. Did they sing _____?
   (bad)
9. The movie began _____.
   (slow)
10. It rained _____ last night.
    (hard)

EXERCISE 3: Adverbs of Manner and Adjectives

(Grammar Notes 1–5)

Complete the conversation. Choose from the words in parentheses. Write the correct adjective or adverbs.

1. **A:** How was the debate?

   B: Good. Both sides spoke _____*well*_____.
   (good / well)
2. **A:** How was the food at the reception after the debate?

   B: It tasted _____.
   (good / well)

(continued on next page)

3. A: There were _____ paintings in the room.
   (beautiful / beautifully)
   B: The artist is from Colombia.

4. A: How did Roger do in his last debate?

   B: Not _____.
   (good / well)

5. A: Please drive _____.
   (slow / slowly)
   B: OK.

6. A: How was the talk?

   B: The first part was very _____, but the second part was better.
   (slow / slowly)

7. A: How did she sound?

   B: _____.
   (Nervous / Nervously)

EXERCISE 4: Editing

Correct the conversations. There are six mistakes. The first mistake is already corrected.
Find and correct five more.

1. A: How did he do?

   B: He did ~~good~~ well.

2. A: Was the food OK?

   B: Everyone loved it. It really tasted well.

3. A: Is Harry a good driver?

   B: I don't think so. He drives too slow.

4. A: How did they do?

   B: They worked hardly and did well.

5. A: Did you hear him?

   B: No, I didn't. He spoke too soft.

6. A: How did she sound?

   B: A little nervously.

EXERCISE 5: Listening

A | *Listen to some tips for giving a speech. Complete the sentences.*

You have a good _____ and _____. You have a couple of good

_____.

B | *Listen again and write the five tips for making a good speech better.*

1. *Look directly at a few people in the audience.* _____

2. _____

3. _____

4. _____

5. _____

EXERCISE 6: Pronunciation

A | *Read and listen to the Pronunciation Note.*

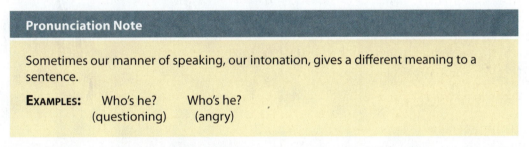

Pronunciation Note

Sometimes our manner of speaking, our intonation, gives a different meaning to a sentence.

EXAMPLES: Who's he?   Who's he?
(questioning)   (angry)

B | *Do you know what the words in boldface mean? If not, use your dictionary. Then listen to the speakers' manner.*

angrily: I love him. He's mine, and you can't have him.

decisively: I love him. I'll love him until I die.

questioningly: Do I love him? Enough to marry him?

sadly: I love him. I miss him so much.

sarcastically: I just love him. His bark wakes me up every day at 5:00 A.M.

C | *Listen again and repeat the sentences.*

D | *PAIRS: Say, "I love him (or her)." Say it angrily, decisively, questioningly, sadly, or sarcastically. Your partner guesses your meaning.*

EXERCISE 7: Writing

A | *PAIRS: Tell about a sports event.*

B | *Write about the event. Use three adverbs of frequency.*

EXAMPLE: It was the final ball game of the season for the Fogville Little League Team. Fogville was up against Lakeville, a very strong team. The score was seven to seven. The bases were loaded. Ron was up at bat. Everyone groaned loudly. Ron never played well. He was the team's worst player. But Ron hit the ball hard. He ran quickly to first base. The man on third ran home. They won. Everyone applauded loudly. It was a great game for everyone, especially Ron.

C | *Check your work. Use the Editing Checklist.*

Editing Checklist

Did you . . . ?
☐ use adverbs of manner correctly
☐ check your spelling

A | *Complete the sentences with the adjectives in parentheses. Use the adverb form.*

1. He drove _____.
      (quick)

2. She speaks Korean _____.
                         (fluent)

3. Did he do _____ on the test?
                  (good)

4. Walk _____ and look at the trees.
            (slow)

5. I spoke _____.
               (clear)

B | *Circle the correct word to complete the sentences.*

1. Both sides gave **good / well** arguments.

2. He listened very **careful / carefully**.

3. She sounded a little **nervous / nervously**.

4. He did **bad / badly** on the last test.

5. I can't understand her because she's talking too **quick / quickly**.

C | *Complete the sentences. Choose from the words in the box.*

briefly clearly fast good honestly

If you want to give a _____ speech, remember these things: Speak
                        1.

_____ and _____. Don't speak too long or swallow your
        2.   **3.**

words. Don't speak too _____. People need time to understand your
                         4.

ideas. Speak _____. Say only what you mean.
              5.

D | *Correct the conversation. There are five mistakes.*

A: I think my speech went good.

B: Did they appreciate your jokes?

A: They laughed polite, but I'm not sure they laughed sincere.

B: It's hard to be funny.

A: I hard worked, and I prepared carefully, but I was nervously.

Before You Read

A prom is a formal school dance. It usually takes place at the end of the senior year of high school. In the United States, proms can include dinner and dancing. Couples often come in limousines. Are there special parties or dances in your country? When are they? What are they like?

Read

Read a conversation between two high school students, Emily and Haley.

> **EMILY:** So Haley—what did you decide? Who's your date for the prom?
>
> **HALEY:** I don't have one. I'm not going.
>
> **EMILY:** What do you mean? You know so many cool guys. . . . How about Mike?
>
> **HALEY:** No—he's **too talkative**. When he's around, no one can get a word in edgewise.
>
> **EMILY:** Oh. He *does* talk a lot. Well . . . how about David? He likes you.

HALEY: David? He's **way too young** for me.

EMILY: He's in **the same** grade **as** we are. What are you talking about?

HALEY: No, Emily. He's a *sophomore*. He's in our Spanish class because he lived in Spain for a while. I can't go with him. People will say I'm a loser if I go with him.

EMILY: Well how about Jake? He's **old enough**, and he's **very cute**.

HALEY: He dresses funny.[1]

EMILY: Oh, come on, Haley, Jake doesn't dress funny. You're just making excuses.

HALEY: OK, OK. But Jake is **too good looking** and **too popular**. I'm not his type.

EMILY: That's not true. My brother says Jake thinks you're awesome.

HALEY: Really? All right. I'll tell you the real reason. I can't dance. I'm a klutz.[2] I look like an idiot on the dance floor. So . . . I'm not going to make a fool of myself.

EMILY: Not a problem. Jake is sort of a klutz too. He broke his foot in art class.

HALEY: What? In *art class*?

EMILY: He tripped over a can of paint. So it'll be perfect. You can go with him and watch the rest of us dance. I'll talk to my brother. Then Jake will ask you. Don't say no.

---

[1] **He dresses funny:** (very informal) He dresses strangely, badly.

[2] **klutz:** a clumsy person

After You Read

A | Practice *PAIRS: Now practice the conversation aloud.*

B | Vocabulary *Circle the letter of the best meaning for the words in* blue.

1. "When he's around, **no one can get a word in edgewise**," means _____.
   a. he never says what he means
   b. he does all the talking

2. "People will say **I'm a loser**" means _____.
   a. I'm unpopular
   b. I get bad grades

3. "You're just **making excuses**," means _____.
   a. you're sorry about something
   b. you aren't telling the truth

4. "**I'm not his type**," means _____.
   a. He's too old for me
   b. He's different from me

5. "**I'm not going to make a fool of myself**," means _____.
   a. I won't do anything that makes me look bad
   b. I'm not stupid

C | Comprehension *Write* **T** *(True) or* **F** *(False) for each statement.*

_____ **1.** Mike is too young for Haley.

_____ **2.** Emily and Haley are sophomores.

_____ **3.** David likes Haley.

_____ **4.** Haley and Emily are in the same Spanish class.

_____ **5.** Haley thinks Jake likes her.

_____ **6.** Haley can't dance well.

_____ **7.** Jake hurt himself in art class.

STEP 2 GRAMMAR PRESENTATION

ENOUGH, TOO / VERY, AS + ADJECTIVE + AS, SAME / DIFFERENT

Adjective + *Enough*			
	Adjective	*Enough*	**(Infinitive)**
The room was	**big**	**enough**	to hold all the students.
It wasn't	**warm**		to go without a jacket.

Very + Adjective		
	Very	**Adjective**
The prom was	**very**	**expensive**.

Too + Adjective				
	Too	**Adjective**	**(Infinitive)**	
His father's tuxedo was	**too**	big	(for him)	to wear.

As + Adjective + *As*				
	As	**Adjective**	*As*	
Jake is	**as**	**tall**	**as**	his dad.
He isn't		**heavy**		his dad is.

The Same As		
My first name is	**the same as**	yours.
My initials are		his.

Different From		
Her dress is	**different from**	mine.
These books are		those.

The Same + Noun (Noun Phrase) + *As*				
	The Same	**Noun**	*As*	
My eyes are	**the same**	**color**	**as**	my brother's. yours.
Max has		**last name**		James.
Jim likes		**kind of food**		I do.

410 UNIT 35

GRAMMAR NOTES

1	*Enough* means that you have the amount you need. It has a positive meaning. Use *enough* after an adjective.	**ADJECTIVE** • He's **old enough** to drive.
	Use *enough* before a noun.	**NOUN** • There are **enough chairs**.

2	*Too* means "more than necessary." It has a negative meaning. Use *too* before an adjective. *Much too* or *way too* makes the meaning stronger. **USAGE NOTE:** We use *way too* in informal speaking and writing.	• The coffee is **too hot**. I burned my tongue. • The suit was **much too big** for him. • The prom was **way too short**. I didn't want to go home.

3	An **infinitive** can follow **adjective** + *enough*. An **infinitive** can follow *too* + **adjective**.	**INFINITIVE** • He's **old enough to drive**. • She's **too tired to drive**.

4	*Very* makes the meaning of an adjective stronger. *Very* comes before an adjective. **BE CAREFUL!** *Too* has a negative meaning, but *very* doesn't.	• He's **very tall**. • He's **very young**. (*He's really young. He's 16, and the other students are 18.*) • He's **too young**. (*He's too young to do something—to drive, to work, etc.*)

5	Use *as* + **adjective** + *as* to show how two people, places, or things are alike. Use *not as* + **adjective** + *as* to show how two people, places, or things are not alike.	• Sally is **as tall as** Paula. They're the same height. • Sally is **not as tall as** Mike. Mike is taller.

6	Use *the same as* for things that are alike. Use *different from* for things that are not alike.	• His family name is **the same as** hers. (*He's Robert Lee, and she's Jennifer Lee.*) • My book is **different from** yours. (*I have a new edition.*)

EXERCISE 1: Discover the Grammar

A | *Circle the adjectives in the sentences. Then underline* **too, as . . . as, enough** *and* **very.** *Draw arrows from the adjectives to the nouns they go with.*

1. Mr. Jones isn't as old as he looks.

2. The food wasn't spicy enough for him.

3. His dress shoes were too tight.

4. Her prom dress was very beautiful.

5. That tuxedo was too expensive.

6. The car wasn't big enough for all of us.

B | *Underline* **the same . . . as** *and* **different from** *in the sentences.*

1. Serena wore the same dress as Jasmin.

2. He has the same voice as his father. It's confusing when I call his home.

3. He's different from his brother. His brother loves to go to parties.

4. Adam Rusk has the same initials as Ali Rogers.

EXERCISE 2: *Enough, Too*   (Grammar Notes 1–2)

Haley is talking to her aunt about the prom. Complete their conversation with **enough** *or* **too** *and the words from the box.*

~~hot~~   ice   salty   seats   sweet

AUNT ANNE: So, Haley. How was the prom?

HALEY: I had a great time, but there were a few problems with the place. The air

conditioner didn't work well, so it was _____*too hot*_____ in the room.
                                                  1.

AUNT ANNE: It was a warm night. I feel bad for the guys in those tuxedos. How was the

music?

HALEY: Good, but the refreshments were so-so. The chips were _____,
                                                              2.

and the desserts were _____. And there wasn't _____
                             3.   **4.**

for the drinks, so the drinks were warm.

Aunt Anne: That's pretty bad.

Haley: Also, there weren't _____. All but a few of us had to stand. Since
5.
Jake hurt his foot, we were able to sit. But I'm really glad I went. Jake's a nice

guy, and we have a lot in common.

Aunt Anne: I'm glad. Your mom sent me your picture. You looked very beautiful in that

dress.

Haley: Thanks.

EXERCISE 3: Word Order Practice; *Enough, Too . . . To*   *(Grammar Notes 1–3)*

Write sentences with the words given.

1. to vote / She isn't / enough / old

   She isn't old enough to vote.

2. warm / that dress / to wear / It isn't / enough

   _____

3. too / This steak / is / to eat / tough / much

   _____

4. to call / him / I'm / busy / too / right now

   _____

5. weren't / the sofa / They / enough / strong / to move

   _____

6. much / restaurant / too / That / expensive / is

   _____

7. too / was / to miss / That class / important

   _____

8. before the movie / have / don't / time / enough / We / to eat

   _____

9. clear / wasn't / to read / His address / enough

   _____

EXERCISE 4: *Too* + Adjective / *The Same . . . As*

(Grammar Notes 2, 6)

A | *Russ Tran, Jean Philippe, and Robert Trent are friends and co-workers. They take turns driving to work. Complete the sentences with the words from the box.*

| too carelessly | too fast | too slowly |

1. Russ thinks Jean drives _____. He thinks Jean will get a

speeding ticket.

2. Jean thinks Russ and Robert drive _____. He complains

that they drive under the speed limit.

3. Russ thinks Robert drives _____. He eats, drinks, and

answers phone calls while driving.

B | *Look at the three licenses. Use the information from the licenses to write similarities among the people. Use* **has**, *the words in parentheses, and* **as**.

1. (the same height) _____

Jean Philippe is the same height as

Robert Trent.

2. (the same color eyes) _____

_____.

3. (the same initials) _____

_____.

4. (the same weight) _____

_____.

Complete the sentences with too or very.

1. Some people think that a black dress is _____*too*_____

    dark to wear to a prom, but I think it's _____

    fashionable.

2. Don't buy those shoes. They're _____ pretty, but

    the heels are _____ high. They will hurt your

    feet.

3. Jake called _____ late to order a limousine, so

    he picked up Haley in his car.

4. He can't reach the shelf. He's _____ short. Ask Ali. He's

    _____ tall.

5. Your composition is _____ well written. You did a great job.

6. I can't lift the box. It's _____ heavy. I'll ask Barry. He's _____

    strong.

7. It's _____ windy outside. Put on a jacket. It's _____ cold to

    go outside without one.

8. It's _____ difficult to get into that school. His grades are

    _____ low. He probably won't get in.

9. This jacket doesn't fit. It's _____ tight in the shoulders.

10. It's _____ early to go to the party. We don't want to be the first to arrive.

11. We had a _____ good time at Joel's graduation party, but there were

    _____ many guests, so it was crowded.

EXERCISE 6: *As* + Adjective + *As*, *The Same* + Noun + *As*   (Grammar Note 5)

Read the conversation between Jake and Haley. Jake applied to an art school but did not get in. Complete the sentences with the phrases from the box.

~~as hard as she does~~	the same art camp as she did
as serious an artist as she is	the same grades as she did
as well as she does	

HALEY: Jake, what's wrong?

JAKE: I'm really angry. Maya got into BCA Art Institute, and I didn't. I work

_____*just as hard as she does*_____.

             1.

HALEY: And you're really talented.

JAKE: Thanks. I think I'm _____.

             2.

HALEY: Yes, you work very hard on your drawings and paintings.

JAKE: And I hand in every project on time. I draw _____.

             3.

HALEY: Why do you think she got into BCA Art Institute then?

JAKE: I don't know. I got _____. We had the same art

             4.

teachers. I even went to _____. Maybe she got in

             5.

because she knows someone at BCA?

HALEY: That happens sometimes.

EXERCISE 7: Editing

Correct the sentences. There are eight mistakes. The first mistake is already corrected. Find and correct seven more.

1. He doesn't have ^{enough} money ~~enough~~ to pay for the limousine.

2. His girlfriend isn't as nice than his old one.

3. She's very different than her sister.

4. We're very young to vote. You have to be 18 years old. We're 17.

5. She has the same dress than I do.

6. I'm as taller as my father.

7. Dan's weight is the same as his brother.

8. Is your new book bag enough big for all your books?

EXERCISE 8: Pronunciation

A | *Read and listen to the Pronunciation Note.*

> **Pronunciation Note**
>
> When an adjective appears between **as . . . as**, stress the adjective and not **as**. **As** is unstressed and reduced to / **əz** / .
>
> **EXAMPLE:** She's as cold as ice.

B | *Listen. Complete the sentences with the words you hear.*

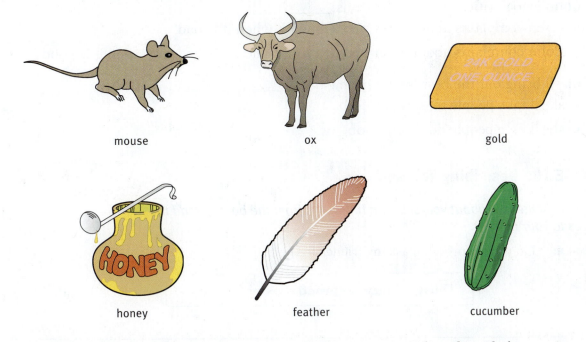

mouse ox gold

honey feather cucumber

1. She's bright, but she never says a word. She just sits and smiles. She's as quiet as a
   _____*mouse*_____.

2. I'm sorry I bought that chair. You have to be as strong as an _____ to lift
   it.

3. He never shows his feelings. He's as cool as a _____.

4. Her sister is nasty, but she's as sweet as _____.

5. She doesn't weigh much at all. She's as light as a _____.

6. I was very upset when she didn't keep her promise. I thought her word was as good as
   _____.

C | *Now listen and repeat each sentence. Remember not to stress the word* **as**.

EXERCISE 9: Listening

A | *Listen to the conversation. Two managers are talking about two young employees, Colin and Maria. Complete the sentence. Circle the correct letter.*

The managers _____.

a. are planning to promote both people

b. promoted one person and didn't promote the other.

B | *Listen again. Then complete the sentences. Circle the correct letter.*

1. "Maria's word is good as gold" means _____.
   a. she does what she says she will
   b. she usually says nice things to others

2. "Colin is too critical of others" means _____.
   a. Colin complains about other people's work when it is bad
   b. Colin complains about other people's work when it is bad *and* when it is good

3. "She'll bring out the best in others" means _____.
   a. she'll take people to nice places
   b. she'll help people do a better job

EXERCISE 10: Describing Yourself

PAIRS: Write sentences about yourself with the words from the boxes. Read the sentences to your partner.

EXAMPLE: I'm not too proud to ask my friends for help.

busy	lazy	proud	shy	tired

I'm too _____ to _____.

I'm not too _____ to _____.

old	smart	strong	tall	young

I'm _____ enough to _____.

I'm not _____ enough to _____.

EXERCISE 11: Similarities

Take five minutes. Walk around your classroom. Find classmates who are like you in some way. Use the chart for suggestions. Take notes. Report to the class. The person who finds the most similarities wins.

EXAMPLES: Cecilia and I were born in the same month.
Julio and I have the same color eyes.
Ming and I like the same kind of movies.
Pierre and I have the same number of sisters.
Jasmine and I have the same lucky number.

Suggestions				
Born	**Looks**	**Likes**	**Families**	**Your Ideas**
same month same day	same color eyes same color hair same height	same kind of movies, music, sports	same number of brothers or sisters	

EXERCISE 12: Writing

A | *Write about two friends or two events. Use three of these structures:* **very, too, as . . . as, the same as,** *and* **different from.** *Underline the examples in your paragraph.*

EXAMPLE: I'm a sophomore in college. I went to two parties this year. I liked the first party. The people were very cool. There were lots of different kinds of students: musicians, artists, but also athletes. Everyone was friendly. The second party was not as good as the first party. The people were not the same—this group wasn't friendly. No one talked to me. The music was too loud.

B | *Check your work. Use the Editing Checklist.*

Editing Checklist
Did you . . . ? ☐ use **very, too, as . . . as, the same as,** and **different from** correctly ☐ check your spelling

Check your answers on page UR-7.

Do you need to review anything?

A | *Circle the words to complete the sentences.*

1. Is that limousine **big enough / enough big** for us to fit in it?

2. His car is the same kind **as / than** mine.

3. He's **very / too** young to get a driver's license. He can't drive legally.

4. He's not as young **from / as** he looks.

5. The new driving test is different **as / from** the old one.

B | *Complete the sentences. Use* **very, enough,** *or* **too** *and the words from the box.*

busy	good	late	short	time	warm

1. The water isn't _____ _____ for swimming.

2. She's taking a taxi because she's _____ _____.

3. I had a lot of work. I was _____ _____ to go to the party.

4. I don't like my hair. The hairdresser cut it _____ _____.

5. We don't have _____ _____ to go out after the prom.

6. He looks _____ _____ in his Dad's tuxedo.

C | *Correct the paragraph. There are nine mistakes.*

   I didn't like the prom this year as much than last year. I usually like parties, but the music at the prom was much very loud. Also, my dress was same as Julia! That was a too big shock. Also, the dinner portions weren't enough large and the servers this year were very rude. Then we tried to dance, but there was no enough room and the room was too much hot. The music was also not good as last year. We had a more better time last year.

The Superlative
PENGUINS

STEP 1 GRAMMAR IN CONTEXT

Before You Read

What do you know about penguins? Write **T** *(***True***) or* **F** *(***False***) for each statement.*

_____ 1. They only live in very cold climates.

_____ 2. They mostly live south of the equator.

_____ 3. They can weigh up to 90 pounds.

_____ 4. English explorers named them.

Read

Read the online article about penguins.

wild nature

WILD NATURE

Animals Home | Animal Facts | Animal Photos | Animal Quizzes | Wild TV

THE PENGUIN

The penguin is one of **the easiest** birds to recognize. Penguins have black backs and white bellies.[1] They look fat. They stand upright, and they waddle.[2] Unlike other birds, most penguins can't fly, but they can swim very fast.

In 1519 Spanish explorers under Ferdinand Magellan saw penguins when they sailed around South America. They thought this type of bird was one of **the strangest** birds in the world. To them, the penguins looked like another strange bird, the Great Auk of Greenland and Iceland. The Great Auk was a large black and white bird that did not fly. The Spanish word for

Fairy Penguin

Great Auk is *pinguis* which means "fat." And that's how penguins got their name.

There are 17 kinds of penguins. They all live below the equator, but they don't only live in very cold climates. Some, like the Little Blue Penguins, (sometimes called Fairy Penguins) live in warmer climates. The Little Blue Penguins are **the smallest** of all. They are 16 inches (about 41 centimeters) tall and weigh only 2.2 pounds (about 1 kilogram). They got their name because of their blue feathers. These penguins live in the warm waters off southern Australia and New Zealand.

---

[1] *belly:* stomach
[2] *waddle:* to walk from side to side like a duck

(*continued on next page*)

The largest penguins are the Emperor Penguins. They are almost 4 feet (about 1.2 meters) tall and weigh from 70 to 90 pounds (about 32 to 41 kilograms). They live on the ice around the Antarctic continent. This is **the coldest** climate on earth.

Of the 17 different species of penguins, the Macaroni Penguins have **the biggest population**, while the Galapagos Penguins have

Emperor Penguin

the smallest. In fact, some scientists worry that the Galapagos Penguins may become extinct.

People say penguins are **the cutest**, **the funniest**, and **the most loved** birds. They also say they're **the most formal**. Do you know why? It's because they look as if they're wearing tuxedos.[3]

_____
[3] *tuxedo:* a formal suit worn at weddings or other very formal occasions

After You Read

A | Practice *PAIRS: Now read the article aloud. Take turns reading each paragraph.*

B | Vocabulary *Complete the sentences with the words from the box.*

centimeters	extinct	inches	pounds
explorer	feathers	kilogram	species

1. One centimeter is equal to .4 _____.

2. 1 millimeter is the same as 0.1 _____.

3. In the United States people usually measure their weight in

   _____.

4. One _____ is the same as 2.2 pounds.

5. There are 17 different _____ of penguins.

6. Some scientists worry that oil spills and global warming may

   cause penguins to become _____.

7. Most penguins' _____ are white and black.

8. The Magellanic Penguin was named after the _____

   Ferdinand Magellan.

millimeter
inch
0 in
1
2
25
24
23
22
21
20
centimeter

C | Comprehension *Complete the information with the words from the box.*

the Antarctic	Galapagos Penguins	Little Blue Penguins
Emperor Penguins	Greenland and Iceland	

1. The biggest penguins: _____

2. The smallest penguins: _____

3. The coldest place on earth: _____

4. Home of the Great Auk: _____

5. Penguin species with the smallest number: _____

The puffin is descended from the Great Auk.

STEP 2 GRAMMAR PRESENTATION

SUPERLATIVE FORMS OF ADJECTIVES

Superlative Forms of Adjectives		
	Superlative Adjective	
The Emperor Penguin	**the biggest**	of all the penguins.
That photo is	**the funniest**	of all.
That program	**the most interesting**	one on TV.

Superlative Forms of Irregular Adjectives			
		Superlative Adjective	
This	is	**the best**	photo of all.
We	had	**the worst**	weather on Saturday.
Her home	is	**the farthest**	of all.

GRAMMAR NOTES

1	Use the **superlative** form of adjectives to compare three or more people, places, or things.	• The Dead Sea is **the lowest** place on earth.

2	To form the superlative of **short (one-syllable) adjectives**, add *the* before the adjective and *-est* to the adjective.
	
	   fast—the fastest
	   long—the longest
	If the adjective ends in *e*, add *-st*.
	   large—the largest
		• The cheetah is **the fastest** animal on earth.
		
		• Alaska is **the largest** state in the United States.

3	To form the superlative of **two-syllable adjectives that end in -y**, add *the* before the adjective, then drop the *-y* and add *-iest* to the adjective. *funny—the funniest*	• The penguin is **the funniest** bird in the zoo.

4	To form the superlative of **long adjectives**, use *the most* before the adjective.
	   interesting—the most interesting
	   dangerous—the most dangerous
		• The bird section was **the most interesting** part of the zoo.

5	These adjectives have **irregular comparative** and **superlative** forms: **ADJECTIVE** **COMPARATIVE FORM** **SUPERLATIVE FORM** *good* *better (than)* *the best* *bad* *worse (than)* *the worst* *far* *farther (than)* *the farthest*	• It is **the best** time of year for bird watching. • That was **the worst** time to visit the zoo. • The Birdhouse is **the farthest** section from the entrance.
6	After the superlative, we often use a **prepositional phrase** to identify the group we are talking about.	• The giraffe is the tallest animal **in the zoo**. • The rhinoceros beetle is the strongest **of all the animals**.
7	*One of the* often comes before a **superlative adjective**. The adjective is followed by a **plural noun**.	• It is **one of the largest animals** in the world. • It is **one of the most intelligent animals** of all. Noт: It is one of the largest ~~animal~~.
8	**BE CAREFUL!** Do not use two superlative forms together.	• It's the biggest. Noт: It's the **most** biggest. • It's the most important. Noт: It's the most ~~importantest~~.

EXERCISE 1: Discover the Grammar

A | *Underline the superlative adjective forms.*

1. Cockroaches are probably the <u>most disliked</u> insect in the world.

2. Cockroaches live everywhere, even in the cleanest kitchens.

3. The world's heaviest cockroach is the Australian Giant Burrowing Cockroach.

4. The best way to kill a cockroach is with boric acid.

5. The most famous cockroach was in a story by Franz Kafka. In it, a man turns into a

   cockroach.

B | *Write the adjectives used in the superlatives in Part A.*

1. _____*disliked*_____   3. _____   5. _____

2. _____   4. _____

C | *Find three more prepositional phrases that go with superlative statements in Part A.*

   in the world, _____

EXERCISE 2: Superlative Form of Adjectives   *(Grammar Notes 1–2, 4)*

*Complete the sentences with the words in parentheses. Use the superlative adjective
form. Then guess the animal from the choices in the box. Write the correct letter.*

a. the African elephant	**c. the hummingbird**	**e. the Macaroni Penguin**
~~**b. the blue whale**~~	**d. the giraffe**	**f. the sailfish**

__*b*__ **1.** It is both ____*the biggest*____ and _____ animal in the world.
                              (big)   **(loud)**

_____ **2.** It is _____ land animal.
                    (large)

_____ **3.** It is _____ animal today.
                    (tall)

_____ **4.** It is _____ bird. It is as small as 2.5 inches (6.2 centimeters) long
                    (small)

and weighs only .06 ounces (1.6 grams).

_____ **5.** It is _____ fish. It swims up to 68 miles per hour (110 kilometers
                    (fast)

per hour).

_____ **6.** It is _____ of all the penguins. It has bright yellow feathers on its
                    (colorful)

head.

EXERCISE 3: Superlative Form of Adjectives

(Grammar Notes 1–4, 7)

Complete the paragraph about two deadly animals: snakes and jellyfish. Use the adjectives in parentheses and the superlative form.

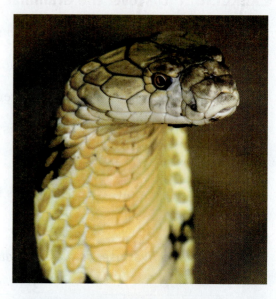

Which snakes are ___the most dangerous___?
       1. (dangerous)

Which snakes are _____?
       2. (deadly)

The country with _____
       3. (high)

percentage of deadly snakes is Australia, but

only three or four people die of snake bites

in Australia each year. The country with

_____ number of fatal snake bites
    4. (large)

is India, and _____ snake in
     5. (scary)

India is the king cobra.

   Do you know _____ creature
       6. (old)

on earth? It's the jellyfish. Jellyfish were around

more than 650 million years ago. They are one of

_____ sea creatures. There are
   7. (frightening)

over 2,000 different kinds of jellyfish. Some are

tiny, and others are big. _____
       8. (heavy)

weigh over 450 pounds (204 kilograms), and

_____ are 120 feet (40 meters).
  9. (long)

   The _____ jellyfish are the
     10. (deadly)

tiny Irukandji jellyfish, which live in the waters off

Australia.

EXERCISE 4: *One of the* + Superlative Adjectives

(Grammar Note 7)

Complete the conversations with **one of the** and the words in parentheses. Use the superlative form of the adjectives and plural form of the nouns.

1. **A:** I'm going to be in San Diego. Is the San Diego Zoo a good place to go?

   B: I think so. It's _____ one of the most popular zoos _____ in the United States.
   (popular / zoo)

2. **A:** I think the peacock is

   _____ in the world.
   (beautiful / bird)

   B: I agree.

3. **A:** Can an octopus open a jar?

   B: Yes, it can. It's _____
   (smart / animal)
   of its type.

4. **A:** Are there any good nature shows on TV?

   B: Yes. _____ is at 8:00 P.M. tonight on the Discovery
   (good / nature show)
   Channel. I saw the show last month.

5. **A:** Are you laughing at that gorilla?

   B: Yes. He's _____ in the zoo.
   (funny / animal)

6. **A:** My son loves dinosaurs. Where can you see

   dinosaur bones?

   B: The Museum of Natural History in New York

   City has _____ of
   (good / collection)
   dinosaur bones in the world.

EXERCISE 5: Comparative and Superlative

(Grammar Notes 1–2, 4, 6)

Complete the sentences with the adjectives in parentheses. Use the comparative or superlative form.

1. African elephants are different from Asian elephants. Asian elephants have

   _____ smaller _____ ears and _____ tusks than African ones. The African
   (small)   (short)
   elephants are _____ and _____.
                      (large)   (tall)

2. Bear's milk is _____ of all milk from animals. It is 46 percent fat. This
                      (rich)
   rich milk allows the tiny bear cub to grow very fast.

(continued on next page)

3. _____ snake in the world is the blind snake. It reaches just slightly more
   (small)

   than 5 inches (13 centimeters) in length and weighs less than 0.1 ounce (less than

   2 grams).

4. _____ snakes are the anaconda and the python. They grow as long as
   (large)

   33 feet (about 10 meters) and can weigh up to 550 pounds (about 250 kilograms).

5. Most female snakes are _____ than male snakes.
   (large)

6. A snake's body temperature is about the same as the temperature outside. When

   the temperature warms up, snakes are _____, and when it gets
   (active)

   _____, they are less active.
   (cold)

7. Many people think the great white shark is _____ of all sharks. Studies
   (dangerous)

   show that it's not true. White sharks mostly attack when they confuse humans with

   seals or sea lions.

EXERCISE 6: Editing

Correct the sentences. There are seven mistakes. The first mistake is already corrected.
Find and correct six more.

1. The Berlin Zoological Garden is the ~~most old~~ *oldest* zoo in Germany. It opened in 1844.

2. It is one of the most popular zoo in the world.

3. The zoo has biggest collection of different species in the world.

4. The zoo is very crowded Sunday afternoons. That is the most bad time to visit.

5. The pandas are the most popular resident of the Berlin Zoological Garden.

6. The Birdhouse is one the most modern bird houses in Europe. There are more than

   500 species of birds, many of them quite rare.

7. The most good time to visit the zoo is in the spring or the fall.

EXERCISE 7: Pronunciation

A | *Read and listen to the Pronunciation Note.*

> **Pronunciation Note**
>
> Be sure to pronounce the -*est* ending of the superlative, but do not stress the ending.
>
> **EXAMPLE:** Long●est

B | *Listen and repeat the sentences.*

1. The biggest is not always the strongest.
2. The loudest is not always the wisest.
3. The funniest is sometimes the saddest.
4. The quietest is sometimes the deepest.

C | *Now listen and repeat the questions.*

1. Is the biggest the best?
2. Is the youngest the fastest?
3. Is the fattest the warmest?
4. Is the slowest the heaviest?

EXERCISE 8: Listening

A | *Listen to a quiz show. Read the questions. Circle the letter of the correct answer.*

1. The first question asks, "Which animal has the longest gestation period?" A gestation period is _____.

   a. the time the baby is carried in its mother   **b.** the time the baby learns to walk

2. The second question asks, "Which animal is _____?"

   a. the fattest   **b.** the fastest

3. The third question asks, "Which animal is _____?"

   a. the loudest   **b.** the proudest

4. The last question asks, "Which animal is _____?"

   a. the deadliest   **b.** the most dangerous

1. What were the answers to the four questions in the quiz show? Choose from the words in the box.

ant	cockroach	horse	mosquito
bear	cow	lion	peacock
cheetah	elephant	monkey	tiger

Answer one: the Asian _____

Answer two: the _____

Answer three: the howler _____

Answer four: the _____

2. How much money did Marcia win? She won _____ dollars.

EXERCISE 9: Survey

A | *Write questions in the superlative. Use the words from the list.*

good / pet to have   interesting / animal to look at

smart / animal you know   beautiful animal / you know

B | *Ask four classmates the questions in Part A. Then ask each student a reason why he or she thinks so. Report results to the class.*

EXAMPLE: **A:** Florian, what's the best pet to have?
           B: Fish.
           A: Why? (. . .)
           (Reporting to class)
           A: According to Florian, fish make the best pets. They're the quietest, the most colorful, and the easiest to take care of, especially for a student who lives in an apartment.

EXERCISE 10: Discussion

PAIRS: Talk about animals or insects that are pests—for example, cockroaches, ants, mice, raccoons, squirrels, deer, or bears.

1. What's the worst pest in your area? Why?

2. What's the best way to handle this pest?

EXAMPLE: **A:** I think one of the biggest problems around here is bears.
           B: Bears? I disagree. There are a lot of bears, and they are big and scary, but they rarely bother people. I think that raccoons are our worst problem. Last summer a raccoon climbed in my attic and made a home there. It was hard to get rid of her.
           A: What did you do?

EXERCISE 11: Game

A | *Make a list from A to Z of as many animals as you can. On the board, write the names of all the animals.*

EXAMPLE: A = Auk
B = bear

B | *GROUPS: Students take turns. Each student asks a question using a superlative about one of the animals on the board.*

EXAMPLES: Which animal has the best memory?
Which animal is the busiest?

C | *GROUPS: Students write their answers. Compare answers.*

EXAMPLE: Ten students think that elephants have the best memory. Three students think that dolphins do.

EXERCISE 12: Writing

A | *Write about one or more animals in the zoo, in books, or in movies. Use a superlative and **one of** plus a superlative in your writing.*

EXAMPLE: Last August I visited the Bronx Zoo. This zoo is one of the best zoos in the world. It covers 265 acres and is home to over 6,000 animals. I enjoyed the Butterfly Zone and the World of Birds, but the most interesting part was the Congo Gorilla Forest. I saw a rain forest and a lot of gorillas. The funniest gorilla imitated one of the visitors. The people laughed a lot. I started to laugh but stopped when I realized I was the one he was imitating!

B | *Check your work. Use the Editing Checklist.*

Editing Checklist
Did you . . . ? ☐ use superlatives correctly ☐ check your spelling

A | Complete the sentences with the adjectives in parentheses. Use the superlative form.

1. Who was _____ monkey in the cage?
     (funny)

2. What is the name of _____ whale?
     (big)

3. What is _____ nature show on TV?
     (good)

4. _____ sharks are not _____.
     (large)   (dangerous)

B | Complete the sentences with the superlative.

1. It's 101 degrees. It's _____ of the year.
     (hot / day)

2. She's 112 years old. She's _____ in town.
     (old / woman)

3. The day after Thanksgiving is _____ of the year.
     (busy / shopping day)

4. It was _____ on TV last month.
     (interesting / show)

5. The pandas are _____ at the zoo.
     (popular / animal)

C | Complete the sentences with **one of** and the words in parentheses. Use the superlative form of the adjectives and the plural form of the nouns.

1. The dolphin is _____ in the world.
     (one of the / intelligent / animal)

2. The Bronx Zoo is _____ in the world.
     (one of the / good / zoo)

3. He has _____ in the stadium.
     (one of the / bad / seat)

4. It was _____ of the year.
     (one of the / long / day)

5. That was _____ in the guidebook.
     (one of the / expensive / trip)

D | Correct the conversations. There are five mistakes.

1. **A:** What is the most good way to get to park?

     B: The shortest route is also the complicated. I'll give you the most direct way.

2. **A:** What's the most hardest part of your job here at the zoo?

     B: Well, the nicer part is taking care of the animals. The most worst part is telling

     people not to feed the animals or bother them.

PART XI

From Grammar to Writing

THE ORDER OF ADJECTIVES BEFORE NOUNS

1 | *Complete the sentences with the words in parentheses.*

1. I saw a _____ on Main Street.
(funny / monkey / brown / little)

2. Maria wore a _____.
(red / dress / beautiful / silk)

2 | *Study this information about the order of adjectives before nouns. When you use adjectives, write them in this order.*

	1. opinion	2. size	3. shape	4. age	5. color	6. origin	7. material	8. noun
1	beautiful	big	square	new	red	French	silk	scarf

2 We use adjectives to describe nouns. Descriptions make writing more lively. They also help the reader form mental pictures. When **several adjectives** come before a noun, they follow a **special order**.
- I saw a **beautiful young** woman.
  Not: I saw a ~~young beautiful~~ woman.

3 Use **and** to connect adjectives from the same category.
- The shirt was *cotton* **and** *polyester*.
- The blouse was *red* **and** *white*.

3 | *Complete the sentences with the words in parentheses. Use the correct order.*

1. He ate a(n) _____ pear.
(brown / big / Asian)

2. His cashmere coat was not as expensive as her _____
(Italian / new / leather / black)

_____ jacket.

3. They bought three _____ bowls.
(silver / beautiful / Mexican)

4 | *Read the story. Then write your own story.*

Detective Work

Several years ago I was walking down the street when I saw my father's brand new shiny blue car. I expected to see my father, but to my surprise a young woman with short, curly bright red hair was behind the wheel of the car. I saw an empty taxi nearby, and I got in quickly. I said dramatically to the driver, "Follow that new blue car." And I told the driver why.

The taxi driver had a cell phone, and I told him to call the police. Soon we heard the siren of the patrol car and a loudspeaker. The police told the woman to pull over. We pulled over too. I immediately said to the woman, "That's not your car. It's my father's."

The woman smiled calmly and said, "Oh. You're Mr. Abbot's younger son. I recognize you from your picture."

Before I could say another word, the woman explained that she was my father's new assistant. My father had asked her to take his computer to the main office to get it fixed. He lent her his car. We called my father, and he confirmed her story. The police laughed, and the taxi driver laughed. I was too embarrassed to laugh. That was the beginning and the end of my career as a detective.

5 | *Exchange papers with a partner. Did your partner follow the directions? Correct any mistakes in grammar and spelling.*

6 | *Talk to your partner. Discuss the mistakes you made. Then rewrite your own paper and make any necessary changes.*

APPENDICES

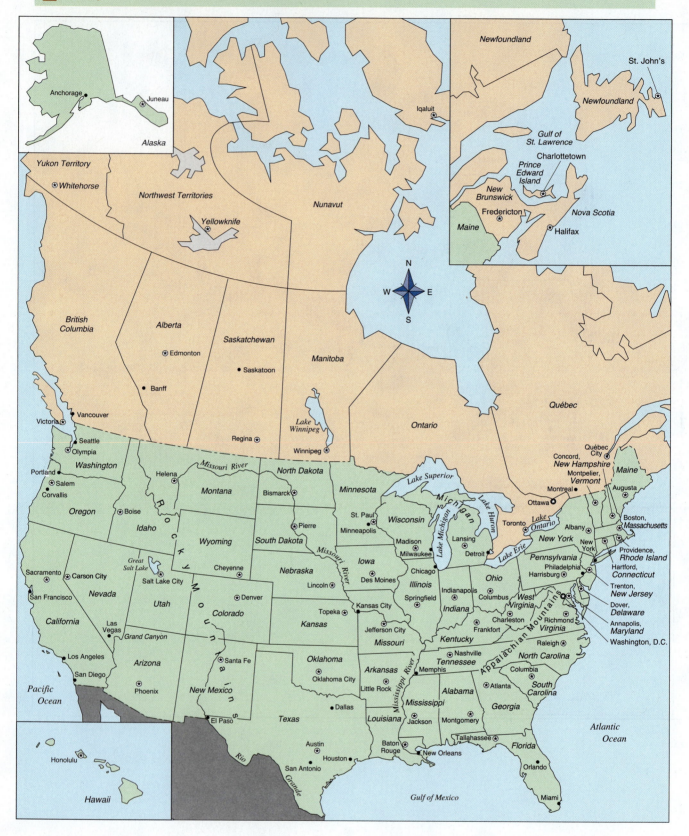

CARDINAL NUMBERS

1 = one	11 = eleven	21 = twenty-one
2 = two	12 = twelve	30 = thirty
3 = three	13 = thirteen	40 = forty
4 = four	14 = fourteen	50 = fifty
5 = five	15 = fifteen	60 = sixty
6 = six	16 = sixteen	70 = seventy
7 = seven	17 = seventeen	80 = eighty
8 = eight	18 = eighteen	90 = ninety
9 = nine	19 = nineteen	100 = one hundred
10 = ten	20 = twenty	101 = one hundred and one
		200 = two hundred
		1,000 = one thousand
		1,000,000 = one million
		10,000,000 = ten million

EXAMPLES

That building has **seventy-seven** pages.
There are **thirty** days in April.
There are **six** rows in the room.
She is **twelve** years old.
He has **four** children.

ORDINAL NUMBERS

1st = first	11th = eleventh	21st = twenty-first
2nd = second	12th = twelfth	30th = thirtieth
3rd = third	13th = thirteenth	40th = fortieth
4th = fourth	14th = fourteenth	50th = fiftieth
5th = fifth	15th = fifteenth	60th = sixtieth
6th = sixth	16th = sixteenth	70th = seventieth
7th = seventh	17th = seventeenth	80th = eightieth
8th = eighth	18th = eighteenth	90th = ninetieth
9th = ninth	19th = nineteenth	100th = one hundredth
10th = tenth	20th = twentieth	101st = one hundred and first
		200th = two hundredth
		1,000th = one thousandth
		1,000,000th = one millionth
		10,000,000th = ten millionth

EXAMPLES

He works on the **seventy-seventh** floor.
It's April **thirtieth**.
He's in the **sixth** row.
It's her **twelfth** birthday.
Bob is his **first** child. Mary is his **second**. John is his **third**, and Sue is his **fourth**.

TEMPERATURE

We measure the temperature in degrees (°).
Changing from degrees Fahrenheit to degrees Celsius:

$$(°F - 32) \times 5/9 = °C$$

Changing from degrees Celsius to degrees Fahrenheit:

$$(9/5 \times °C) + 32 = °F$$

DAYS OF THE WEEK

Weekdays	Weekend
Monday	Saturday
Tuesday	Sunday
Wednesday	
Thursday	
Friday	

MONTHS OF THE YEAR

MONTH	ABBREVIATION	NUMBER OF DAYS
January	Jan.	31
February	Feb.	28*
March	Mar.	31
April	Apr.	30
May	May	31
June	Jun.	30
July	Jul.	31
August	Aug.	31
September	Sept.	30
October	Oct.	31
November	Nov.	30
December	Dec.	31

*February has 29 days in a leap year, every four years.

(continued on next page)

THE SEASONS

NORTHERN HEMISPHERE

Spring: March 21–June 20

Summer: June 21–September 20

Autumn or Fall: September 21–December 20

Winter: December 21–March 20

SOUTHERN HEMISPHERE

Spring: September 21–December 20

Summer: December 21–March 20

Autumn or Fall: March 21–June 20

Winter: June 21–September 20

TITLES

Mr. (Mister)	/ mɪstər /	unmarried or married man
Ms.	/ mɪz /	unmarried or married woman
Miss	/ mɪs /	unmarried woman
Mrs.	/ mɪsɪz /	married woman
Dr. (Doctor)	/ dɑktər /	doctor (medical doctor or Ph.D.)

4 Time

It's one o'clock.
(It's 1:00.)

It's five after one.
(It's 1:05.)

It's one-ten.
It's ten after one.
(It's 1:10.)

It's one-fifteen.
It's a quarter after one.
(It's 1:15.)

It's one twenty-five.
It's twenty-five after one.
(It's 1:25.)

It's one-thirty.
It's half past one.
(It's 1:30.)

It's one forty-five.
It's a quarter to two.
(It's 1:45.)

It's one-fifty.
It's ten to two.
(It's 1:50.)

TALKING ABOUT TIME

1	You can talk about time this way:	**A: What time is it?** **B:** It's one o'clock.
2	**A.M.** means before noon (the hours between midnight and noon). **P.M.** means after noon (the hours between noon and midnight). **BE CAREFUL!** When people say 12:00 A.M., they mean midnight. When people say 12:00 P.M., they mean noon.	It's 10:00 A.M. It's 10:00 P.M.
3	We often write time with numbers.	It's one o'clock. = It's **1:00**. It's two-twenty. = It's **2:20**.

PLURAL NOUNS: SPELLING RULES

1	Add **-s** to form the plural of most nouns.	student chief picture	student**s** chief**s** picture**s**
2	Add **-es** to form the plural of nouns that end in **ss**, **ch**, **sh**, and **x**. (This ending adds another syllable.)	class watch dish box	class**es** watch**es** dish**es** box**es**
3	Add **-es** to form the plural of nouns that end in **o** preceded by a consonant. **EXCEPTION:** Add **-s** to plural nouns ending in **o** that refer to music.	potato piano soprano	potato**es** piano**s** soprano**s**
4	Add **-s** to form the plural of nouns that end in **o** preceded by a vowel.	radio	radio**s**
5	To form the plural of words that end in a consonant + **y**, change the **y** to **i** and add **-es**.	dictionary fly	dictionar**ies** fl**ies**
6	To form the plural of words that end in a vowel + **y**, add **-s**.	boy day	boy**s** day**s**
7	To form the plural of certain nouns that end in **f** or **fe**, change the **f** to **v** and add **-es**.	half loaf knife wife	hal**ves** loa**ves** kni**ves** wi**ves**
8	Some plural nouns are **irregular**.	woman child person mother-in-law man foot tooth	women children people mothers-in-law men feet teeth
9	Some nouns **do not have a singular form**.	(eye) glasses clothes pants scissors	
10	Some plural nouns are the same as the singular noun.	Chinese fish sheep	Chinese fish sheep

1	The **final sounds** for regular plural nouns are / s /, / z /, and / ɪz /.	boots	boys	horses
2	The plural is pronounced / s / **after** the **voiceless sounds** / p /, / t /, / k /, / f /, and / θ /.	cups hats works	cuffs myths	
3	The plural is pronounced / z / **after** the **voiced sounds** / b /, / d /, / g /, / v /, / m /, / n /, / ŋ /, / l /, / r /, and / ð /.	crabs cards rugs	doves drums fans	rings girls stores
4	The plural *s* is pronounced / z / **after** all **vowel sounds**.	day toe	days toes	
5	The plural *s* is pronounced / ɪz / **after** the **sounds** / s /, / z /, / ʃ /, / tʃ /, and / dʒ /. (This adds another syllable to the word.)	races causes dishes	churches judges	

6 The Simple Present: Spelling and Pronunciation Rules

THE THIRD-PERSON SINGULAR AFFIRMATIVE: SPELLING RULES

1	Add **-s** to form the third-person singular of most verbs. Add **-es** to words that end in **ch**, **s**, **sh**, **x**, or **z**.	Pete work**s**. I work too. Doug wear**s** sweatshirts. I wear shirts. Norma teach**es** Spanish. I teach English. Lulu wash**es** her clothes on Tuesday. Elenore and Pete wash their clothes on Sunday.
2	When a base-form verb ends in a **consonant** + **y**, change the **y** to **i** and add **-es**. Do not change the **y** when the base form ends in a **vowel** + **y**. Add **-s**.	I study at home. Carol stud**ies** at the library. Dan play**s** tennis. I play tennis too.
3	*Have*, *do*, and *go* have **irregular forms** for the third-person singular.	I have. He **has**. I do. She **does**. I go. It **goes**.

1	The **final sound** for the third-person singular form of the simple present is pronounced / s /, / z /, or / ɪz /. The final sounds of the third-person singular are the same as the final sounds of plural nouns. See Appendix 9 on pages A-8 and A-9.	/ s / / z / / ɪz / talk**s** love**s** danc**es**
2	**Do** and **say** have a change in vowel sound.	I say. / seɪ / He say**s**. / sɛz / I do. / du / He do**es**. / dʌz /

7   Possessive Nouns

1	Add **'s** to form the possessive of singular nouns.	Lulu**'s** last name is Winston.
2	To form the possessive of plural nouns ending in **s**, add only an **apostrophe (').**	The girl**s'** gym is on this floor. The boy**s'** locker room is across the hall.
3	In hyphenated words (*mother-in-law, father-in-law*, etc.) and in phrases showing joint possession, only the last word is possessive in form.	My sister-in-law**'s** apartment is big. Elenore and Pete**'s** apartment is comfortable.
4	To form the possessive of plural nouns that do not end in **s**, add **'s**.	The men**'s** room is next to the water fountain.
5	To form the possessive of one-syllable singular nouns that end in **s**, add **'s**. To form the possessive of words of more than one syllable that end in **s**, add an **'** or an **'s**.	**James's** apartment is beautiful. **McCullers'** novels are interesting. OR **McCullers's** novels are interesting.
6	**BE CAREFUL!** Don't confuse possessive nouns with the contraction of the verb **be**.	**Carol's** a student. = **Carol is** a student. **Carol's** book is open. = **Her** book is open.

8 The Present Progressive: Spelling Rules

1	Add *-ing* to the base form of the verb.	drink see eat	drink**ing** see**ing** eat**ing**
2	If a verb ends in a silent *e*, drop the final *e* and add *-ing*.	smil**e**	smil**ing**
3	If a one-syllable verb ends in a consonant, a vowel, and a consonant (**CVC**), double the last consonant before adding *-ing*. However, do not double the last consonant if it is a *w*, *x*, or *y*.	**CVC** sit run se**w** mi**x** pla**y**	si**tt**ing ru**nn**ing se**w**ing mi**x**ing pla**y**ing
4	In words with two or more syllables that end in a consonant, a vowel, and a consonant (**CVC**), double the last consonant only if the last syllable is stressed.	admit′ whis′per	admi**tt**ing *(stressed)* whisper**ing** *(not stressed)*

9 Direct and Indirect Objects

		Group One						
Subject	**Verb**	**Direct Object**	**To**	**Indirect Object**	**Subject**	**Verb**	**Indirect Object**	**Direct Object**
She	sent	a gift it	to	us.	She	sent	us	a gift.

		Group Two						
Subject	**Verb**	**Direct Object**	**For**	**Indirect Object**	**Subject**	**Verb**	**Indirect Object**	**Direct Object**
They	found	a towel it	for	him.	They	found	him	a towel.

		Group Three		
Subject	**Verb**	**Direct Object**	**To**	**Indirect Object**
He	repeated	the question	to	the class.

		Group Four		
Subject	**Verb**	**Direct Object**	**For**	**Indirect Object**
He	fixed	the shelves	for	me.

Group One Verbs (*to*)		Group Two Verbs (*for*)	Group Three Verbs (*to*)	Group Four Verbs (*for*)
email	sell	build	explain	cash
give	send	buy	prove	close
hand	show	find	repeat	fix
lend	teach	get	say	pronounce
owe	tell	make	whisper	translate
pass	throw			
read	write			

RULES FOR DIRECT AND INDIRECT OBJECTS

1 With **Group One** and **Group Two verbs**, there are **two** possible **sentence patterns** if the **direct object** is a **noun**.

	DIRECT OBJECT	TO/FOR	INDIRECT OBJECT
I gave the	**money**	**to**	**him**. =

	INDIRECT OBJECT	DIRECT OBJECT
I gave	**him**	**the money**.

	DIRECT OBJECT	TO/FOR	INDIRECT OBJECT
We bought	**the book**	**for**	**him**. =

	INDIRECT OBJECT	DIRECT OBJECT
We bought	**him**	**the book**.

If the **direct object** is a **pronoun**, it always comes **before the indirect object**.

	DIRECT OBJECT	TO/FOR	INDIRECT OBJECT
I gave	**it**	**to**	**him**.
Please get	**them**	**for**	**me**.

NOT: I gave ~~him it~~.
NOT: Please get ~~me them~~.

2 With **Group Three** and **Group Four verbs**, the **direct object** always comes **before the indirect object**.

	DIRECT OBJECT	TO/FOR	INDIRECT OBJECT
Explain	**the sentence**	**to**	**John**.
She translated	**the letter**	**for**	**us**.

NOT: Explain ~~John the sentence~~.
NOT: She translated ~~us the letter~~.

THE SIMPLE PAST: SPELLING RULES

1	If the verb **ends in an e**, add **-d**.	arrive like	arrive**d** like**d**
2	If the verb **ends in a consonant**, add **-ed**.	rain help	rain**ed** help**ed**
3	If a **one-syllable verb** ends in a consonant, a vowel, and a consonant (**CVC**), double the last consonant and add **-ed**. However, do not double the last consonant if it is a **w**, **x**, or **y**.	**CVC** hug rub bow mix play	 hu**gged** ru**bbed** bow**ed** mix**ed** play**ed**
4	If a **two-syllable verb** ends in a consonant, a vowel, and a consonant (**CVC**), double the last consonant only if the last syllable is stressed.	re•fer en•ter	refe**rred** *(stressed)* ente**red** *(not stressed)*
5	If the verb ends in a **consonant** + **y**, change the **y** to **i** and add **-ed**.	worry carry	worr**ied** carr**ied**
6	If the verb ends in a **vowel** + **y**, do not change the **y** to **i**. Add **-ed**. There are **exceptions** to this rule.	play annoy pay lay say	play**ed** annoy**ed** **paid** **laid** **said**

THE SIMPLE PAST: PRONUNCIATION RULES

1	The **final sounds** for regular verbs in the simple past are / **t** /, / **d** /, and / **ɪd** /.	walk**ed**	plann**ed**	wait**ed**
2	The final sound is pronounced / **t** / **after** the **voiceless sounds** / **f** /, / **k** /, / **p** /, / **s** /, / **tʃ** /, and / **ʃ** /.	laug**hed** lic**ked**	si**pped** mi**ssed**	wat**ched** wi**shed**
3	The final sound is pronounced / **d** / **after** the **voiced sounds** / **b** /, / **g** /, / **dʒ** /, / **l** /, / **m** /, / **n** /, / **r** /, / **ŋ** /, / **ð** /, / **ʒ** /, / **v** /, and / **z** /.	ru**bbed** hu**gged** ju**dged** pu**lled**	hu**mmed** ba**nned** occu**rred** ba**nged**	ba**thed** massa**ged** li**ved** surpri**sed**
4	The final sound is pronounced / **d** / **after vowel sounds**.	pl**ayed** sk**ied**	t**ied** sn**owed**	arg**ued**
5	The final sound is pronounced / **ɪd** / after / **t** / and / **d** /. / **ɪd** / adds a syllable.	want instruct rest attend	wan**ted** instruc**ted** res**ted** atten**ded**	

11   Base Forms and Past Forms of Common Irregular Verbs

Base Form	Past Form	Base Form	Past Form	Base Form	Past Form
become	became	give	gave	say	said
begin	began	go	went	see	saw
bite	bit	grow	grew	send	sent
blow	blew	hang	hung	shake	shook
break	broke	have	had	shoot	shot
bring	brought	hear	heard	shut	shut
build	built	hide	hid	sing	sang
buy	bought	hit	hit	sit	sat
catch	caught	hold	held	sleep	slept
choose	chose	hurt	hurt	speak	spoke
come	came	keep	kept	spend	spent
cost	cost	know	knew	stand	stood
do	did	lead	led	steal	stole
draw	drew	leave	left	swim	swam
drink	drank	lend	lent	take	took
drive	drove	lose	lost	teach	taught
eat	ate	make	made	tear	tore
fall	fell	meet	met	tell	told
feed	fed	pay	paid	think	thought
feel	felt	put	put	throw	threw
fight	fought	quit	quit	understand	understood
find	found	read*	read*	wake	woke
fly	flew	ride	rode	wear	wore
forget	forgot	ring	rang	win	won
get	got	run	ran	write	wrote

*Pronounce the base form / rid /. Pronounce the past form / rɛd /

A-11

COMMON NON-COUNT NOUNS*

Liquids		Food		Too Small to Count		School Subjects	
milk	soda	bread	ketchup	sugar	baking powder	math	biology
coffee	water	cheese	jam	salt	cereal	history	chemistry
oil	beer	lettuce	jelly	pepper	spaghetti	geography	music
juice		broccoli	fish	cinnamon	wheat		
		ice cream	meat	rice	corn		
		butter	sour cream	sand			
		mayonnaise	soup				

City Problems	Weather	Gases	Abstract Ideas		Others	
traffic	snow	oxygen	love	advice	money	jewelry
pollution	rain	carbon dioxide	beauty	help	mail	garbage
crime	ice	nitrogen	happiness	noise	furniture	toothpaste
	fog	air	luck	time	homework	paper
					information	

*Some nouns can be either count or non-count nouns.

I'd like some **chicken**. (non-count)   Did you eat any **cake**? (non-count)
There were three **chickens** in the yard. (count)   I bought a **cake** at the bakery. (count)

QUANTIFIERS: CONTAINERS, MEASURE WORDS, AND PORTIONS

a bottle of (milk, soda, ketchup)	a pair of (pants, skis, gloves)
a bowl of (cereal, soup, rice)	a piece of (paper, cake, pie)
a can of (soda, beans, tuna fish)	a pint of (ice cream, cream)
a cup of (hot chocolate, coffee, tea)	a quart of (milk)
a foot of (snow, water)	a roll of (film, toilet paper, paper towels)
a gallon of (juice, gas, paint)	a slice of (toast, cheese, meat)
a head of (lettuce)	a tablespoon of (flour, sugar, baking soda)
an inch of (snow, rain)	a teaspoon of (sugar, salt, pepper)
a loaf of (bread)	a tube of (toothpaste, glue)

METRIC CONVERSION

1 liter	= .26 gallons or 1.8 pints	1 mile	= 1.6 kilometers	1 ounce	= 28 grams
1 gallon	= 3.8 liters	1 kilometer	= .62 mile	1 gram	= .04 ounce
		1 foot	= .30 meter or 30 centimeters	1 pound	= .45 kilogram
		1 meter	= 3.3 feet	1 kilogram	= 2.2 pounds
		1 inch	= 2.54 centimeters		

These are the pronunciation symbols used in this text. Listen to the pronunciation of the key words.

VOWELS

Symbol	Key Word
i	beat, feed
ɪ	bit, did
eɪ	date, paid
ɛ	bet, bed
æ	bat, bad
ɑ	box, odd, father
ɔ	bought, dog
oʊ	boat, road
ʊ	book, good
u	boot, food, student
ʌ	but, mud, mother
ə	banana, among
ɚ	shirt, murder
aɪ	bite, cry, buy, eye
aʊ	about, how
ɔɪ	voice, boy
ɪr	ear, beer
ɛr	bare
ɑr	bar
ɔr	door
ʊr	tour

CONSONANTS

Symbol	Key Word	Symbol	Key Word
p	pack, happy	ʃ	ship, machine, station, special, discussion
b	back, rubber	ʒ	measure, vision
t	tie	h	hot, who
d	die	m	men
k	came, key, quick	n	sun, know, pneumonia
g	game, guest	ŋ	sung, ringing
tʃ	church, nature, watch	w	wet, white
dʒ	judge, general, major	l	light, long
f	fan, photograph	r	right, wrong
v	van	y	yes, use, music
θ	thing, breath	t̬	butter, bottle
ð	then, breathe		
s	sip, city, psychology		
z	zip, please, goes		

GLOSSARY OF GRAMMAR TERMS

action verb   A verb that describes an action. It can be used in the progressive.
- *Sachiko **is planning** a big party.*

adjective   A word that describes (or modifies) a noun or pronoun.
- *That's a **great** idea.*

adverb   A word that describes (or modifies) an action verb, an adverb, an adjective, or a sentence.
- *She drives **slowly**.*

adverb of frequency   A word that tells the frequency of something.
- *We **usually** eat lunch at noon.*

adverb of manner   A word that describes a verb. It usually answers the question *how*.
- *She speaks **clearly**.*

affirmative statement   A sentence that does not use a negative verb form (*not*).
- ***I have a car**.*

apostrophe   A punctuation mark used to show possession and to write a short form (contraction).
- ***He's** in my father's car.*

base form   The simple form of the verb without any ending such as *-ing*, *-ed*, or *-s*. It is the same as the infinitive without *to*.
- *Arnold will **come** at 8:00. We should **eat** then.*

be going to future   A verb form used to make predictions, express general facts in the future, or talk about definite plans that were made before now.
- *Mei-Ling says it**'s going to be** cold, so she**'s going to take** a coat.*

capital letter   The big form of a letter of the alphabet. Sentences start with a capital letter.
- ***A**, **B**, **C**, etc.*

comma   Punctuation used to separate single things in a list or parts of a sentence.
- *We went to a restaurant**,** and we ate chicken**,** potatoes**,** and broccoli.*

common noun   A noun for a person, place, or thing. It is not capitalized.
- *The **man** got a **book** at the **library**.*

comparative form   An adjective or adverb ending in *-er* or following *more*. It is used in comparing two things.
- *My sister is **older** and **more intelligent** than my brother.*
- *But he studies **harder** and **more carefully**.*

consonant   The letters *b, c, d, f, g, h, j, k, l, m, n, p, q, r, s, t, v, w, x, y, z*.

contraction   A short form of two words. An apostrophe (') replaces the missing letter.
- ***It is** late and **I am** tired. I **should not** stay up so late.*
- ***It's** late and **I'm** tired. I **shouldn't** stay up so late.*

count noun   A noun you can count. It usually has a singular and a plural form.
- *In the **park**, there was a **man** with two **children** and a **dog**.*

definite article   *The*; It makes a noun specific.
- *We saw a movie. **The** movie starred Sean Penn.*

demonstrative adjective   An adjective used to identify the noun that follows.
- ***This** man is resting, but **those** men are busy.*

demonstrative pronoun   A pronoun used in place of a demonstrative adjective and the noun that follows.
- ***This** is our classroom, and **these** are my students.*

direct object   A noun or pronoun used to receive the action of a verb.
- *She sold a **car**. He bought **it**.*

exclamation point   A punctuation mark (!) used at the end of a statement. It shows strong emotion.
- *Help**!** Call the police**!***

formal language   Language we usually use in business settings, academic settings, and with people we don't know.
- ***Good morning**, ladies and **gentlemen**. **May** we begin?*

gerund   The *-ing* form of a verb. It is used as a noun.

- *Skiing is fun, but we also enjoy swimming.*

imperative   A sentence used to give an instruction, a direction, a command, or a suggestion. It uses the base form of the verb. The subject (you) is not a part of the sentence.

- *Turn right at the corner. Drive to the end of the street. Stop!*

indefinite article   *A* and *an*; used before singular, nonspecific non-count nouns.

- *Jaime brought a sandwich and an apple for lunch.*

infinitive   *To* + the base form of a verb.

- *To travel is my dream. I want to see the world.*

informal language   The language we usually use with family and friends, in email messages, and in other informal settings.

- *Hey, Doug, what's up?*

inseparable phrasal verb   A phrasal verb that cannot have an object between the verb and the particle.

- *She ran into John.*

irregular verb   A verb that does not form the simple past by adding *-d* or *-ed*.

- *They ate a fancy meal last night. The boss came to dinner.*

modal   A word that comes before the main verb. Modals can express ability, possibility, obligation, and necessity.

- *You can come early, but you mustn't be late, and you should wear a tie.*

negative statement   A statement with a negative verb form.

- *He didn't study. He wasn't ready for the test.*

non-action verb   A verb that does not describe an action. It can describe an emotion, a state, a sense, or a mental thought. We usually don't use non-action verbs in the progressive.

- *I like that actor. He is very famous, and I believe he won an Oscar.*

non-count noun   A noun we usually do not count. We don't put *a*, *an*, or a number before a non-count noun.

- *All you'll need is rice, water, salt, and butter.*

noun   A word that refers to a person, animal, place, thing, or idea.

- *Paula has a friend at the library. She gave me a book about birds.*

noun phrase   A phrase formed by a noun and words that describe (modify) it.

- *It was a dark brown leather jacket.*

object   A noun or pronoun following an action verb. It receives the action of the verb.

- *I sent a letter. He read it.*

object pronoun   A pronoun following a verb or a preposition.

- *We asked him to show the photos to them.*

period   A punctuation mark (.) used at the end of a statement.

- *I'd like you to call on Saturday. We need to talk.*

phrasal verb   A two-part (or three-part) verb that combines a verb and a particle. The meaning of the parts together is often different from the meaning of the verb alone.

- *We put on our gloves and picked up our umbrellas.*

phrase   A group of words that can form a grammatical unit.

- *She lost a red hat. He found it under the table.*

plural   The form that means more than one.

- *We sat in our chairs reading our books.*

possessive   An adjective, noun, or pronoun that shows possession.

- *Her book is in John's car. Mine is at the office.*

preposition   A small word that goes before a noun or pronoun object. A preposition often shows time or place.

- *Maria saw it on the table at two o'clock.*

prepositional phrase   A phrase that consists of a preposition followed by a noun or a noun phrase.

- *Chong-Dae saw it under the black wooden table.*

present progressive   A verb form that shows an action happening now or planned for the future.

- *I'm working hard now, but I'm taking a vacation soon.*

pronoun   A word that replaces a noun or a noun phrase. There are subject pronouns, object pronouns, possessive pronouns, and demonstrative pronouns.

- *He is a friend—I know **him** well. **This** is his coat; **mine** is black.*

proper noun   The actual name of a person, place, or thing. A proper noun begins with a capital letter.

- ***Tom** is living in **New York**. He is studying **Russian** at **Columbia University**.*

quantifier   A word or phrase that comes before a noun and expresses an amount of that noun.

- *Jeannette used **a little** sugar, **some** flour, **four** eggs, and **a liter of** milk.*

question mark   A punctuation mark (?) used at the end of a question.

- *Where are you going**?** When will you be back**?***

quotation marks   Punctuation marks (" . . . ") used before and after the actual words a person says.

- *I said, **"Where are you going?"** and **"When will you be back?"***

regular verb   A verb that forms the simple past by adding -d or -ed.

- *We **lived** in France. My mother **visited** us there.*

sentence   A group of words with a subject and a verb.

- ***We opened the window.***
- ***Did they paint the house?***

separable phrasal verb   A phrasal verb that can have an object between the verb and the particle.

- *She **put on** her coat. She **put** it **on** before he **put** his coat **on**.*

simple past   A verb form used to show a completed action or idea in the past.

- *The plane **landed** at 9:00. We **caught** a bus to the hotel.*

simple present   A verb form used to show habitual actions or states, general facts, or conditions that are true now.

- *Kemal **loves** to ski, and it **snows** a lot in his area, so he**'s** very happy.*

singular   The form that means only one.

- *I put on my **hat** and **coat** and closed the **door**.*

small letter   The small form of a letter of the alphabet. We use small letters for most words except for proper nouns and the word that starts a sentence.

- ***a**, **b**, **c**, etc.*

subject   The person, place, or thing that a sentence is about.

- ***The children** ate at the mall.*

subject pronoun   A pronoun used to replace a subject noun.

- *Irene works hard. **She** loves her work.*

superlative form   An adjective or adverb ending in -est or following *most*. It is used in comparing three or more things.

- *We climbed the **highest** mountain by the **most dangerous** route.*
- *She drives the **fastest** and the **most carelessly** of all the drivers.*

syllable   A group of letters with one vowel sound. Words are made up of one or more syllables.

- *One syllable—**win***
- *Two syllables—**ta ble***
- *Three syllables—**im por tant***

verb   A word used to describe an action, a fact, or a state.

- *He **drives** to work now. He **has** a new car, and he **is** a careful driver.*

vowel   The letters a, e, i, o, or u, and sometimes y.

wh- question   A question that asks for information. It begins with *what, when, where, why, which, who, whose,* or *how*.

- ***What**'s your name?*
- ***Where** are you from?*
- ***How** do you feel?*

will future   A verb form used to make predictions, to talk about facts in the future, to make promises, to offer something, or to state a decision to do something at the time of speaking.

- *It **will** probably rain, so I**'ll take** an umbrella. I**'ll give** you my extra one.*

yes/no question   A question that has a *yes* or a *no* answer.

- ***Did you arrive on time?** Yes, I did.*
- ***Are you from Uruguay?** No, I'm not.*
- ***Can you swim well?** Yes, I can.*

UNIT REVIEW ANSWER KEY

Note: In this answer key, where a short or contracted form is given, the full or long form is also correct (unless the purpose of the exercise is to practice the short or contracted forms).

UNIT 1

A 1. are 3. am 5. are
  2. is 4. is

B 1. 'm 3. 're 5. 're
  2. 's 4. 's

C 1. He isn't (He's not) 3. We aren't (We're not)
  2. They're 4. She's

D My father and mother are from India, but they're in Canada now. My parents are doctors.

My father *is* a sports doctor and my mother ~~she~~ is a foot doctor. My parents and I love sports. My father ~~are~~ *is* a soccer fan, and my mother *is* a baseball fan. I'm a soccer fan. My father and I ~~am~~ *are* fans of Lionel Messi and Nuno Gomes. My sister ~~no is~~ *isn't* good at sports. She's not a sports fan. She loves movies.

UNIT 2

A 1. Where's 3. What's 5. Is
  2. How's 4. Are

B 1. I am
  2. it isn't (it's not)
  3. they aren't (they're not)
  4. we are
  5. you aren't (you're not)

C 1. What's today's date?
  2. Where's the men's room?
  3. Why is he absent? (Why's he absent?)
  4. When's your first class?
  5. Who's your teacher?

D 1. ~~She~~ *Is she* your teacher?
  2. What *is* your name?
  3. Where *is* your class?
  4. ~~Is~~ *Are* Bob and Molly good friends?
  5. Why *are* you late?

UNIT 3

A 1. was 3. Were 5. Was
  2. was 4. were

B 1. c 3. d
  2. b 4. a

C 1. was 5. were
  2. was 6. wasn't
  3. Were 7. was
  4. was

D John ~~is~~ *was* at a job interview yesterday. It ~~were~~ *was* for a job at a bank. The questions ~~no were~~ *weren't* easy, but John's answers were good. He was happy. It a *was* good day for John.

UNIT 4

A 1. a 3. Ø 5. Ø
  2. an 4. Ø

B 1. cities 3. clothes 5. people
  2. watches 4. fish or fishes

C lin = Lin london = London
  ali = Ali thanksgiving = Thanksgiving

D Melanie Einzig is *an* artist and ~~an~~ *a* photographer. She was born in Minnesota, but lives in New ~~york~~ *York*. Einzig captures moments in time. Her ~~photograph~~ *photographs* are striking. They are in ~~museum~~ *museums* in San ~~francisco~~ *Francisco*, Chicago, and Princeton.

UNIT 5

A 1. a 3. Ø 5. Ø
  2. Ø 4. an

B 1. c 3. b 5. b
  2. a 4. c

C 1. I'm at the new museum.
  2. It is full of interesting things to see.
  3. It has unusual bowls from long ago.
  4. It has beautiful carpets too.
  5. The museum is a great place to visit.

D The Grand Canyon National Park in Arizona is ~~a~~ *an* awesome place to visit. Almost five million people visit this ~~park unusual~~ *unusual park* each year. The weather is good in the late spring and summer, but it *is* crowded ~~is~~ during those months. There are seven ~~differents~~ *different* places to stay in the park. I like El Tovar. It is ~~a~~ *an* old hotel with a great view.

UR-1

UNIT 6

A 1. on   3. behind   5. in front of
     2. under   4. next to

B 1. at   3. at, on the
     2. at

C

```
 _____
|    ____                            |
|   /    \      /\                    |
|  |  X   |    /  \      _____      |
|   \____/    / Y  \    |       |     |
|            /_____\   |   Z   |     |
|                       |_____|     |
|_____|
```

D **A:** Is Jon at ~~the~~ school?

     B: No. He's ~~in~~ *at* home.

     A: Where does he live?

     B: He lives ~~at~~ *on* Oak Street, between First and
          Second Avenue ~~at~~ *in* Lakeville.

     A: Does he live in an apartment?

     B: Yes. He lives ~~in~~ *on* the third floor.

UNIT 7

A 1. Let's get   4. Let's not meet
     2. Why don't we invite   5. Don't touch
     3. Don't buy

B 1. Wear   4. Don't bring
     2. Don't wear   5. pay
     3. Bring

C 1. Let's go to the gym.
     2. Let's watch a movie this afternoon.
     3. Why don't we take a trip together?
     4. Why don't we hang out with Pietro this
         weekend?

D 1. Why ~~you~~ *you* don't ask Andrij for help?

     2. You look really tired. ~~You~~ *Why don't you* take a short nap?

     3. Let's ~~to~~ walk to work. Let's not drive.

     4. Don't ask Boris to fix the car. ~~Asks~~ *Ask* Mickey.

     5. I'm on a diet, so buy yogurt at the store. Don't ~~to~~ buy sour cream.

UNIT 8

A 1. shops   3. don't like   5. has
     2. likes   4. go

B 1. don't need   3. play
     2. need   4. doesn't like

C 1. is   3. wears   5. are
     2. works   4. don't wear

D 1. My son doesn't ~~has~~ *have* a suit.

     2. He always ~~wear~~ *wears* jeans, T-shirts, and hoodies.

     3. He ~~need~~ *needs* a suit for my brother's wedding.

     4. Suits ~~is~~ *are* expensive and my son ~~don't~~ *doesn't* like to wear them.

     5. We ~~wants~~ *want* to rent or borrow a suit for him.

UNIT 9

A 1. Do   3. Does   5. Am
     2. Is   4. Are

B 1. Do / have   3. Does / watch   5. Are
     2. Does / speak   4. Is

C 1. Are the neighbors noisy?
     2. Does the apartment building have an elevator?
     3. Is the apartment near trains or buses?
     4. Does the bedroom have two closets?
     5. Is the bedroom big?

D 1. **A:** Does he have a big TV in his room?

         B: Yes, he ~~has~~ *does.*

     2. **A:** Does she ~~needs~~ *need* help?

         B: No, she ~~don't~~ *doesn't.*

     3. **A:** ~~Do you are~~ *Are you* friends?

         B: Yes, we ~~aren't~~ *are*. (OR No, we aren't.)

UNIT 10

A 1. Why   3. Who   5. Where
     2. When   4. How

B 1. Who snores in your family?
     2. What do you dream about?
     3. What time does your mother get up?
     4. What time do you go to bed?
     5. Where does your brother sleep?

C 1. Who meets his uncle at the diner (on Saturdays)?
     2. Who does John meet at the diner (on Saturdays)?
     3. Where does John meet his uncle (on Saturdays)?
     4. When does John meet his uncle at the diner?

D 1. Where *do* you live and who *do* you live with?

     2. Why *does* he daydream in class?

     3. When does she ~~gets~~ *get* up?

     4. How *do* they feel about sleeping pills?

     5. Who ~~does~~ *do* you dream about?

UNIT 11

A 1. **A:** Are there   **B:** there are
     2. **A:** Are there   **B:** there aren't
     3. **A:** Is she   **B:** she is

4. A: Are they   **B:** they aren't

5. A: Is there   **B:** there isn't

B 1. There's / It's

2. There are / They're

3. There's / She's

C Visit the new Shopper's Mall on Route 290.

~~There's~~ *There are* over 100 stores. ~~There~~ *There's* a movie theater, and ~~they~~ *there* are ten great places to eat. Come early.

Every morning at 10:30 ~~there are~~ *there's* a free show for children. The mall is three miles from the Tappan Bridge on Route 290.

UNIT 12

A 1. Their   3. Its   5. Her

2. His   4. Their

B 1. **A:** mine   **B:** yours   **A:** your

2. **A:** Whose   **B:** Ali's

3. My / Its

4. **A:** Her / yours   **B:** Mine

C **A:** ~~Who's~~ *Whose* bag is that on the floor?

B: I think it's ~~Maria~~ *Maria's*.

A: No. Her bag is on her arm.

B: Well, it's not ~~mine bag~~ *mine* (OR *my bag*). Maybe it's ~~Rita~~ *Rita's*.

A: Rita, is that ~~bag your~~ *yours* (OR *your bag*)?

UNIT 13

A 1. couldn't understand / can understand

2. can't run / could run

3. couldn't drive / can drive

B 1. **A:** Can   **B:** can

2. **A:** Could   **B:** couldn't / can

3. **A:** Can   **B:** can

C **A:** Can you ~~to~~ get online?

B: No, I can't ~~not~~. I couldn't ~~got~~ *get* online last night either.

A: My brother is good with computers. Maybe he can ~~helps~~ *help*.

B: Great. I ~~can no~~ *can't* figure out what's wrong.

A: I ~~no can~~ *can't* reach him now, but I can ~~to~~ call him after 6 P.M.

UNIT 14

A 1. may eat   4. may not use

2. can't eat   5. may drink

3. can have

B 1. When can I return to work?

2. When can I take a shower?

3. Can I go to the gym?

4. Can I ride my bike?

C 1. You may not eat. (You may not bring food.)

2. You may not use a pencil.

3. You may not make phone calls.

4. You may bring a bottle of water.

5. You may use a black or blue pen.

6. You may use a dictionary.

D **A:** May I ~~sees~~ *see* a menu?

B: ~~Sure, you might~~ *Sure.* Here you go.

A: And can we ~~to~~ have some water?

B: I'll be right back with the water. . . . Ready?

A: Yes. I want the chicken with mushroom sauce. But may I ~~has~~ *have* the sauce on the side?

B: ~~You may not.~~ *I'm sorry.* We cook the chicken in the sauce.

A: Oh? Well, then I'll have grilled chicken with rice.

UNIT 15

A 1. 'm not getting   4. 're doing

2. 're preparing   5. 's feeling

3. isn't playing

B 1. is listening to

2. are standing and talking

3. are running

4. is driving

5. is carrying

C 1. is texting / isn't ('s not) calling

2. are working / aren't giving up

3. is swimming / 's trying

D My classmates and I ~~am~~ *are* sitting in a computer lab.

One student ^is writing a composition. Two students are ~~check~~ *checking* their email. A teacher is ~~helps~~ *helping* a student. The other students are surfing the Internet.

UNIT 16

A 1. **A:** Are / watching   **B:** they are

2. **A:** are / doing   **B:** 'm listening

3. **A:** 's happening   **B:** is putting

B 1. Are you working?

2. Is he buying tickets online?

3. Are they watching a mystery?

4. Is she enjoying the movie?

C 1. Where are they going?

2. What music group is performing?

3. Where are they playing?

4. Why is Bob staying home?

D 1. **A:** Is ~~it's~~ *it* raining outside?

B: Yes. I hope it stops.

2. A: Are they playing soccer?

B: No, they 're not. They're playing rugby.

3. A: ~~You~~ *Are you* watching a good movie?

B: It's OK.

4. A: What *are* they doing?

B: They're fixing the cabinets.

UNIT 17

A 1. don't own   4. needs
2. doesn't like   5. want
3. has

B 1. is using   3. 's getting   5. wants
2. is surfing   4. has

C 1. is / doing   4. don't know
2. 's trying   5. Does / need
3. 's

D **1. A:** Where *are* you calling from?

B: Downtown. ~~I walk~~ *I'm walking* along Second Street.

2. A: Is she ~~play~~ *playing* tennis at West Park?

B: No, she's not. She ~~no~~ *doesn't* like those courts.

3. A: Does he ~~understands~~ *understand* Greek?

B: Yes, he does. He was in Greece for a year.

UNIT 18

A 1. watched   4. Last night
2. visited   5. didn't land
3. an hour ago

B 1. helped   4. didn't ask
2. stayed   5. didn't want
3. didn't snow

C 1. canceled   4. played
2. didn't stay   5. didn't enjoy
3. didn't rain

D Hello from London. Our friends ~~did~~ invited us here for a week. We're having a great time.

Yesterday we ~~visit~~ *visited* Big Ben, and we ~~tour~~ *toured* the Royal Palace. This morning we ~~watch~~ *watched* the Changing of the Guard. We wanted to shop this afternoon, but we didn't. The prices were high, but we ~~are~~ enjoyed looking at the store windows.

UNIT 19

A 1. saw   3. tried
2. was / wanted   4. got / didn't want

B A lucky man **found** a pot of gold. He **kept** the pot of gold in a hole in the ground of his garden. A jealous worker **stole** the gold from the man.

The man **became** upset. But a neighbor laughed because the man **didn't use** the gold. He just enjoyed counting it.

C 1. didn't stay   3. ran   5. took
2. lost   4. didn't see

D 1. William Sidney Porter *was* born in North Carolina in 1862.
2. He was a famous American short story writer. He wrote under different names, but he ~~did~~ became best known as O. Henry.
3. His stories ~~were~~ had surprise endings.
4. O. Henry had many talents, but he ~~did get~~ *got* into trouble and spent time in prison.

UNIT 20

A 1. Did they go to the theater?
2. Did she get there by bus?
3. Did you have good seats?
4. Did he understand everything?
5. Did we miss the beginning?
6. Did it have a happy ending?

B 1. What play did you see?
2. Where did you see it?
3. How long was the show?
4. Did you enjoy the performance?
5. Who were the stars?
6. Did you go out after the show?
7. Where did you go?
8. What did you order?

C 1. Where ~~he did~~ *did he* go last night?
2. What ~~saw he~~ *did he see*?
3. Did he ~~enjoyed~~ *enjoy* it?
4. Who *did* he ~~met~~ *meet*?
5. When *did* they go?
6. Who ~~did pay~~ *paid* for it?

UNIT 21

A 1. was born   5. started
2. grew up   6. became
3. attended   7. expanded
4. went

B 1. When did she go to college?
2. Who did they meet?
3. Where did he study?
4. How long did they live in Canada?

C 1. Were   3. Was   5. Did
2. Did   4. Did

D Steve Paul Jobs ~~did start~~ *started* college in 1970, but he ~~no did~~ *didn't* finish it. In 1976 Jobs and his friend ~~begin~~ *began* to make their own computers. They worked in the Jobs' garage. That was the beginning of Apple® Computers. Their company ~~become~~ *became* a big success. Apple® changed the field of computers, and by the age of 30, Jobs was a multimillionaire.

UNIT 22

A 1. starting
2. to sell
3. to return
4. to become
5. flying / seeing
6. to help

B 1. to work
2. to change
3. quitting / going
4. to study
5. doing

C Carol volunteers at a hospital. She enjoys ~~to take~~ *taking* care of patients. Some patients refuse ~~do~~ *to* exercise, but Carol keeps ~~to push~~ *pushing* them. Carol intends ^*to* study physical therapy in college. She needs ~~taking~~ *to take* a lot of science courses. She expects to ~~went~~ *go* to college next fall. She hopes ^*to* get a degree in physical therapy in five years. She prefers ~~to~~ working with teenagers, but she will work with adults too.

UNIT 23

A 1. is taking
2. make
3. made
4. likes

B 1. invented
2. didn't work
3. wanted
4. became
5. started
6. use
7. are sewing

C 1. Where did you go last weekend?
2. How did you get there?
3. What did you see at the museum?
4. How was the museum?
5. Do you go there often?

D 1. Last night I ~~did watch~~ *watched* a movie about fish.
2. I thought the fish were beautiful, and I ~~enjoy~~ *enjoyed* the movie.
3. My brother is watching the movie now, but he ~~don't~~ *doesn't* like it.
4. He ~~is only liking~~ *only likes* action films.

UNIT 24

A 1. is going to build
2. 's going to cost
3. 's going to have
4. are going to be
5. isn't going to begin

B 1. are not going to increase
2. aren't going to play
3. 're going to visit
4. 's going to retire
5. 'm not going to do

C 1. **Q:** When is she going to the dentist? **A:** On Monday at 5:30.
2. **Q:** Where is she meeting Yu Chen? **A:** At Pappa Pizza.
3. **Q:** Is she meeting Yu Chen on Monday? **A:** No, she isn't.

D This city ^*is* going to change under our new mayor. ~~People's~~ *People are* going to ride bikes and they're ~~gonna~~ *going to* use public transportation. They're ~~no~~ *not* going to drive big cars. There are probably going to be higher tolls on bridges and more bike paths on the roads.

UNIT 25

A 1. Where will people travel in twenty years?
2. Will people fly to the moon?
3. How will they get around?
4. Will the climate change?
5. Will people look different?

B 1. won't
2. won't
3. will
4. will
5. won't

C 1. Will / be hot
2. Will / have a test
3. Will / be a storm
4. Will / rain
5. Will / work late

D I usually bring my lunch to work, but tomorrow I ~~no will~~ *won't* bring it because it's my birthday. My co-workers will ~~takes~~ *take* me out to a restaurant. We'll ~~to~~ order a few different dishes, and we'll share them. They'll ~~singing~~ *sing* "Happy Birthday," and they'll give me a small gift. I'm sure it will ~~is~~ *be* a lot of fun.

UNIT 26

A 1. go
2. buy
3. might not
4. may
5. Will

B 1. may (might) snow
2. may (might) not get
3. may (might) need
4. may (might) not see
5. may (might) stay

C 1. There may (OR There might) be a restroom in the library.
2. He may (OR might) be the director.
3. The plane might (OR may) be late.
4. They may (OR might) be cousins.
5. It might (OR may) be his coat.

D 1. He might ~~goes~~ *go* on vacation next week.
2. He may ~~works~~ *work* late tomorrow.
3. They might ~~to~~ visit him tomorrow. Are you free?
4. I might not help him. I might ~~to~~ help her instead.
5. She ~~maybe~~ *may* take a yoga class.

UNIT 27

A 1. a few   3. an
   2. the   4. any

B 1. many   3. a little
   2. much   4. a few

C 1. a   4. the
   2. a   5. a
   3. the   6. a

D 1. A: What are you looking for?
       B: I need a ~~little~~ *few* stamps. I wrote ~~any~~ *some* postcards, and I want to mail them.
   2. A: There isn't ~~some~~ *much* yogurt in the refrigerator. There's only half a container.
       B: There ~~isn't much~~ *aren't many* eggs either. We need to go shopping, but we don't have ~~many~~ *much* time.

UNIT 28

A 1. How many   4. How much
   2. How much   5. How many
   3. How many

B 1. How often do you go to the movies?
   2. How many close friends do you have?
   3. How much time do you spend online?
   4. How many people live in your home?
   5. How often do you check email?

C 1. I usually bake a few times a week.
   2. They never have enough food in the house.
   3. Every weekend we play soccer in the park.
   4. He spilled a glass of grape juice.
   5. She added a little salt to the soup.

D 1. ~~Never I~~ *Never* eat breakfast at home.
   2. ~~She once in a while~~ *Once in a while she* bakes.
   3. Do you have ~~milk enough~~ *enough milk*?
   4. How ~~much~~ *many* tomatoes did they buy?
   5. I rarely ~~don't~~ cook.

UNIT 29

A 1. too long
   2. too much homework
   3. too much milk
   4. too many trucks
   5. too much time

B 1. too / too little
   2. too few
   3. too much
   4. too many

C 1. There's too little rain.
   2. There are too few subways.
   3. There's too little sunlight.
   4. There are too few traffic lights.
   5. There is too little water.

D The climate here is terrible. It gets too ~~much~~ hot in the summer and too cold in the winter. There's too ~~many~~ *much* snow and ice. Winters are ~~to~~ *too* long. There are too ~~little~~ *few* comfortable days with mild temperatures and blue skies. Also, there's too ~~many~~ *much* air pollution from all the traffic on the streets. I want to move.

UNIT 30

A 1. should   4. ought to
   2. had better   5. better not
   3. shouldn't

B 1. had better not   3. had better not
   2. had better   4. had better

C 1. should   3. should
   2. shouldn't   4. shouldn't

D 1. Where should we ~~meets~~ *meet* after work?
   2. We*'d* better take an umbrella tonight. It's going to rain.
   3. Should I ~~to~~ make a reservation now for my flight? I think I ~~outta~~ *ought to* buy it soon.
   4. What ~~I should~~ *should I* see during my business trip to Uruguay?
   5. Should we ~~leaves~~ *leave* Brazil tonight or tomorrow?
   6. You ought *to* bring flowers to your hostess to thank her for dinner.

UNIT 31

A 1. Would you like   4. We'd like
   2. Could you pass   5. Can you
   3. I'd like

B 1. Of course.   4. Sorry, I need it.
   2. Sure.   5. I'd be glad to.
   3. Thanks.

C 1. Could you please
2. I'd like
3. Could you please
4. Would you like
5. I'd like

D 1. A: Could ~~please~~ you _please_ move my car at 11:00?

B: ~~No, I wouldn't.~~ _Sorry._ I'll be at work then.

2. A: ~~I like~~ _I'd like_ to see you this weekend. Would you like to go to the park?

B: ~~I could.~~ _Yes, I would._

3. A: Would you like ~~have~~ some more ice cream?

B: No, thanks. I'm full.

UNIT 32

A 1. don't have to   4. doesn't have to
2. have to   5. have to
3. must not

B 1. mustn't   3. don't have to
2. has / has to   4. has to

C 1. had to work
2. have to read / answer
3. had to give OR have to give
4. didn't have to bring

D The test starts at 8:10. You must ~~to~~ be in the room at 8:00. You mustn't ~~came~~ _come_ late. You have to ~~has~~ _have_ two number two pencils and an eraser. You ~~musts~~ _must_ ~~brings~~ _bring_ proper identification, such as a photo ID or a passport. You must leave your cell phone in the front of the room.

UNIT 33

A 1. much   5. higher
2. than   6. better
3. more popular   7. brother's
4. worse

B 1. A bus ride is more expensive in Sun City than in New City.
2. A cup of coffee is cheaper in New City than in Sun City.
3. The average home is less expensive in New City than in Sun City.
4. The average income is higher in Sun City than in New City.

C We moved to the countryside, and we're much ~~more~~ happier. Our home is ~~more~~ larger, and the air is cleaner and polluted ~~less~~ _less_. It _is_ less

expensive than the city too. Fruits and vegetables are ~~more cheap~~ _cheaper_. The people are ~~friendler~~ _friendlier_. Of course our commute is ~~more bad~~ _worse_; it's much ~~more long~~ _longer_, but we listen to Spanish tapes, and our Spanish is ~~more good~~ _better_.

UNIT 34

A 1. quickly   3. well   5. clearly
2. fluently   4. slowly

B 1. good   3. nervous   5. quickly
2. carefully   4. badly

C 1. good   3. clearly (briefly)   5. honestly
2. briefly (clearly)   4. fast

D A: I think my speech went ~~good~~ _well_.

B: Did they appreciate your jokes?

A: They laughed ~~polite~~ _politely_, but I'm not sure they laughed ~~sincere~~ _sincerely_.

B: It's hard to be funny.

A: I ~~hard worked~~ _worked hard_, and I prepared carefully, but I was ~~nervously~~ _nervous_.

UNIT 35

A 1. big enough   3. too   5. from
2. as   4. as

B 1. warm enough   4. too short
2. very late   5. enough time
3. too busy   6. very good

C I didn't like the prom this year as much ~~than~~ _as_ last year. I usually like parties, but the music at the prom was much ~~very~~ _too_ loud. Also, my dress was the same as ~~Julia~~ _Julia's_! That was a ~~too~~ _very_ big shock. Also, the dinner portions weren't ~~enough large~~ _large enough_ and the servers this year were very rude. Then we tried to dance, but there was ~~no~~ _not_ enough room and the room was ~~too much~~ _much too_ hot. The music was also not _as_ good as last year. We had a ~~more~~ better time last year.

A 1. the funniest
   2. the biggest
   3. the best
   4. The largest / the most dangerous

B 1. the hottest day
   2. the oldest woman
   3. the busiest shopping day
   4. the most interesting show
   5. the most popular animals

C 1. one of the most intelligent animals
   2. one of the best zoos
   3. one of the worst seats
   4. one of the longest days
   5. one of the most expensive trips

D 1. **A:** What is the ~~most good~~ *best* way to get to the park?

   B: The shortest route is also the ^*most* complicated. I'll give you the most direct way.

   2. **A:** What's the ~~most~~ hardest part of your job here at the zoo?

   B: Well, the ~~nicer~~ *nicest* part is taking care of the animals. The ~~most~~ worst part is telling people not to feed the animals or bother them.

CREDITS

INDEX

This index is for the full and split editions. All entries are in the full book. Entries for Volume A of the split edition are in black. Entries for Volume B are in red.